RACING POST
ANNUAL 2022

Racing Post Floor 7, The Podium, South Bank Tower Estate, 30 Stamford Street, London, SE1 9LS. 0203 034 8900

Editor Nick Pulford
Art editor David Dew
Cover design Duncan Olner
Chief photographers Edward Whitaker, Patrick McCann
Other photography Mark Cranham, Getty, John Grossick, Caroline Norris
Picture artworking Stefan Searle
Feature writers Mark Boylan, Scott Burton, David Carr, Steve Dennis, Andrew Dietz, Richard Forristal, Matt Gardner, Jonathan Harding, Sam Hendry, David Jennings, Lee Mottershead, Julian Muscat, Lewis Porteous, Nick Pulford, John Randall, Brian Sheerin, James Stevens, Peter Thomas

Archant Dialogue
Advertising Sales
Gary Millone, 07843 369124, gary.millone@archantdialogue.co.uk
Advertising Production Manager
Kay Brown, 01603 772522, kay.brown@archantdialogue.co.uk
Prospect House, Rouen Road, Norwich NR1 1RE. 01603 772554
archantdialogue.co.uk

Distribution/availability
01933 304858 help@racingpost.com

Published by Pitch Publishing on behalf of Racing Post, A2 Yeoman Gate, Yeoman Way, Worthing, Sussex, BN13 3QZ

A CIP catalogue record is available for this book from the British Library.

ISBN 978-1839500879 [UK]
ISBN 978-1839500893 [Ireland]

Printed in Great Britain by Buxton Press.

racingpost.com/shop

WELCOME to the Racing Post Annual horses and races of 2021 in a pac of what the next year might hold.

There was no bigger racing story Blackmore's seismic Grand Natio her historic feat deservedly domi newspapers across the globe after that famous day in April.

Blackmore was also part of another historic achievement for Henry de Bromhead, riding Honeysuckle to victory in the Champion Hurdle to kickstart the trainer's unique big-race treble at the Cheltenham Festival. Gold Cup hero Minella Indo, who completed the set, is another of our cover stars.

So too is Adayar, the first horse in 20 years to do the Derby-King George double as he led a tremendous campaign for Godolphin and Charlie Appleby alongside dual Classic winner Hurricane Lane.

Our fourth cover star is St Mark's Basilica, who won two Classics in France and added the Eclipse and Irish Champion Stakes to make a unique collection of big-race triumphs.

Many others left their mark in the record books too. From Aidan O'Brien to Colin Keane and from Snowfall to Stradivarius, they are all celebrated in these pages.

The racing year also produced great stories of comeback and redemption, including those of Jack Kennedy and Kieran Shoemark, as well as triumph against the odds for the likes of Germany's Arc hero Torquator Tasso and Irish Grand National outsider Freewheelin Dylan.

There were many other heartwarming moments, from Lady Bowthorpe's emotional Group 1 triumph to Celerity's unlikely win in a lowly Haydock race, as well as the uplifting initiative of National Racehorse Week.

Of course, this was also the year crowds were allowed back on racecourses in ever increasing numbers to enjoy at least some of these delights.

Whether or not you were lucky enough to be there when Stradivarius won at York or St Mark's Basilica triumphed at Leopardstown, we hope the Annual will bring those stories to life and rekindle happy memories.

Nick Pulford
Editor

CONTENTS

16

BIG STORIES

82

RACHAEL THE FIRST

By Richard Forristal

B Y THE time Aintree rolled around in April, Rachael Blackmore had already conquered the world once. For jump racing's most luminescent star, however, the world was not enough.

Blackmore had bossed the Cheltenham Festival in March. She plundered the Champion Hurdle on the opening day en route to a final tally of six winners that only Ruby Walsh can match, and departed with the sort of international acclaim that tends to be the preserve of the planet's most revered sportspeople.

For those invested in jump racing, be it the stakeholders who make it happen or the devout fans who obsess over it every day, Prestbury Park in March is the axis upon which everything turns and Blackmore owned the week. But for the casual observer who dips in once a year for a novelty, the Grand National is the race that captures the imagination. It transcends the sport.

For all that it might not be the fearsome test it once was, the National still retains an exotic allure to an
▸ *Continues page 6*

Rachael Blackmore crowned her incredible year by making Grand National history on Minella Times

otherwise oblivious public. Once a year, then, there is the potential for racing to reverberate far beyond its own confines. In 2021, arguably for the first time since Sir Anthony McCoy banished his hoodoo in the race after a decade and a half of disappointment in 2010, Blackmore catapulted the sport into another galaxy. After nearly two centuries, the slight 31-year-old boldly thrust the Grand National where no man had ever taken it before, to uncharted territory in far-flung corners of the cosmos.

Blackmore's flawlessly synchronised performance on Minella Times – and it was an utterly impeccable exhibition – produced one of the definitive sporting moments of our time. Her triumph saw her become the first female jockey to win the Grand National, scaling the summit of a mountain that for so long women weren't even allowed to set foot upon at base camp.

It was 1977 before the daunting Aintree event embraced the idea of female riders. Eleven years earlier, women in Britain had won the right to hold trainers' licences, and in 1983 Jenny Pitman made the National breakthrough when Corbiere seized a slice of history under Ben de Haan.

They were all seismic landmarks in their own right but, in all the time since then, the prospect of a female jockey getting the opportunity to emerge on top in such a formidable and demanding assignment continued to be something of a utopian ideal. It felt about as likely as 007 being played by a woman; never going to happen.

The sense of it being a romantic notion was reinforced by Elizabeth Taylor's star turn in National Velvet. It was a movie fantasy in 1944 and remained a halcyon pipedream for decades. Bridging that cinematic divide is what enthralled the watching world.

NBC New York, Al Jazeera and The Washington Post all hailed Blackmore's singular success, while The Age, Melbourne's daily paper, duly reached for the National Velvet analogy. "A Hollywood fantasy turned into reality when Rachael Blackmore became the first female jockey to win Britain's gruelling Grand National, breaking down one of the biggest

gender barriers in the sport," it effused.

"Fantasy no more: Blackmore 1st Woman to win Grand National," boomed NBC New York's headline. Japan Today, the South China Morning Post and The West Australian were other outlets to acknowledge the moment, as did Ringo Starr when he lauded her feat to his two million Twitter followers. Blackmore had gone global.

✦✦✦✦

FOR reasons few will need reminding about, horse racing had found itself in defensive mode for much of the previous 12 months, and the National didn't even happen in 2020. All of a sudden, with much of the world confined to barracks in lockdown, it was gifted the sort of authentic, feelgood exposure that no marketing department or scriptwriter could conjure.

Fact, in this instance, was greater than fiction, and the authenticity of it

▸▸ *Continues page 8*

▲ Dream come true: Rachael Blackmore passes the post on Minella Times

'Phenomenal'

Rachael Blackmore on her historic National triumph

I had such a beautiful passage through the race. Minella Times jumped fantastically and didn't miss a beat anywhere. You need so much luck to get around with no-one else interfering. You need so much to go right and things went right for me.

I heard the commentator say I was four lengths in front as we came back on to the racecourse proper. I knew Minella Times would gallop to the line and you start believing it then. Jumping two out I was trying to hold on to a bit as it's a long way home. We all know what can happen on the run-in here.

When I crossed the line, I don't know how I felt – it's incredible. It's absolute elation, it really is. It's just so massive, such a special race. It's just phenomenal. To actually fulfil something like this is unbelievable. I didn't dream about making a career as a jockey because I didn't think it could happen. Keep your dreams big, that's the inspiration I have for you.

all was what resonated so loudly. Blackmore's ascent, in a traditionally male-dominated, punishing sporting realm, was built on skill and endeavour. She hadn't the privilege of a racing pedigree or wealth to promote her. There were no concessions, just merit.

"Racing went through a difficult time and she put it on the front pages," McCoy reflected of her exploits. "She's a great credit to herself and racing has been very lucky to have her. We talk about gender a lot in the world today, but it's about results – and she's getting results. Whether I say she's great, or someone else says she's great, is irrelevant. Her statistics speak volumes, they're top class and she was the best jockey riding at Cheltenham.

"Why have we never had a woman driving a Formula 1 car? It's even more mechanical than a racehorse. She has been able to do what no other female has been able to do in any sport."

Of course, merit has always played a part in female jockeys' chequered National history, but within certain parameters. Katie Walsh, for example, had a memorable dalliance with glory in 2012, when the gambled-on Seabass eventually wilted into third. Her gallant turn, though, seemed to epitomise the lot of female riders in the race up to that point. She was riding for her father Ted, and such intimate links were usually the basis for a female jockey's National opportunities.

Regardless of a woman's quality as a rider, winning the trust of the most exalted owners and trainers remained a rarity. Gradually, long after the groundwork had been laid by the pioneers who paved the way, that sentiment began to turn. Then along came Blackmore. A bit like Hemingway's line about first going broke gradually and then suddenly, she took that incremental touchpaper of progression and obliterated it with an inexorable fireball that could not be repelled.

Granted, it was a slow burn for her early on as well. However, since being crowned Ireland's champion conditional in 2017 Blackmore's graph had been on a steep upward curve, and her association with Henry

'A day in history'

What they said about Blackmore's achievement

Katie Walsh This is a day we'll never forget – it's a day in history. I've always hoped a woman would pass the line in front one day and I'm absolutely delighted it's Rachael. She's a phenomenal woman who is great for racing and sport. She's an inspiration to males and females alike.

Sir Anthony McCoy It's amazing for her and for racing. She's got it all. You have to have so much talent to be in her position. She's brought riding to a new level in terms of how far a female jockey can go.

Henry de Bromhead She's a fantastic rider, a great team player and a lovely person to work with. They broke the mould after her. She's breaking through all the records.

de Bromhead gave her a platform no other female rider had before.

★★★★

SHE arrived at Aintree on the crest of a wave. When De Bromhead confirmed to the Racing Post on the Tuesday of National week that she was due to ride the JP McManus-owned Minella Times in the Saturday showpiece, the news commanded Wednesday's front page splash. It also moved the market.

Minella Times promptly plunged from 14-1 to 8-1 as punters latched on to the girl with the golden touch. The Paddy Power and Leopardstown Chase runner-up had the right profile for the race, as he was an experienced operator who was in form but not exposed, with an ideal National weight of 10st 3lb. He also represented a yard that had won each of the marquee championship races at Cheltenham and an owner synonymous with plundering the sport's most illustrious handicaps. The booking of the irresistible force that was Blackmore put the cherry on top.

On the day, Blackmore's mount's

▲ Inside track: Rachael Blackmore and Minella Times are perfectly placed as they jump the water
▼ The Racing Post front page three days before the race with the news that Blackmore would ride Minella Times, and the day after her momentous win

odds eased back to 11-1, as Any Second Now, Ted Walsh's McManus-owned runner, was the subject of strong support. However, their respective fates demonstrated that the National still possesses that capricious sliding doors potential.

When they took the 12th fence, which would be the third last with a circuit to go, Mark Walsh had what seemed the box seat on the rail in behind the leaders aboard Any Second Now. Blackmore had taken a slightly wider path to give herself the option of going left or right for light. Both were tracking Double Shuffle, who made an uncharacteristic mistake before falling heavily. By and large, horses fall out, away from the inside rail.

This time, though, Double Shuffle rolled in. In doing so, he brought Any Second Now's momentum to a shuddering halt. He went from the plum position behind the leaders to having 17 horses in front of him. In an instant, while he ran his heart out to be third in the end, his prospects of victory were ruined. Inches away, Blackmore ghosted by Double

Shuffle's flailing legs and carried on unimpeded.

★★★★

IT WAS a vignette that illustrated the charmed experience Blackmore enjoyed on Minella Times, for they demonstrated an utterly symbiotic rhythm around Aintree's unique course. From the moment the flag fell, Blackmore always looked happy with her position.

"A lot's down to Rachael – she was just brilliant on him today," said De Bromhead, who had achieved an unprecedented feat by winning the Champion Hurdle, Queen Mother Champion Chase, Gold Cup and Grand National in the same season. He also emulated his Gold Cup one-two thanks to Balko Des Flos' gallant National second behind Minella Times, yet it tells you all you need to know of Blackmore's incomparable tour de force that such epochal accomplishments were relegated to footnotes.

"She got a great passage all the way round," De Bromhead added. "We had a lot of luck on our side and he

winged fences for her. And Balko Des Flos was brilliant as well. I'm over the moon."

Minella Times certainly relished the whole experience, pinging fences and travelling with consummate ease. When the long-time leader Jett cried enough as they swung towards the final two fences, Blackmore's destiny rolled out in front of her. Immortality beckoned. She shaded the lead two out, as Balko Des Flos kept them company. Blackmore, though, was just marking time.

Once they cleared the final fence, she gave her mount his orders and they surged towards the Elbow with a clear lead that never looked like being diminished. The composure she demonstrated over those last two obstacles, when there was so much at stake, had become her trademark. Here was someone at the peak of their sport who was now

▼ Ultimate prize: Blackmore adds the National trophy to her glittering collection

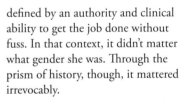

defined by an authority and clinical ability to get the job done without fuss. In that context, it didn't matter what gender she was. Through the prism of history, though, it mattered irrevocably.

"I can't believe we've just won the Grand National," Blackmore beamed after her epic victory. "He gave me an absolutely sensational spin. I don't feel male or female right now – I don't even feel human. This is just unbelievable."

That out-of-body sense of incredulity didn't wear off in a hurry, later prompting a soundbite that seemed to fully convey the year she was having. "Yeah, I can't believe I am Rachael Blackmore – genuinely," she responded when it was put to her on ITV that she was inspiring kids all over the world. "I still feel like that little kid and I can't believe I'm me. This race is the one that catches every young person with a pony's imagination. It's just phenomenal. To actually fulfil something like this is unbelievable."

Not anymore it's not. Never say never again.

Honeysuckle's victory in the Champion Hurdle was the start of a glorious spring for Rachael Blackmore and her ally Henry de Bromhead

THE BLOOMING

By Richard Forristal

GIVEN all that followed, it is easy to forget how seismic Honeysuckle's emphatic Champion Hurdle triumph was in the moment it occurred. Indeed, it is maybe not too outlandish to wonder just how much of what followed would have happened if things hadn't worked out for Henry de Bromhead's indomitable mare. Remember, the Rachael we now know, recognisable by her first name and utterly unflappable on the big occasion, isn't the Rachael Blackmore we knew before March 16, 2021.

As a three-time Cheltenham Festival-winning rider who had already been crowned champion conditional, challenged for the Irish jockeys' championship and landed some of the domestic scene's most coveted Grade 1s, the then 31-year-old was firmly established as one of jump racing's most prolific riders. However, there is a distinct difference between then and now, and it was Honeysuckle's barnstorming display on the opening day in the Cotswolds that was the catalyst for Blackmore's transformation from a cult star into a global superstar.

When the partnership arrived at the start for the two-mile championship event, no female jockey had ever won one of Cheltenham's marquee races. Honeysuckle was at that stage unbeaten in ten starts under rules and a dual Irish Champion Hurdle heroine, and she was the 11-10 favourite to bring up the hat-trick of shorties in the festival's first three Grade 1s after the victories of Appreciate It and Shishkin. The expectation was off the scale.

If it went pear-shaped, it could have left Blackmore second-guessing herself for the week. A year earlier, although the duo had combined to win the Mares' Hurdle, they needed the bounce of the ball to do so, and things generally didn't fall for Blackmore.

Defeat on Honeysuckle would have been the worst possible start to the 2021 festival, but, in what would become a trademark of hers in the weeks that followed, the County Tipperary native rode with such imposing conviction that the outcome seemed a formality. When the need was greatest, under what should have been an overwhelming weight of pressure, Blackmore bloomed. It is the stamp of a rare talent, the sort of inherent authority for so long synonymous with a certain Ruby Walsh.

★★★★

IN THE Champion Hurdle, with Silver Streak setting strong fractions, Blackmore tore up the script that had yielded those ten previous victories. Honeysuckle was accustomed to racing bang on the pace, which allowed her to use her long stride and mobilise her abundant stamina. This time, though, Blackmore settled her in. She promptly recognised the gallop was too strong and let Honeysuckle find her rhythm in behind, a shade closer to the trailing Saldier than the pacesetting Silver Streak as they went by the winning post the first time.

"I'd be used to seeing her sitting second or third, but there she was in fifth or sixth passing the stands at Cheltenham," De Bromhead reflected later. "I was thinking 'that's not normal', but I was very comfortable seeing her there, and I would usually be nervous watching races."

De Bromhead was comfortable because he had by now come to trust Blackmore implicitly in a way that maybe many viewing on their television screens that week hadn't yet. Those watching at home, confined to barracks during the Covid-19 lockdown, were about to understand what infused that trust.

As the field traversed the back straight, with Goshen careering away on the outside, Honeysuckle gradually ghosted closer to the front end. Blackmore had her snapping at the heels of Silver Streak and Aspire Tower crossing the fourth-last. They pinged the next and all of a sudden Honeysuckle was visibly in command.

Cutting in from the outside as they swung for home, Blackmore closed the door on Aspire Tower and made for the inside as they seized the lead. It was the sort of ruthless manoeuvre that won her an array of plaudits from the game's most revered names throughout the week, and in this instance gave her mount the platform to surge up the hill to a historic success.

"Every experience in life is a lesson, and I'd say Rachael left the 2020 festival after learning a good few lessons," Ruby Walsh mused later. "When she went to the last in the RSA Chase on Minella Indo in 2020, she let him pop; this time, Honeysuckle was home and hosed but she still rode her to the last."

Honeysuckle powered across the line six and a half lengths clear of Sharjah to post one of the most impressive Champion Hurdle performances in recent times. That she arrived there with such a flawless record spoke volumes of her potential. But in extending that sequence, beating Sharjah and Epatante, she accounted for the 2020 Champion Hurdle runner-up and winner. To brush them off with such disdain was reminiscent of some of the division's most exalted names. Suitably, Honeysuckle emulated the mighty Faugheen, for he is the only other horse in recent times to carry such an unblemished record into the Champion Hurdle and maintain it.

Not even Istabraq could match that enduring precocity, and it is hardly premature now to say that, along with Annie Power, Honeysuckle is as good a National Hunt mare as we've seen since Dawn Run. She would add to her remarkable run with another decisive win at Punchestown, by which point Blackmore and De Bromhead held the whole world in their hands. However, it was that seminal Cheltenham rout that set the tone for their sensational spring tide.

"To me, this was never even a dream," Blackmore beamed. "It was so far from what I ever thought could happen in my life. To be in Cheltenham, riding the winner of a Champion Hurdle, it's so far removed from anything I ever thought could be possible. Maybe there's a lesson in that for everyone out there."

★★★★

HER work ethic, and that tendency to do rather than dream, would reap the richest of rewards. The following day, Blackmore was again at her uncompromising best on Bob Olinger when not giving Willie Mullins' Gaillard Du Mesnil an inch in the curtain-raising Ballymore Novices' Hurdle en route to another barnstorming win, and De Bromhead added the

▸ Continues page 12

HONEYSUCKLE

Queen Mother Champion Chase with the Aidan Coleman-ridden Put The Kettle On.

Blackmore then took the bull by the horns on Sir Gerhard for Mullins in the Champion Bumper. When everyone else was looking around waiting for someone else to go on, she bounced out and set the fractions to suit herself, pinching it before they swung for home. That initiative, with Paul Townend left cursing her acumen as Kilcruit powered home to be second, was the mark of a jockey in the zone.

Granted, Blackmore had to pick herself up off the ground a few times, but even then she never seemed to break stride. Come the Ryanair Chase on Thursday, she absolutely bossed the race on Allaho, another masterclass in making things happen rather than waiting for them to happen.

Shortly afterwards, she and De Bromhead took the mares' novice hurdle with the patiently ridden Telmesomethinggirl, and Blackmore rounded off her week with Quilixios in the Triumph Hurdle on Friday. She must have felt bulletproof going to the start on A Plus Tard in the Gold Cup, but Cheltenham's indiscriminate nature had the final say, as ever.

For while De Bromhead would crown the week with Gold Cup glory, becoming the first trainer ever to plunder the holy trinity of the Champion Hurdle, Champion Chase and Gold Cup in the same year, Blackmore was left to rue what might have been. She didn't make many poor decisions all week, but opting for A Plus Tard over Minella Indo turned out to be one.

As they swung down the hill and began the last turn for home, she once again bottled up Townend on the hat-trick-seeking Al Boum Photo. At that point, it looked like it was written, but she ultimately couldn't get A Plus Tard close enough to eyeball Minella Indo.

Jack Kennedy, who at 21 years of age became the youngest jockey to win the Gold Cup since Tim Hamey (20) on Koko in 1926, simply had too much horse under him in Minella Indo. While A Plus Tard rallied, the fairytale climax wasn't to be for Blackmore.

Having eschewed the winning mount on a Gold Cup horse, it was a sore end to the week. Nonetheless, she had made her mark. A weighing room that had lost totemic figures such as Sir Anthony McCoy, Ruby Walsh, Barry Geraghty and Richard Johnson all of a sudden had a readily identifiable female icon carrying the sport into uncharted territory.

Blackmore, so inherently unassuming, might not relish the clamour for a big personality to fill those esteemed boots, but what she lacks as an extrovert she makes up for as a role model. Deeds, not words, are her thing, and she is not dissimilar to her ally De Bromhead in that respect.

They are a formidable, no-nonsense duo who crowned an epic season with Minella Times at Aintree. That was a crescendo to end all crescendos, but it was Honeysuckle's sublime turn that served as the release valve for what was to come.

The only pity was that Blackmore wasn't able to soak up what would have been a raucous reception on her return to that hallowed winner's enclosure after such an epochal feat. Still. She ended the unique behind-closed-doors festival clutching the Ruby Walsh Leading Rider Award with a tally of six wins that only Walsh has ever matched. That's the realm in which she now belongs. A class apart.

Super six

RACHAEL BLACKMORE became the first woman to be top jockey at the Cheltenham Festival and only the second rider after Ruby Walsh to have six winners at a single festival. Here's how she did it:

Horse	Race	Trainer	Odds
Honeysuckle	Champion Hurdle	Henry de Bromhead	11-10f
Bob Olinger	Ballymore Novices' Hurdle	Henry de Bromhead	6-4f
Sir Gerhard	Champion Bumper	Willie Mullins	85-40
Allaho	Ryanair Chase	Willie Mullins	3-1f
Telmesomethinggirl	Mares' Novices' Hurdle	Henry de Bromhead	5-1
Quilixios	Triumph Hurdle	Henry de Bromhead	2-1

▲ A week to remember: top from left, Sir Gerhard, Allaho, Telmesomethinggirl and Quilixios, and below, Bob Olinger

The middle leg of Henry de Bromhead's historic big-race treble at Cheltenham came with the tenacious mare Put The Kettle On in the Queen Mother Champion Chase

KETTLE ON THE BOIL

HISTORY was in the making for Henry de Bromhead throughout an incredible spring campaign and there was another huge slice of it with Put The Kettle On, the "crackers" mare with a deep love of Cheltenham. Her victory in the Queen Mother Champion Chase made her the first mare to put her name on the illustrious roll of honour and by the end of the week she had also taken her place as the middle leg of De Bromhead's clean sweep of the festival's big three championship races.

It almost didn't happen, as De Bromhead explained later. "In mid-February I was probably leaning towards the Mares' Chase," he admitted, "but then I spoke to the owners and we looked at the stats of the Arkle winners, which seemed ridiculous, and it's her trip and she loves the Old course, so we thought we'd give it a lash."

Put The Kettle On was up for the challenge, even though it meant taking on hot favourite Chacun Pour Soi, who had beaten her more than eight lengths into third place at Leopardstown over Christmas. The chance of a turnaround in that form lay in their respective records at Cheltenham: Put The Kettle On had won on all three starts there, including the previous year's Arkle Chase, while Chacun Pour Soi's only visit had ended in late withdrawal from the 2020 Champion Chase.

That was a source of great hope, as the mare's jockey Aidan Coleman confirmed afterwards. "Chacun Pour Soi looked pretty solid coming into the race and there weren't many question marks about him, only the track," he said. "That was the only thing we had massively in our favour. If you're going to have form around the track, this is where you want it."

When she turned up for the Champion Chase, Put The Kettle On had won nowhere but Cheltenham since the autumn of 2019. It was clearly her track, as she had proved by winning the Arkle trial and then the big race itself, before returning early in the 2020-21 season to land the Grade 2 Shloer Chase. Yet it would be wrong to say the mare comes alive at Cheltenham; in truth, this kettle is always on the boil.

"She's a bit crackers the whole time," De Bromhead said. "She's quite wild, but a real character. Andrea, who looks after her at home and puts up with her antics every day, does a really good job with her. She wouldn't be the easiest ride and you'd want to have your wits about you. She's nuts, but in a great way."

De Bromhead had done the Arkle-Champion Chase double with Sizing Europe – one of 12 to achieve the feat before Put The Kettle On – and he made sure his mare was freshened up for her return to her favourite track. He was hopeful, but no more than that, as he admitted later. "I felt we were always up against it with Chacun Pour Soi. He looked so good at Leopardstown – he is so good – but you have to take your chances. Her record on the Old course is incredible. But did I think she would come here and win? Probably not."

★★★★

THEY say you should never be scared of one horse, and De Bromhead wasn't. Nor was Coleman, who felt he had unfinished business in the race after his narrow defeat by the De Bromhead-trained Special Tiara in 2017. "I got beat a head [on Fox Norton] and it really annoyed me as I thought I should have won that day," he recalled. "I was a bit slow through the middle part of the race and Special Tiara got away from me. Up until Paisley Park it was the only Grade 1 I was close to winning. It always bugged me a bit as I thought I should have won it."

Coleman, older and more experienced, was determined to give himself every chance this time and Put The Kettle On disputed the lead with Rouge Vif from the outset. Pressing the pace down the far side on the final circuit, Coleman had the lead coming down the hill but it was still congested behind, so much so that Sceau Royal was badly squeezed against the rail and almost came down.

Chacun Pour Soi was second on the inner coming to the penultimate fence but it was already clear this was going to be more of a battle than he was used to facing in Ireland. The favourite jumped the last in front but Put The Kettle On fought back tenaciously, getting to his flank, then to his withers and finally forcing herself back into the lead. Still the issue was not settled, as Nube Negra and Harry Skelton also powered past Chacun Pour Soi, but the mighty mare hung on gamely by half a length.

"This mare is something else. Whether she's the best or not, it doesn't matter, if you've got a heart like she has, I don't have to do a lot," Coleman said. "I beat Chacun Pour Soi off, then Harry came and she went again. If I could bottle what she has I wouldn't have to ride again, I could sell it and be a rich man."

Having wiped away his previous Champion Chase disappointment, the jockey treasured the moment. "When you ride something who loves it and wants to win as much as this, it's a pleasure. It brings you back to your roots and why you wanted to get into the game, and that's for the love of the animal. You can't watch this race and the jumps she put in and her attitude from the last [and not] really appreciate what they do for us."

For De Bromhead, better still was to come in the Cheltenham Gold Cup and Grand National but Put The Kettle On played a vital part in his remarkable story. He will have appreciated what she did for him too.

HOLY TRINITY

RACING POST

KING OF THE HILL

Gold Cup victory for Minella Indo gives Henry de Bromhead stunning first ever clean sweep of the festival's big three races

PLUS Brilliant Blackmore crowned Cheltenham top jockey. page 8

Henry de Bromhead became the first trainer to win Cheltenham's big three in the same year when Minella Indo held off stablemate A Plus Tard in a famous one-two

By David Jennings

AN EMPTY grandstand but a Cheltenham Gold Cup packed full of quality. The average rating of the delicious dozen was 165 and, but for a global pandemic, there would have been some palaver at preview nights up and down the country trying to sort it all out. It was everything the Cheltenham Festival showpiece should be.

Al Boum Photo was favourite, of course he was. You don't win two Gold Cups in a row and not be the market leader for the next one. But the fact that he was as big as 9-4 told you all you need to know about the magnitude of the task he was facing in trying to emulate Arkle, Golden Miller, Cottage Rake and Best Mate.

His preparation was predictable. The traditional trip to Tramore on New Year's Day resulted in a wide-margin win at 2-9, although there was a fleeting moment when Acapella Bourgeois looked like he might have him in trouble. That soon passed and he put 19 lengths between himself and his stablemate at the line.

The two horses Al Boum Photo
▸ *Continues page 18*

MINELLA INDO

held off in the 2020 Gold Cup were back for more, but Santini was 12-1 and Lostintranslation was 40-1. It was a better race in 2021, a much better race.

Champ, who defied a high of 599-1 in running to win the previous year's RSA Chase, had been seen only once since that astonishing late surge but his jumping was electric over two miles at Newbury in the Game Spirit and Nicky Henderson was convinced he was cherry ripe for the big day.

There was the King George winner, the fabulous Frodon. The 2019 Ryanair hero was finally given his chance on the main stage. There was the 2018 winner Native River, who had turned 11 but suggested he retained a raging appetite for a battle with his triumph in the Cotswold Chase, transferred to Sandown from Cheltenham. There was the novice Royale Pagaille, who had won the Peter Marsh by 16 lengths, and Kemboy, the winner of four Grade 1s.

But the race, in keeping with the week, was all about one man – Henry de Bromhead. The Knockeen trainer thought he might have four runners at one stage, but neither the previous year's fourth Monalee nor Chris's Dream made it for one reason or another and it was left to A Plus Tard and Minella Indo to fly his flag.

He couldn't pick between the pair beforehand, saying: "I genuinely couldn't split them. A Plus Tard was really good in the Savills Chase at Christmas. There aren't many horses who can win a Grade 1 over two miles and be in the Gold Cup picture – Kauto Star would be one. Minella Indo is in mighty form and loves Cheltenham. He comes alive there and his record is brilliant. They both have good chances, I hope, but I wouldn't be able to pick between them."

Rachael Blackmore had to. She went for A Plus Tard, who had won the Savills Chase at Leopardstown on only his second try over three miles. Jack Kennedy was snapped up for the spare on Minella Indo. And so to 3.05pm on Friday, March 19.

★★★★

BY 3.06pm Champ was cooked. His challenge lasted less than a minute as a horrible jump at the first set the trend

for mistakes at the third, fifth and sixth. He was pulled up before the seventh. It was too bad to be true.

Frodon did what Frodon does. Bryony Frost bowled along merrily at the head of affairs and remained in front with three to jump. Native River tried to go in pursuit but age caught up with him. Santini and Lostintranslation were long gone by that stage.

"A Plus Tard is moving forward menacingly," commentator Simon Holt told us, but as he was picking them off one by one, stablemate Minella Indo was lobbing along on the tail of Frodon. Everything was effortless. Al Boum Photo was creeping into contention too. The hat-trick was on.

Frodon's heart got him as far as the home turn. He had given his all and the Irish challenge was just too strong. It had been a recurring theme all week. Minella Indo kicked first, with A Plus Tard in his slipstream. Al Boum Photo had to wait for daylight and, when it arrived, the acceleration wasn't instant. And then there were two.

Henry was going to win it, but the big question now was with which one? "Coming to the last I was watching Al Boum Photo and thinking he was going to come and nab both of ours. I

▲ Golden handshake: Jack Kennedy on Minella Indo (left) is congratulated by Rachael Blackmore aboard A Plus Tard; opposite page, Kennedy celebrates with Henry de Bromhead; below, the winning rider and trainer savour their success

was sure of it," De Bromhead admitted. "Then, halfway up the hill, I realised Al Boum Photo wasn't getting to them. It was an incredible thing to see the two of them battling it out. Surreal, I suppose you could say. I don't really remember what I was thinking or what I was shouting. I didn't have a preference at all. I didn't mind which one of them won."

There was always the suspicion Minella Indo would be the stronger stayer; an Albert Bartlett winner, an RSA runner-up, a five-time winner over three miles. Stamina was his strong suit. A Plus Tard tried to get by, but this was one of those rare occasions when Blackmore couldn't make a rabbit appear from her hat.

They tried, they pulled away from Al Boum Photo, but Minella Indo was not for passing. He held on gamely by a length and a quarter. There were four and a quarter lengths back to the defending champion in third and a further 24 lengths to Native River, who did best of the British in fourth.

★★★★

NOT only was it a one-two for De Bromhead, it also completed the holy trinity for the trainer. The Champion Hurdle, Champion Chase and Gold Cup had never been won by the same trainer in the same year. It had now.

Minella Indo completed the incredible feat that had been made possible by Honeysuckle and Put The Kettle On earlier in the week.

"It's massive," said De Bromhead of the feat. "I can't tell you what it means to win it – or what winning any of these races means. I feel like I'm going to wake up and it will be Monday evening." De Bromhead didn't wake up. It was real. Unbelievable, but most definitely real.

The man of the moment added: "It's incredible. I've been coming here a lot of years now and there have been plenty of tough years and tough results, but also some great ones. To do this is a credit to everyone that's working with us, everyone at home and here, and we couldn't do any of it without our clients supporting us. They give us the opportunity to buy these good horses and I just feel extremely lucky."

So, then, what of Minella Indo? Was De Bromhead in any way surprised by what he witnessed? "A Plus Tard had the Savills form and that looked the best trial. [Minella] Indo had been so good early on, but I did start to worry about the novice form from last season after the Irish Gold Cup. It was him, Allaho and Champ. Him and Allaho had raced against each other over hurdles and fences and I started to question it.

"Then, when Allaho did what he did in the Ryanair, that changed everything. Indo is just a different beast at Cheltenham too. He's so laid-back, but the morning of the race I sent Barry [Maloney, owner] a video. He was kicking his door and really psyched up. He started kicking the wall when I was saddling him. I loved it when I saw him doing that."

He must have loved seeing him winging fences too. This was the Minella Indo we had seen for 19 of the 20 fences in the previous year's RSA. In fact, it was an older, stronger and more powerful version. A staying chaser who looks like he is going to be around for quite a while.

Minella Indo did not just win the Cheltenham Gold Cup, he won the most competitive renewal in a decade and he did so in emphatic fashion. He was the best horse in the best race of the week.

'Definitely the best day of my life'

IT WAS the moment jump racing's next big thing transformed into the sport's latest star. In guiding Minella Indo to victory, Jack Kennedy became the youngest jockey to win the Cheltenham Gold Cup since 20-year-old Tim Hamey won on Koko way back in 1926.

Kennedy, whose talents were spotted by Gordon Elliott when he was a fresh-faced 16-year-old, was winning jump racing's most prestigious prize at the tender age of just 21. But, boy, had the Dingle native been through the mill to get there. He missed the 2020 festival after breaking his leg for a fourth time. Yes, you read it right, a fourth time. He had also suffered three fractured collarbones. Yes, three.

His luck turned for the Gold Cup, picking up the ride on Minella Indo when Rachael Blackmore opted for A Plus Tard out of Henry de Bromhead's pair, and he made the most of it. So it was hardly surprising to see some rare emotion from jump racing's coolest customer after winning his first Gold Cup. There are surely more to come.

"It's definitely the best day of my life," he beamed, while trying to fight back the tears at the same time. "I can't believe it's happening. I was emotional after it because it means the world to me. This is what I've dreamed of since I was a child. I'm just so grateful to Henry and Barry Maloney for giving me the opportunity to ride him. I can't thank them enough and I will owe them forever. This is what I live for. I just can't believe it.

"I thought my horse had as good a chance as any in the race. I was fairly confident going out, and the fact that Rachael picked A Plus Tard probably took some of the pressure off. He travelled and jumped great and there wasn't really any point where I wasn't happy."

Happiness is something Kennedy deserved more than most. A precocious talent who has the potential to be one of the greats. The next decade should pen a fascinating tale.

'I still think I'm going to wake up some day and realise it wasn't real'

At the end of his amazing run Henry de Bromhead took time to reflect on what he had achieved

By David Jennings

OUR annus horribilis was Henry de Bromhead's annus mirabilis. The year we want to forget is the one he wants to remember. As lockdowns lingered he was looting every big prize going and if becoming the first trainer to win the three championship races at the Cheltenham Festival in the same week wasn't enough, he only went and won the Grand National a few weeks later too. Oh, and he trained the runner-up at Aintree as well, just like he did in the Gold Cup.

This, of course, is still all very surreal to the man himself. He is a self-confessed pessimist, a glass-half-empty sort of guy, so you won't be surprised to hear he is convinced a large slice of luck was the main ingredient in his greatest campaign.

"I keep saying how lucky our season was and how lucky those few weeks, in particular, were for us," he begins. "Like in the Grand National you need so much luck and halfway around on the first circuit a horse [Double Shuffle] fell. Any Second Now was on his left-hand side and we were on his right. He fell and rolled over to his left and he almost brought down Any Second Now. He could just as easily have brought us down, or hampered us, and our race would have been lost there and then. That's how fine the margins are. That summed up the season we had. We just had luck on our side."

E.S.B. was a lucky Grand National winner, Henry; Minella Times wasn't. He was an emphatic winner of the world's most famous jumps race and put the finishing touches to an audacious plan by his trainer. A plan that involved running him over three miles only twice in his career up to that point; a plan that involved a warm-up over 2m5f at Leopardstown; a plan that saw him run only three times in more than a year. This, no matter which way you looked at it, was a terrific training performance even if the man himself won't admit it.

"Aintree was just a brilliant day,"

▸ *Continues page 22*

De Bromhead says. "I've watched Grand Nationals since I was a kid and I just feel so lucky to have actually won it. And to have Rachael [Blackmore] as well. She was brilliant. It was a super ride from start to finish, she never left the rail and got a great passage the whole way round. He winged fences for her. We're very lucky to have her."

We rewind a few weeks to Cheltenham and those heady days in the Cotswolds when everything De Bromhead and Blackmore touched turned to gold.

"We actually thought we had a similar sort of team going over the previous year," he says. "We thought we could get plenty of winners. We got two, but there were plenty of disappointments – Indo getting caught, A Plus Tard in the Ryanair. They would have been strongly fancied. So you can never get too high because that makes it easier to take the lows.

"Going over, I just wanted one [winner] and see where we go from there. They seemed in good form going over, but they were all in good form going over the previous year too. You can never expect to get anything handed to you at Cheltenham, it's so competitive, so tough. The previous year was a bit deflating, so I didn't want to get too hopeful."

When Honeysuckle is on your team you can dare to dream, though. She arrived unbeaten and departed unbeaten, this time beating the boys in the Champion Hurdle 12 months on from inflicting a shock defeat on Benie Des Dieux in the Mares' Hurdle. Was it tough to turn down a repeat and sidestep the easier option?

"We were always leaning towards the Champion Hurdle, but if she was disappointing or got beaten in the Irish Champion Hurdle we would have had to have a rethink," he explains. "But she told us at Leopardstown where she wanted to go. She made our minds up for us. That was that. Decision made. She made it very simple."

It is put to him that the performance in the Irish Champion

▶ *Continues page 24*

'Premier League versus Championship'

HENRY DE BROMHEAD was in the vanguard as Ireland dominated the Cheltenham Festival in unprecedented fashion with 23 winners to Britain's five and then had ten of the first 11 home in the Grand National, led by De Bromhead's one-two with Minella Times and Balko Des Flos.

Ireland had all but two of the Grade 1 winners and seven of the nine handicap scorers at Cheltenham, prompting much soul searching and gnashing of teeth on the home side. Dan Skelton, who finished second in the British jumps trainers' championship, called it a "drubbing" and Gold Cup-winning trainer Colin Tizzard said "we need to up our game".

Both had ideas for how to redress the balance – with Skelton saying a better programme was needed for the top-end horses and Tizzard favouring a British version of the Dublin Racing Festival – and many others said poor prize-money was at the root of the problem.

By the autumn, alongside the BHA's ongoing Quality Jumps Review, there was a change to the way British horses are handicapped to correct a perceived imbalance in ratings with Ireland, including giving older horses bigger drops after being beaten and reassessing the approach to handicapping novice hurdlers. The hope is that British handicappers will become more competitive against Irish raiders as a result.

In Ireland, meanwhile, there was simple satisfaction with their near monopoly of the spring's big events. "I think it proves beyond doubt that we simply have the best horses," said senior Irish jumps handicapper Andrew Shaw. "Back in the 1980s, when we were lucky to come out with one winner at Cheltenham, it used to be the other way around. But it has turned on its head now. It's a bit like the Premier League versus the Championship."

▼ First leg: Honeysuckle starts Henry de Bromhead's historic run with victory in the Champion Hurdle; previous page, De Bromhead with Honeysuckle (left) and Gold Cup winner Minella Indo

Hurdle was the first time she really wowed us. "I felt she had done some wows before that," he counters. "The Hatton's Grace the year before was a wow, I thought. When Willie Mullins says Benie Des Dieux is one of the best mares he's ever trained and she beats her, that's a wow. Benie Des Dieux was odds-on and the fact we could beat her was incredible. I'm not saying I expected her to go and do what she did at Leopardstown, but she definitely had wowed us before. Cheltenham is a turbulent place, though. It's all your best horses and a lot of them don't usually win."

Honeysuckle is different. She always wins. "Honey was our big one the first day, there was a lot of pressure. Fair play to Rachael, she was brilliant. She was further back than I expected her to be but I had so much confidence in them both as a team. To see her travelling as well as she was turning in was just unreal. She just needed to jump the last. For a fella who does get very wound up during races, they didn't really give me too many nervous moments."

It was more nerve-racking watching Put The Kettle On, the star mare who followed up the previous year's Arkle win with a typically tenacious triumph in the Queen Mother Champion Chase.

De Bromhead says: "She's an incredible mare, the stuff you dream about. She's so tough and Aidan [Coleman] was brilliant on her. I don't know what it is about Cheltenham that she loves. A couple of weeks before the race she just wasn't herself, but we freshened her up as much as we could. It was all down to everyone at home, but especially Andrea who looks after her and puts up with her antics every day, it's special for her. She's quite wild at home, she's a great character.

"Around mid-February I was probably leaning towards running in the Mares' Chase, but we all discussed it and I looked at the stats for the previous year's Arkle winner in the race and they're ridiculous, so we said we'd give it a lash."

The two mares had done their bit and now it was all down to Minella Indo or A Plus Tard in the Gold Cup to complete the unprecedented championship hat-trick for De

▲ History man: Henry de Bromhead with the Gold Cup trophy; inset, Champion Chase winner Put The Kettle On

Bromhead. They only went and finished first and second.

"Sure, it was just unbelievable," he says, seemingly still in mild shock that it actually happened. "Indo just comes alive when he gets to Cheltenham every year. He's an amazing horse and A Plus Tard ran an absolute cracker too. I still think I'm going to wake up some day and realise it wasn't real. It was an amazing season."

Amazing indeed. The year we will remember for all the wrong reasons will never be forgotten by De Bromhead for all the right ones. He came, he saw and he conquered all the big races. An outrageous feat that might never be repeated.

Truly historic feats

HENRY DE BROMHEAD'S achievements in the spring were truly historic, but even now he has not received the credit he deserves, *writes John Randall.*

He became the first trainer to win all three top jumps races in one season (Champion Hurdle, Gold Cup, Grand National), the first to win all three top Cheltenham Festival races in one season (Champion Hurdle, Champion Chase, Gold Cup), and only the second to have the first two in the Grand National, following Fred Withington in 1908.

Several trainers have won two of the Champion Hurdle, Gold Cup and Grand National in one season, but De Bromhead's treble with Honeysuckle, Minella Indo and Minella Times is unique.

Vincent O'Brien, perhaps the greatest jumps trainer as well as the greatest Flat trainer of all time, holds the record of ten career wins in those three races, but not even he won all three in one season. In 1953 he won the Gold Cup with Knock Hard and initiated his unique Grand National hat-trick with Early Mist, but came second in the Champion Hurdle with Galatian.

Before this year the last trainer to win two of the three was Paul Nicholls with Rock On Ruby and Neptune Collonges in 2012. Only one jockey has ever achieved that treble – Tommy Cullinan in 1930.

De Bromhead also achieved a unique Cheltenham Festival treble with Honeysuckle, Put The Kettle On and Minella Indo. Several trainers had won two of the Champion Hurdle, Champion Chase and Gold Cup in one season, including Nicholls and Nicky Henderson, but none had won all three. No jockey has ever done so.

Training the first two in the Gold Cup, as De Bromhead did with Minella Indo and A Plus Tard, is rare in itself, being surpassed only by Michael Dickinson's famous five in 1983 and Nicholls' first three – Denman, Kauto Star and Neptune Collonges – in 2008.

His feat of training the first two in the Grand National, with Minella Times and 100-1 shot Balko Des Flos, is even rarer, having been achieved before only by Withington in 1908.

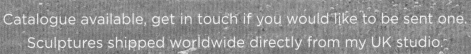

THE
BIGGER
PICTURE

Donagh Meyler gets ready before his winning
ride on Scarlet And Dove in the Grade 2
Charleville Cheese Irish EBF Mares Novice
Chase at Limerick on March 14

PATRICK McCANN (RACINGPOST.COM/PHOTOS)

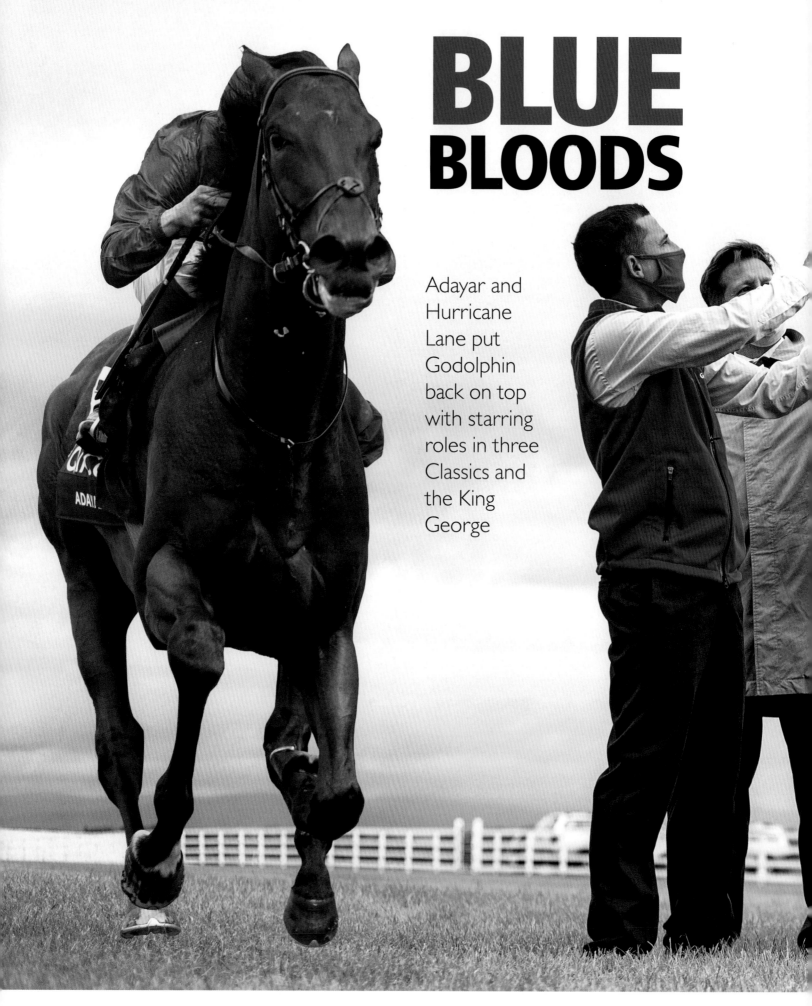

BLUE
BLOODS

Adayar and Hurricane Lane put Godolphin back on top with starring roles in three Classics and the King George

By Peter Thomas

THE world in 2021 was no place for anybody seeking restoration of their trust in the old order of things. If there was a God at work, he must have been one with either a dark sense of humour or a deep-seated desire to test our faith, as he swept away the certainties of life with one devastating sweep of a pandemic and dared us to guess what might come next.

Racing people of a certain age, mind you, may have been better prepared than most for this virus-led sea change. The past couple of decades have seen the erosion of many of the old rhythms of the turf year, to the point where it has been hard to recall which country we were in, let alone which month. It's

▶ *Continues page 30*

IMAGE COURTESY OF ITV RACING

November so it must be Cheltenham, or maybe Bahrain via Melbourne.

It was all so much simpler a while back, when a promising domestic two-year-old might emerge from any number of sources, plot its course through the Classics in Britain and Ireland, then climb selected domestic peaks in high summer before rounding off the year with an audacious tilt at the Arc, accompanied by a small army of travelling turfistes.

Since 2001, however, the princely total of zero winners of Epsom's formerly pre-eminent Derby had gone on to emulate Galileo by landing the King George VI and Queen Elizabeth Stakes in the same year. They surely can't have been put off by the glittering later career of the horse who went on to become one of the greatest stallions in history before his death in July at the satisfactory age of 23; but year by year, the winners of the blue riband either declined the challenge or accepted and failed. Where once Nijinsky, Mill Reef, Grundy, The Minstrel, Troy, Shergar, Reference Point, Nashwan, Generous and

Lammtarra lit up Ascot on the last Saturday in July, there suddenly appeared a drought of biblical proportions.

★★★★

IT WAS a conundrum to which Adayar wasn't supposed to be the answer. With a Nottingham maiden win under his belt as a two-year-old, he was subsumed beneath the traditional host of Ballydoyle contenders in the winter betting for the Derby, with his reputation hardly elevated by second places in trials at Sandown and Lingfield in the spring.

When Aidan O'Brien cherry-picked Bolshoi Ballet as his number one for Epsom – in fact his only one, which has often been seen as a sign of great confidence emanating from the yard – it's unlikely he was quaking in his boots at the prospect of meeting Adayar, who was a 50-1 shot come race morning. Hurricane Lane, Adayar's stablemate carrying the first colours of Godolphin blue, looked the danger at 6-1 second favourite.

For those whose idea of a great

▲ Winning move: Adam Kirby takes the Derby on Adayar after squeezing through on the inside in the straight (inset)

Derby is a triumph of the obvious over the forces of romance, O'Brien's six-length Derrinstown Stud Derby Trial winner was a perfect fit; but out there in the land of fairytales lurked a story to warm the cockles.

When Adam Kirby committed himself to ride John Leeper for Ed Dunlop at Epsom, there were thoughts that the horse named after the trainer's father, the late John Leeper Dunlop, might involve him in an emotional journey that would lead to poignant victory. When Kirby was jocked off John Leeper in favour of Frankie Dettori, there were many who felt he had been shabbily treated. When Charlie Appleby instantly called Kirby to offer him the ride on the horse he had broken and nurtured at his farm near Newmarket, a little faith was restored in the integrity of the game – and so began the perfect denouement to a neat racing fable.

John Leeper never threatened to be involved in the finish of the Derby; Bolshoi Ballet, sent off 11-8 favourite, finished 17 lengths seventh; but Kirby, belying his misplaced reputation as

'A first-class rider who reads a race and is a supreme judge'

ADAM KIRBY had to overcome a difficult passage through Derby week and in the big race to claim Classic glory on Adayar for Godolphin and Charlie Appleby. It all made for one of the most popular and heartwarming stories of the year.

First there was losing the ride on the Ed Dunlop-trained John Leeper to Frankie Dettori less than 72 hours before the Derby. "It can all be said now," the 32-year-old said after Adayar's triumph. "I was asked to ride John Leeper, which was an exciting moment. Five minutes later Charlie rang and asked me to ride this lad. I told him I was sorry but I had just committed myself to John Leeper. I'm a man of my word and I had put my name to him.

"Then came the day when Ed rang and said, 'I'm very sorry Adam, but you've lost John Leeper – Frankie's on him. I was angry and must have been like a pit bull when I got back to the house. I rang Charlie and he said, 'You can ride mine. I've spoken to Oisin [Murphy, who was booked for Adayar] and he's been an absolute gentleman'."

Kirby then had to play his part on only his second ride in the Derby – and it was far from easy. "I really had to stoke him up early as he's a big horse to get into gear and I was worried about that early climb, so I had to ask him for plenty. In fact, I had to burn him for a furlong and a half, but he was more than up to it," he said.

"I wasn't happy at the top of the hill and found myself following Ben Curtis [on Gear Up] and the last thing I wanted was a 50-1 chance coming back suddenly and landing in my lap. I didn't want to switch him out because it can affect heartbeat, rhythm and screw their stride pattern.

"There was just enough room up the rail. I thought I needed to get in or get out. I knew I had to make a decision, so I went in. When that little sliver opened up I didn't think twice about getting in there. Luckily the horse was brave enough to go through the gap. And God did he pick up – he really surprised me just how very, very good he was."

Some people were surprised by how good Kirby was in his Derby-winning ride, but not his fellow professionals. "Adam is a natural horseman and you can put him on any type of horse," Appleby said. "He can settle them, he can send them and when I first got my licence Adam rode winners for us from very early on. I don't need to say what he does – he's just done it."

Lambourn trainer Clive Cox has long been Kirby's biggest supporter. "Adam came to me when he was 17 and he was very special right from the start," he said. "His first ride for me was on a difficult, hard-pulling horse and as a 7lb claimer Adam got on him and did exactly the same as Pat Eddery, who used to have the best hands in the business. He's an amazing horseman with the strength of a lion – a first-class rider who reads a race and is a supreme judge."

Kirby's fellow jockeys paid their own tribute as he returned to Epsom's hallowed winner's circle. "Coming into the winner's enclosure and seeing all the boys from the weighing room coming outside to clap and congratulate me was a great feeling. Usually it happens when you retire and I don't mind admitting it touched me very much. You usually have to wait for your funeral to find out how good people thought you were but I imagine you don't really take it in then!" said Kirby, whose phone was flooded with congratulatory messages in the minutes, hours and days that followed. "There were quite a lot of them!" he said. "I'm privileged to have had so much support and people saying 'well done'."

Every single one of those messages was well deserved.

merely an 'all-weather jockey' – "run of the mill" was his own piece of self-deprecation – had Adayar in prime position throughout, tracking the leaders on the inside rail and biding his time.

He had the option to wait for matters to unfold, to put his fate in the hands of the gods, but in typically forthright and uncomplicated fashion, he sensed Gear Up drifting off the fence before the two-furlong pole, identified his opportunity and burrowed through the gap on a partner who was both willing and able to carry out instructions. The rest was simply an unchallenged march into the history books for the man in the Godolphin blue with the red cap.

Four and a half lengths was the gap back to Mojo Star, with Hurricane Lane and William Buick a further three and a quarter lengths back in third. Adayar had won and won convincingly, at starting odds of 16-1, but as with all the best Derbys of yore – yore really was a great place to live, back in the day – this was just the

▶ *Continues page 32*

ADAYAR
Owner Godolphin
Trainer Charlie Appleby
Sire Frankel
Starts 8
Wins 3
Group 1 wins Derby, King George
Earnings £1,453,832
RPR 129 (King George)

HURRICANE LANE
Owner Godolphin
Trainer Charlie Appleby
Sire Frankel
Starts 8
Wins 6
Group 1 wins Irish Derby, Grand Prix de Paris, St Leger
Earnings £1,980,001
RPR 125 (Grand Prix de Paris & Arc)

beginning of a thrilling tale with not one hero but two.

★★★★

CHARLIE APPLEBY admitted after the Derby that he'd had Adayar marked down as a St Leger horse and that only the unanswerable insistence of Sheikh Mohammed had led him to Epsom. Hurricane Lane was presumably more of a Derby horse after his win in the Dante, but racing's a funny old game.

Whatever the pecking order at Moulton Paddocks, it was something of a revelation – a game-changer as it turned out – to see Godolphin with two horses in the first three in a race that had been annexed no fewer than seven times by the might of Ballydoyle and Coolmore since their success with Galileo. Aided by Sheikh Mohammed's

refusal to buy the produce of Coolmore stallions at the sales, they had become dominant, pre-eminent, practically unstoppable, with the 2001 winner proving the linchpin of their success in his role as a sire.

Now, however, there was Frankel. Quite possibly the best racehorse ever, as his advertising slogan might have read, he was a publicly available sire with the potential to give a tectonic nudge to the bloodstock world, and here were two of his sons out to prove the point.

Hurricane Lane was a daughter of the French Listed winner Gale Force, bred by Normandie Stud and bought for 200,000gns by Sheikh Mohammed at Tattersalls in October 2019. As a Derby third he was already a triumph for the 'boys in blue', but when he went on to land the Irish

▼ Classic force: Hurricane Lane lands the Irish Derby at the Curragh

Derby and the Grand Prix de Paris (by no less than six lengths) he became part of a tremor that rumbled through the breeding world.

Registering even higher on racing's Richter scale was the homebred Adayar, out of the Dubawi mare Anna Salai, who went to Ascot for the King George to restore a sense of what should be and what always was. Reunited with Buick, he carried the torch for the Classic generation and carried it with flair and distinction, dismissing O'Brien's 13-8 favourite Love with ease and putting a length and three-quarters between himself and runner-up Mishriff (albeit in receipt of that old conversation piece, the 11lb age allowance).

It was a triumph that seemed to suggest a new order, one in which the
▶▶ *Continues page 34*

EVERY RACING MOMENT

HORSE RACING IRELAND

2021 MAJOR FESTIVALS

LEOPARDSTOWN
Dublin Racing Festival
5th – 6th February

CORK
Easter Festival
16th – 18th April

FAIRYHOUSE
Easter Festival
16th – 18th April

PUNCHESTOWN
National Hunt Festival
26th – 30th April

KILLARNEY
Spring Festival
15th – 17th May

CURRAGH
Guineas Festival
20th – 22nd May

DOWN ROYAL
Ulster Derby
17th – 18th June

CURRAGH
Irish Derby Festival
24th – 26th June

BELLEWSTOWN
Summer Festival
30th June – 2nd July

KILLARNEY
July Festival
11th – 15th July

CURRAGH
Irish Oaks Weekend
16th – 17th July

GALWAY
Summer Festival
25th – 31st July

TRAMORE
August Festival
11th – 14th August

KILLARNEY
August Festival
18th – 20th August

LEOPARDSTOWN & CURRAGH
Longines Irish Champions
Weekend 10th – 11th September

LISTOWEL
Harvest Festival
18th – 24th September

GALWAY
October Festival
29th – 31st October

DOWN ROYAL
Festival of Racing
4th – 5th November

PUNCHESTOWN
November Winter Racing
19th – 20th November

FAIRYHOUSE
Winter Festival
3rd – 4th December

LEOPARDSTOWN
Christmas Festival
26th – 29th December

LIMERICK
Christmas Festival
26th – 29th December

HRI.ie

navy blue faced a serious threat from the royal blue army that had for so long sat in its turbulent wake.

★★★★

HURRICANE LANE'S Leger win may not have possessed quite the same va-va-voom as the Derby-King George double of Adayar, but it capped a memorable and quite possibly significant season for Godolphin.

His Grand Prix de Paris romp on very soft ground had marked him down as high class and full of stamina, which made him a natural for the Doncaster Classic, and despite taking a while to unfurl his full, raking stride, he eventually wore down and pulled away from the Derby runner-up Mojo Star, prompting Appleby to suggest that, when the dust had settled and he'd had a word with the big boss, this was a horse that might well emerge as a handy second string to his Arc bow.

Adayar was top dog, undoubtedly, but he missed his trial after a setback, and by the time the first Sunday in October rolled along, with the weekend's weather proving acceptable only to ducks, it was Hurricane Lane who emerged the punters' pick of the pair, being sent off the 3-1 favourite in a competitive field.

After a few years of a decent surface for the Arc, 'terrain lourd' prevailed in France, which translates roughly as 'bring your wellies'. Although the early pace was middling, there would certainly be no hiding place for those who couldn't skate over or plough through the Parisian mud, for a full, unforgiving mile and a half – and the opposition to the Godolphin pair was none too shabby either.

There were eight Group 1 winners in the 14-strong field, from five different countries, with Chrono Genesis and Deep Bond seeking to end the lengthy Japanese drought in a race they treasure, Tarnawa, Snowfall and Broome batting for Ireland, Sealiway, Raabihah, Bubble Gift and Baby Rider offering resistance on behalf of the home team, Alenquer and Mojo Star accompanying the Godolphin pair for Britain and the 72-1 outsider Torquator Tasso carrying the German flag like a lonely one-man team at the Olympics.

The form book went out of the window, unless you believed winning the Grosser Preis von Baden the time before was good form, which with hindsight may well have been the case. Anyway, the same market that had ignored Star Appeal and Danedream in the past also overlooked this German outsider, who registered his offence in the best possible way.

Adayar made his own running in the absence of any other takers, then quickened off the final turn, into what briefly looked a decisive lead, but with 300m to go, Tarnawa and the running-on Hurricane Lane shot past him, only to both be unceremoniously dismissed by the decisive final challenger, the upstart Torquator Tasso, the charge of trainer Marcel Weiss, ridden by an ecstatic Rene Piechulek.

If ever a trio tripped off the tongue, it certainly wasn't these, but the win was as incontrovertible as it was poorly received by those who hate to see a longshot have its day in a championship race. The immediate talk was of moving the Arc to a slot a week earlier, to make an autumnal quagmire marginally less likely, but in the Godolphin camp there was less of a clamour to dismiss the result.

Appleby contented himself with the

▲ Hurricane Lane storms home in the St Leger; below, William Buick celebrates his third win in the race after Arctic Cosmos (2010) and Masked Marvel (2011)

fact that he had already bagged five Group 1s with his two sons of Frankel, and hoped against hope that at the end-of-season debrief, Sheikh Mohammed would see his way clear to declaring the three-year-old stars set fair for another year on the track.

After all of which expectant chat, it came as a minor surprise to see Adayar line up for a last hurrah of 2021 in the Champion Stakes, dropping back to ten furlongs for what represented a very different test to his brace of Group 1 wins.

When Buick unleashed him off the final turn it seemed for a moment as though the 'afterthought' might prove to be a masterstroke. It wasn't to be. As in the Arc, Adayar raced prominently, perhaps a little too boldly, and found himself ultimately vulnerable, fading rather tamely in the straight to finish fifth behind French mudlark Sealiway, who had been three-parts of a length behind him in the Arc.

It was a defeat that left questions unanswered. Was soft ground again a detrimental factor? Was ten furlongs a step too far in the wrong direction? Had a hard race in the Arc simply left its mark on his constitution?

Appleby had already said he would be a force to be reckoned with on better going and spoke warmly also of Hurricane Lane, who looks set to go wherever his emerging stamina will be seen to best advantage.

The pair, described lovingly as "big old units" by Appleby as he ruled them out of the sharper test of the Breeders' Cup, have already dragged Godolphin, and an expectant racing public, into what may be a new era of competition with their fiercest rivals, and that's a prospect to relish.

What we saw this year was a return to classic British racing values. Next year may bring more and more of the same.

Double winners

ADAYAR was the 14th Derby winner to go on to King George VI and Queen Elizabeth Stakes success in the same year, becoming the first in 20 years to join the illustrious list.

1952 **Tulyar** 1953 **Pinza** 1970 **Nijinsky** 1971 **Mill Reef**
1975 **Grundy** 1977 **The Minstrel** 1979 **Troy** 1981 **Shergar**
1987 **Reference Point** 1989 **Nashwan** 1991 **Generous**
1995 **Lammtarra** 2001 **Galileo** 2021 **Adayar**

IN THE PICTURE

Superstar stallion and Derby winner Galileo dies at 23

GALILEO, the sire of sires who won the 2001 Derby during a glorious Classic campaign and was hailed by Aidan O'Brien as "a thoroughbred we will never see the like of again", died in July at the age of 23. He was euthanised on humane grounds due to a "chronic, non-responsive, debilitating injury to the near-fore foot".

The 12-time champion sire is the most prolific source of Group 1 winners in history, numbering 91 at the time of his death with three full crops still to come. His covering fee at Coolmore Stud in County Tipperary had been listed as 'private' since 2008 but was believed to be in excess of €500,000. The best of his offspring was the mighty Frankel, the best racehorse in modern-day rankings with an unbeaten 14-race career that spanned three seasons and featured ten Group 1 victories, including a jaw-dropping display in the 2,000 Guineas and wide-margin wins in the Queen Anne Stakes and Juddmonte International.

John Magnier, owner of Coolmore and many of Galileo's finest sons and daughters, said: "We all feel incredibly fortunate to have had Galileo here at Coolmore. He was always a very special horse to us and was the first Derby winner we had at Ballydoyle in the post-Vincent O'Brien era. The effect he is having on the breed through his sons and daughters will be a lasting legacy and his phenomenal success really is unprecedented."

A son of the multiple champion sire Sadler's Wells out of the 1993 Arc winner Urban Sea, Galileo was a racehorse of the highest calibre with wins in the Derby, Irish Derby and King George in 2001, before finishing second to Fantastic Light in one of the most memorable runnings of the Irish Champion Stakes.

However, his achievements on the track were outshone by his career as a stallion, which saw him overhaul every record set by Sadler's Wells to become even more dominant than his father. He has sired a record five Derby winners, with New Approach, Australia, Ruler Of The World, Anthony Van Dyck and Serpentine emulating their sire, and other notable offspring include Nathaniel, Waldgeist, Found, Love, Magical, Highland Reel, Teofilo and Minding. At the time of his death 20 of his sons at stud had produced Group 1 winners, ensuring a lasting legacy, and in 2021 Frankel had Derby winner Adayar and Irish Derby winner Hurricane Lane.

O'Brien, who trained Galileo as well as many of his best offspring, said: "He was our first Derby winner and who could ever have imagined what was going to happen after that. The legacy he's left is just incredible."

Picture: PATRICK McCANN (RACINGPOST.COM/PHOTOS)

FAB FOUR

By Steve Dennis

TO bring criticism to bear on the remarkable training career of Aidan O'Brien is a little like pointing out a loose tile on the Taj Mahal, or grumbling about the frame surrounding The Night Watch. It can be done, of course, but to what purpose? It is the whole, not the particular, that really matters.

O'Brien has won the lot, has time to win a lot more of the lot, but the one omission on his resume is an all-time great, a universal champion in the mould of a Frankel, a Sea The Stars, a Dancing Brave, a Nijinsky. He has trained so many top-class horses but never yet one whose deeds will live on as part of the collective memory. His best horse ever, if Racing Post Ratings are taken as a guide, is Hawk Wing, whose stature rests on

▶ *Continues page 40*

St Mark's Basilica flashed through the year to win two French Classics, the Eclipse and Irish Champion Stakes before being retired to stud

his 11-length demolition of the 2003 Lockinge Stakes, for which he was allotted a Racing Post Rating of 134, a one-off performance 7lb higher than his previous best. And no-one sings songs about Hawk Wing.

Every year the capacity for wonder is there, every year there is the potential of unearthing from the golden treasury at Ballydoyle that elusive 24-carat nonpareil, the horse of O'Brien's lifetime. It says something about the scale of the task that his 2021 superstar, the brilliant, exhilarating St Mark's Basilica, champion European two-year-old, dual Classic winner, five-time Group 1 winner, was not the answer to the quest.

That is not to muddy the lustre of St Mark's Basilica, who flashed through the year like a bright bay arrow, hitting the bullseye every time. Indeed, the son of Siyouni offered O'Brien the opportunity to try something unusual, something inventive, and it worked like a charm.

Most often, O'Brien runs his best

non-Derby horse in the 2,000 Guineas, as he did with St Mark's Basilica's half-brother Magna Grecia. This year was different. There were three horses from Ballydoyle at Newmarket in May – Battleground, Wembley and Van Gogh – but they performed like second-division types and between them didn't win a race all season. This year the best horse was somewhere else.

St Mark's Basilica is a French-bred, and that may have been one of the persuasions that led O'Brien to send him to Longchamp for the Poule d'Essai des Poulains, although he had been earmarked for a cross-Channel trip on Arc weekend 2020 only to be denied through an episode of feed contamination, and springtime in Paris was no more than a continuation of that policy, a necessary separation of the perceived powers at the yard.

Just as pertinently, there are hefty prize-money premiums for French-breds winning French races, and although the Coolmore crew is not short of dough, they didn't get where

▲ Three steps to heaven: St Mark's Basilica produces his best performance in the Eclipse at Sandown, beating Addeybb and Mishriff; previous page, his winning career finale in the Irish Champion Stakes

▼ The front pages of the Racing Post following two of St Mark's Basilica's Group 1 victories

they are today by passing up opportunities like that. St Mark's Basilica justified their hopes and plans with a scintillating success, finishing off his race with a dazzling turn of foot to win by a length and three-quarters.

"He has that acceleration you only see with the cracks," said jockey Ioritz Mendizabal, entrusted with the ride when pandemic travel regulations meant shopping local for jockeys was required. "When you're sitting on a Formula 1 car like him 250 metres from the winning post in a Classic it's a great feeling."

★★★★

VA-VA-VOOM, n'est ce-pas? Mendizabal was behind the wheel next time too in the Prix du Jockey Club, when he put his foot down a little earlier and St Mark's Basilica strode clear of his field, dominant beyond the winning margin of a length and three-quarters on a sunny day at Chantilly. Now there was no question which was the best colt at

'Against just three rivals, a shortfall partly explained by the sheer quality on offer, St Mark's Basilica produced the performance of his life'

Ballydoyle, and in victory St Mark's Basilica had given O'Brien his first success in the French Derby, a landmark as notable as the Venetian church that provides the colt's name.

There are so few of the world's major races that do not have O'Brien's name written against them – on turf only the Melbourne Cup and the Japan Cup now come to mind – and his absence from the Jockey Club roll of honour had seemed perverse. O'Brien had won the Eclipse Stakes at Sandown five times, including with the aforementioned Hawk Wing, and that was the next objective for St Mark's Basilica.

Against just three rivals, a disconcertingly low turnout for one of Britain's great races, a shortfall partly explained by the sheer quality on offer, St Mark's Basilica produced the performance of his life. The race was run at a dawdle, always a pitfall in a small field, but off that leisurely gallop he quickened so dramatically that the seasoned stars Addeybb and Mishriff were made to look slow. He cleared

away up the hill to win by three and a half lengths, the abruptness of his dominance its most striking aspect.

It was a little like Frankel, a little like Sea The Stars, a bit like Dancing Brave, yet not quite, and elevation to the pantheon of those paragons was neither anticipated nor forthcoming, with an RPR of 128 indicating that here was a very good colt but not a great one.

"I can't remember that we've had one like this," said O'Brien, anxious for the nuances of his colt's brilliance to be understood. "We've had horses get into battles and fight and brawl it out but he's very happy to follow horses and quicken. He puts races to bed very quickly - that's what he did again today and he's just a bit different."

★★★★

O'BRIEN'S words were worth remembering. Like all star pupils, St Mark's Basilica had the summer off, missing the Juddmonte International after sustaining a minor injury to his

▶ *Continues page 42*

Far and wide

THERE is an old saw that goes along the lines that if a trainer thinks he has more than one Derby horse, he probably doesn't have any. This, like many received 'wisdoms', doesn't apply to Aidan O'Brien.

Some years he runs six in the race and has the winner. This year he ran just one and didn't, Bolshoi Ballet finishing seventh behind Adayar. O'Brien wins the Derby so often – eight times, a record – that when he doesn't it colours the season indiscriminately and leaves a misleading impression of a poor campaign.

O'Brien nevertheless enjoyed a hugely successful season, and although he wasn't going to beat his own world record of 28 Group 1 wins in a calendar year, set during 2017 and arguably his greatest achievement, in this regard he still far outstripped the Derby-winning empire overseen by Charlie Appleby.

St Mark's Basilica aside, the master of Ballydoyle won Classics in 2021 with Snowfall, Mother Earth, Empress Josephine and Joan Of Arc. He raided Grade 1s in the US with the ill-fated Santa Barbara and the aforementioned Bolshoi Ballet, landed marquee events with Broome (Grand Prix de Saint-Cloud) and Love (Prince of Wales's Stakes), and struck a blow with the younger generation through the blisteringly fast Tenebrism.

Most of this glory came from the distaff side of the stable, another reason why the achievements of St Mark's Basilica are so important, so prized in the wider scheme of Ballydoyle and Coolmore. Even in a year when many of his colts and older horses – notably Japan and Mogul – failed to impress, when his two-year-olds were slow in showing their customary sparkle, O'Brien delivered big-race success after big-race success, business as usual.

near-hind leg on the gallops, before returning to business in early September in the Irish Champion Stakes at Leopardstown, a contest renowned over the years for producing the sort of races old men tell their grandchildren about. Prick up your ears, here's another.

In another star-strewn four-runner field, off another languid saunter that turned into a sprint, St Mark's Basilica proved he had the stomach for a fight. Not only did he have the speed to whistle past crack miler Poetic Flare, he also had the grit to turn back the sustained challenge of mile-and-a-half star Tarnawa, although the angle of his charge to the line did carry that filly off a straight course sufficiently for the stewards to examine the matter. Tarnawa was beaten only three-quarters of a length, and her trainer Dermot Weld muttered darkly about winning jockey Ryan Moore "edging his horse over, knowing exactly what he was doing". The stewards left it alone, but perhaps the horse was feeling that recent injury under the stress of race conditions and hanging away from the discomfort.

This performance was rated 2lb shy of St Mark's Basilica's tour de force at Sandown, but away from the dry diligence of the numbers the magnitude of the colt's achievements came into focus. O'Brien's secondary role as a trainer – or his primary role, depending on which end of the telescope you're looking through – is to make stallions to stand at Coolmore. That ravenous empire demands at least one a year, one superstar to sow the seeds of a new dynasty, and thus far O'Brien's supply of embryo embryo-makers would make a perpetual motion machine look inefficient by comparison. We heard which way the wind was blowing in the winner's enclosure at Leopardstown.

"He's a wonderful horse, we're so lucky to have him, and it's to keep him safe now and have him to go off to stud, which is going to be very exciting for us all," said the trainer, adroitly walking the ancient line that divides the feuding territories of breed to race, race to breed, uncannily clairvoyant of the statement that would come two weeks later when St Mark's Basilica was retired.

▼ Aidan O'Brien with St Mark's Basilica in the winner's enclosure after the Irish Champion

At a moment in time when the great Galileo pipeline has ceased to provide, Coolmore needs to find the next daddy of them all. There are of course several stalwarts in situ, but St Mark's Basilica represents something different, speed on the top line of the pedigree from Siyouni and the old Galileo magic underneath. Five Group 1s including the Dewhurst as a two-year-old, two Classics, three top-level victories at the stallion-making distance of a mile and a quarter, speed and guts and class and brilliance . . . St Mark's Basilica has the lot.

O'Brien does not yet have the lot, because for all St Mark's Basilica's many attributes, he was not a legend in his own lifetime like the horses mentioned in the second paragraph. But he was a very good horse. And O'Brien has plenty of time to find a better one.

Classic collection

Aidan O'Brien won half of the major European Classics he contested in 2021, five of them with fillies. St Mark's Basilica was his only successful colt.

Race	Best runner	Position
1,000 Guineas	Mother Earth	**WON**
2,000 Guineas	Van Gogh	8th
Derby	Bolshoi Ballet	7th
Oaks	Snowfall	**WON**
St Leger	The Mediterranean	3rd
Irish 1,000 Guineas	Empress Josephine	**WON**
Irish 2,000 Guineas	Van Gogh	3rd
Irish Derby	Wordsworth	3rd
Irish Oaks	Snowfall	**WON**
Irish St Leger	King Of The Castle	4th
French 1,000 Guineas	Mother Earth	2nd
French 2,000 Guineas	St Mark's Basilica	**WON**
French Derby	St Mark's Basilica	**WON**
French Oaks	Joan Of Arc	**WON**

The list shows the best finishing position achieved in each race by O'Brien's runners

South Africa's
leading auction house

BloodStock
· SOUTH AFRICA ·

Leading by
innovation & service

2022 SALES CALENDER

Cape Yearling Sale
Kenilworth Racecourse, Cape Town, South Africa
27th February 2022

National Yearling Sale
TBA complex, Johannesburg, South Africa
28th & 29th April 2022

KZN Yearling Sale
Suncoast, Durban, South Africa
30th June & 1st July 2022

August 2YO Sale
TBA complex, Johannesburg, South Africa
26th & 27th August 2022

November 2YO Sale
TBA complex, Johannesburg, South Africa
27th November 2022

RAINBOW BRIDGE *5x Gr1 winner*
(Ideal World (USA) ex Halfway To Heaven by Jet Master)
2016 National Yearling Sale graduate
& 2021 Equus Champion Horse Of The Year

www.bsa.co.za

MONEY SPINNER

Mishriff proved his worth with valuable successes, both financial and reputational, from Saudi Arabia in February to York in August

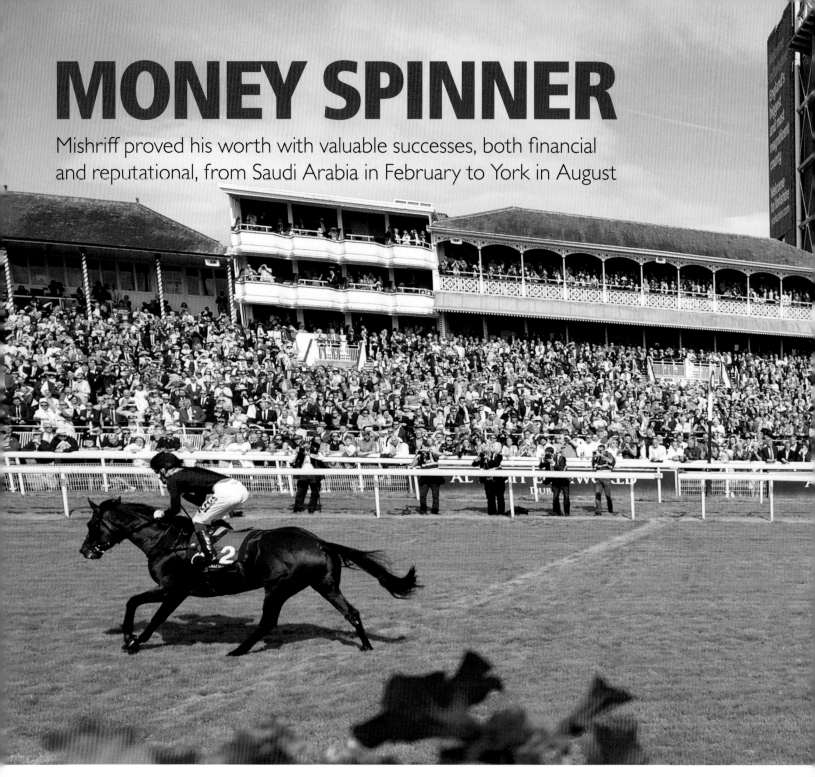

By Steve Dennis

VERSATILITY is a highly prized commodity in the world of horse racing, although hand in hand with that goes the phrase 'Jack of all trades', with its pejorative sub-clause.

Sometimes the yearning for versatility is commercially driven, as when stallion masters contrive to wring a ten-furlong race out of their mile-and-a-half champion, to show he has speed to pass on to his offspring. That's

understandable; money makes the world go round.

But sometimes the impulse seems driven more out of boredom, the passive armchair urge for change, for example the doomed movement to see Altior turned into a three-mile chaser or – as touched upon elsewhere in the Annual – Palace Pier into a mile-and-a-quarter horse.

We want it all and we want it now. And in 2021, we got it from Mishriff. Mishriff is the horse who can do almost

anything. This year the four-year-old son of Make Believe won major races in three different countries, at three different distances, on two different surfaces, in the process setting a new earnings record for a British-trained horse and becoming the world's best older horse. Truly, Mishriff has it all.

He is a very modern horse, the epitome of progress. Where Frankel, say, was campaigned upon lines that barely differed from those of Brigadier Gerard 40 years earlier, Mishriff has torn up the

rule book and rewritten it as he went, expanding the parameters of possibility. Innovation has been his friend, as there was no $20 million Saudi Cup when Frankel strode the earth, but Mishriff – named, like Frankel, in memory of a fine trainer – nevertheless seized his opportunities as few have done before.

The Saudi Cup, run on dirt over nine furlongs in Riyadh in February, is the world's richest race and from 2022 will hold Group 1 status. The trip, the surface and the timing are all designed to lure the

▼ World class: Mishriff hits his peak with a six-length win in the Juddmonte International

best horses from America, but Mishriff struck a resounding blow for the Old World when producing the best performance of his life up to that point, skipping over the unfamiliar dirt surface on his way to an authoritative one-length victory and a winner's purse of £7.3 million.

Money and prestige do not always go together, though. The Saudi Cup has been run only twice and has not had time to build up the depth of renown afforded to many of the world's other great races. Seven million nicker goes a

long way towards assuaging the race's current novelty status, mind, and Mishriff's success – as opposed to a local winner, or even a US-trained winner – will have gone a long way towards metaphorically putting it on the map.

★★★★

NEXT in the colt's I-Spy book of the world's biggest races – the Prix du Jockey Club was ticked off the year before – was the Dubai Sheema Classic at Meydan in March, worth 'only' £2.2m to the

winner but blessed with a far greater freight of prestige. Back on familiar turf, but stepping up three furlongs to a distance he had never yet tried, Mishriff demonstrated that everything came as one to him with a tenacious display lit from within by staying power hitherto only guessed at.

Brought very wide on the turn by young jockey David Egan, whose career Mishriff has done so much to promote, he came with a sustained run to lead inside the final furlong and turn back the persistent challenge of the star

Japanese mare Chrono Genesis by a neck.

"Full marks to the horse, to be able to do that under two very different codes," said trainer John Gosden, recognising the ability and adaptability that have come naturally to Mishriff, who then proceeded to do what any seasoned traveller would do after two remarkably successful excursions abroad – he went home and put his feet up.

At that moment, despite having almost £10m in his bank account,

▶ *Continues page 46*

▼ Warming down: Mishriff at Clarehaven Stables after exercising up Warren Hill

Mishriff was not particularly well known in Britain, where his finest hour had come when winning a little Listed race at Newmarket in June 2020. Since then he had won twice in France and in Saudi Arabia and Dubai, but the most recent impression he had left on British racegoers was when finishing out with the washing in the Champion Stakes at Ascot.

★★★★

TO the cognoscenti, Mishriff was magnificent. To the local, parochial racegoer, he was a vaguely exotic obscurity. In a global society, we are still most preoccupied with what happens on our own doorstep. But Mishriff would soon knock, and we would let him in.

That didn't happen on his reappearance in the Eclipse Stakes at Sandown, where he was compromised by a lack of peak fitness, undone by a dawdling gallop, skewered by the savage turn of foot displayed by St Mark's Basilica. He finished third of four, his versatility not stretching to

the ability to make other horses set a faster pace.

Gosden – now joined as licence-holder by son Thady – entertained the idea of dropping him in class, considered a Group 2 affair at York, but decided instead, with the sense of adventure that had characterised his previous treatment of Mishriff, to send him for the King George at Ascot over the mile and a half at which he was less experienced, in a hot contest in which he was fourth favourite in a field of five. As omens they were not propitious, but this was the horse who could do almost anything.

Almost. In conceding the Derby winner Adayar 11lb and running him to a length and three-quarters, Mishriff finished second but emerged the best horse in the race. It was a superlative performance, the best run of his life, and one that brought his great strength into the light. Nine furlongs on dirt in Riyadh, ten furlongs in the mud at Deauville, a mile and a half on fast turf at

▶▶ *Continues page 48*

Money, money, money

Prize-money records, like track records, are not a reliable indicator of the ability of the horses who set them, but they do provide an excellent prism through which to observe the changing face of the sport. In winning the Saudi Cup and earning £7.3 million for 110 seconds' worth of distance run, more than £66,300 per second, Mishriff made a mockery of all the European prize-money records ever set.

Where horses such as Highland Reel and Cirrus Des Aigles accumulated their bankrolls through long perseverance, step by step up a financial Everest, Mishriff did it in one giant leap for horse-kind, taking a helicopter to the summit.

At the beginning of the 20th century, the earnings record for a horse trained in Britain and Ireland was held by Isinglass, winner of the 1893 Triple Crown, who banked £58,655 during his 12-race career. Mishriff knocked that off in less than a second, a stride or two.

Isinglass was overtaken in 1952 by Tulyar, who was in turn outearned by Ballymoss, who was surpassed by Ragusa, until soon the record was held by Brigadier Gerard, who earned £253,000 during his incomparable career.

From then on, the increasing value of the world's top races made comparison both difficult and redundant. Troy earned more than £300,000 in one season (1979), and the inauguration in the early 1980s of the Arlington Million, the Japan Cup and the Breeders' Cup meant that all bets were off.

At time of writing, and using the Racing Post's database for clarity in a minefield of foreign currency and exchange rates, the biggest earner of all time is the magnificent Australian mare Winx, with a bankroll of £14,564,743. Sooner rather than later, this record too will be broken.

▼ Mishriff and David Egan win the Saudi Cup

Ascot – Mishriff was the horse for all seasons.

★★★★

FOR his next trick, he reinforced that impression in the most lapidary fashion. The Juddmonte International at York is truly one of the world's greatest races in a way that the Saudi Cup and Sheema Classic are not. Victory on the Knavesmire, in a race the aforementioned Brigadier Gerard didn't win but the likes of Frankel, Sea The Stars, Dahlia and Sakhee did, confers immense prestige on a horse, the sort of respect that neither the Arab petro-dollars nor the half-million of Yorkshire prize-money can buy.

Here was his first domestic Group 1, Mishriff scorching off the green, green grass of home in the manner of a true champion, turning the final quarter-mile of the race into a procession, a parade, the perfect illustration of his all-embracing brilliance. He won eased down by six lengths, and his stature was sealed in a Racing Post Rating of 128 that confirmed him the best older horse in the world. This win mattered more, much more than the others.

"I'm so thrilled for the horse to be able to do it on British soil," Egan said. "He's proved he can do it elsewhere and some people had doubts whether he could do it here. To do what he has done is phenomenal."

The cash rewards for Mishriff's York tour de force took his career earnings past those of his illustrious former stablemate Enable, past the £11 million mark, a record for a horse trained in Europe. Dual Dubai World Cup winner Thunder Snow, trained by Saeed bin Suroor, banked more, but was trained in the UAE for a substantial part of each year.

What came next did not overlay what came before. On Champions Day at Ascot, the stage for his worst performance of 2020, Mishriff ran his most lacklustre race of 2021 in the Champion Stakes. Not helped by morning rain that turned the ground gluey, he lacked the scintillating zip of Meydan and York and finished a weary fourth behind the surprise French-trained winner Sealiway. He did at least gain revenge on the well-beaten Adayar, added a few thousand to his bank account, but it was disappointing, although it is not what we'll remember him for.

As a snapshot of the capabilities of a horse, Mishriff's four-year-old season is unparalleled. The ability has to come first, of course, for without that there is no opportunity to showcase the versatility, but even the most brilliant of horses may not possess the aptitude for the multi-faceted that has been demonstrated so generously by Mishriff. There he is, the horse who can do almost anything, this Jack of all trades, master of all he surveys.

Sealiway strikes Champion blow

"THE Arc did him the world of good." Not many have been able to say that on Champions Day at Ascot, but Sealiway's trainer Cedric Rossi did after the mud-loving star of his Marseille stable ground out victory in the showpiece race.

On a soggy surface where Adayar and Snowfall failed to sparkle after their Arc efforts 13 days earlier, Sealiway stepped forward from his Longchamp fifth to take the Champion Stakes by a hard-fought three-quarters of a length from Dubai Honour. Adayar, fourth in the Arc, was fifth here, just over an hour after Snowfall had followed her Arc sixth with third place at odds-on in the Fillies & Mares Stakes.

Sealiway, though, had followed the classic French route of resting through the summer after his second to St Mark's Basilica in the Prix du Jockey Club in June and he was ready for the autumn. After a career-best run in the Arc, he improved again at Ascot to take his second Group 1 victory, having won the Prix Jean-Luc Lagardere on heavy ground as a two-year-old.

He had been trained then by Rossi's uncle, Frederic, before switching stables over the summer. "He's only been in my yard for three and a half months," his new trainer said. "The Arc did him the world of good and he was ready for this. He recovered really well from Longchamp and we came here with the thought of winning it."

That confidence infused Mickael Barzalona's riding as he took on Adayar early in the straight and, once in front, repelled the challenges of first Mishriff and then Dubai Honour.

"The team were very confident and they were saying he'd improved a lot from the Arc," Barzalona said. "He showed stamina in the Arc but speed today and I just think he's a good horse. It was a tough race but he did it well. When I felt the other horse [Dubai Honour] coming beside me and he didn't pass me straight away, I thought it would be hard for him to get past me."

So soon after a testing Arc, it was a mighty effort.

IN THE PICTURE

'He was a natural' – Brigadier Gerard's rider Joe Mercer dies

JOE MERCER, the legendary rider who was crowned champion Flat jockey in 1979 and partnered Brigadier Gerard throughout his career, died in May aged 86. Mercer was also memorably involved in the epic 1975 King George VI and Queen Elizabeth Stakes, finishing runner-up on Bustino in his duel with Grundy that became known as the 'Race of the Century'.

Mercer, who recorded his first success in 1950, rode 2,810 winners in 36 seasons, which ranks him among the top ten most prolific winning jockeys of all time in Britain, and was stable jockey in turn to Dick Hern and Henry Cecil. Champion apprentice in 1953, he had to wait almost 30 years more to become champion for the only time in 1979. At 45, he remains the oldest jockey ever to win the title for the first time.

Easily the best horse Mercer ever rode, Brigadier Gerard landed a dazzling series of victories as a three- and four-year-old. He beat Mill Reef in the 1971 2,000 Guineas and also won the Queen Elizabeth II and Champion Stakes twice each, as well as the Eclipse and King George. Roberto (at York) was the only horse to beat him in 18 races.

Mercer also won two Classics on the Queen's Highclere and his other stars included Song, Sallust and Kris, exceptional stayers Buckskin and Le Moss, and King George-winning filly Time Charter. He was 18 when he won the first of his eight British Classics on Ambiguity in the 1953 Oaks and the last came on Cut Above in the 1981 St Leger. Mercer, who was made an OBE in 1980 for his services to racing, won on the final ride of his career in 1985, taking the November Handicap at Doncaster on Bold Rex.

After retiring from the saddle, Mercer spent 19 years as racing manager to Maktoum Al Maktoum's Gainsborough Stud and guided the careers of Zilzal and Kris Kin.

Bruce Raymond, Mercer's great friend and contemporary, was among those to pay tribute. "He was not only a great jockey but an even nicer man," he said. "He was always very punctual all the way through his life and when he was riding he was the first to put his cap on, first to leave the weighing room, first into the gate and often first home."

Jimmy Lindley, who rode alongside Mercer and later became a BBC racing pundit, said: "He had a wonderful life and was a man with a lot of talent. He was a natural and did everything correct on a horse. All through his life he was a great ambassador for the game."

Picture: EDWARD WHITAKER (RACINGPOST.COM/PHOTOS)

Palace Pier filled up his CV with top honours over a mile
at Royal Ascot, Deauville and Newbury before signing off

MR RELIABLE

By Steve Dennis

IF HE were human, working in an office somewhere, Palace Pier would win employee of the month every month, though half the workforce wouldn't know who he was.

He'd be whispered about at the watercooler, stared at in the canteen, where he would sit peacefully eating the same lunch as he'd eaten the day before and the same as he would eat the following day, idly discussed by the smokers outside the main entrance. Yet he would be oblivious to this and would simply go unhurriedly, unworriedly about his work in his habitually efficient, hugely competent and thoroughly unspectacular fashion. His bosses would love him, although the woman at the next desk would find him almost impossible to describe to her friends.

Palace Pier. One of the best horses in the world. Praised by rider Frankie Dettori with the words "he's the best miler I've ridden", praise salted with the knowledge of past glories such as Mark Of Esteem, Dubai Millennium and Barathea. Crowned champion three-year-old colt at the 2020 Cartier Awards, rated that year's best three-year-old in Europe by the International Federation of Horseracing Authorities. Palace Pier eats his lunch, while new employees are told of his immaculate brilliance, encouraged to emulate him, before struggling to recall his name an hour later.

In 2020 Palace Pier won easily on his seasonal reappearance, then won Group 1s at Royal Ascot and Deauville. This year Palace Pier won easily on his seasonal reappearance, then won Group 1s at Royal Ascot and Deauville, this time putting in a little overtime with victory in a Group 1 at Newbury. Give him a job and he'll do it at 100 per cent, even when joint-trainer John Gosden admits he's only at 80 per cent, as when winning his second Prix Jacques le Marois in August.

His record shows only two defeats in 11 starts, both defeats coming in the Queen Elizabeth II Stakes at Ascot, first when losing a shoe, then when narrowly thwarted in a slowly run race. In defeat he can be forgiven, in victory he was applauded but rarely lauded, the least starry superstar in the game.

Perhaps this is because he has always laboured in the shadow of more glamorous stablemates. While he was working his way to the top, all the headlines and all the gossip belonged to Enable and Stradivarius. This year Mishriff muscled into centre stage, he and the old 'Cups King' sharing the spotlight. Palace Pier shrugged, got on with the job, not bothered that there are no posters of him on the nation's bedroom walls.

Perhaps it's because the miling division has lost some of the dazzle it had in Frankel's era, when there was a 'duel on the Downs' every year, with the ten-furlong brigade now hogging all the glitter. Perhaps we're too obsessed by flash and finesse and not equally charmed by efficiency and excellence. To paraphrase the old heartbreaker: look, it's not you, it's us. How can it be anything else? Look at the facts.

Palace Pier, a good-looking son of Kingman – see, even his old man was more appreciated by the masses – began his 2021 campaign in the Group 2 bet365 Mile at Sandown in April, a race that was Group 2 in name only, a four-runner Listed race in effect, and even though Gosden admitted that the colt was only at 80 per cent for his reappearance, as anyone might expect, he could have got it done at 25 per cent, with one hoof tied behind his back, possibly two.

He brushed aside Bless Him
▶ *Continues page 54*

PALACE PIER

with the insouciance of a peer marching past a panhandler, eight lengths, the perfect warm-up for the major tests to come.

That walk in the Sandown Park whetted an edge on Palace Pier for the Lockinge Stakes at Newbury the following month, not one of the year's blockbuster Group 1s, an important race but one that any champion should expect to win. Palace Pier won it easily, like a champion, posting his joint-top Racing Post Rating of 127 in so doing, yet again we contrived to be mealy-mouthed about it.

Much of the aftermath centred upon the runner-up Lady Bowthorpe, who possesses a much more accessible backstory, the sort of smalltown boy/girl saga upon which racing unfailingly seizes. This time, though, it was more a case of taking the eye off the ball, looking around the subject rather than at it.

Because Palace Pier was expected to win, there was less of a feeling of 'wow', an easy length and a half, Frankie looking from side to side like a five-year-old crossing the road, those in behind working hard while Palace Pier was hardly working, and more of a feeling of 'okay', even in the face of that 127 rating.

Dettori described him as a "really good horse who went 'whoosh' and just took off", but then everyone turned the conversation to whether Palace Pier should step up to a mile and a quarter, which is something that racing folk are prone to do, again looking around the subject rather than at it.

Sometimes it seems that we'd clamour for Sir Donald Bradman to be given a bowl, plead for Lionel Messi to be allowed to play at centre-back, argue that Helen of Troy could have made a bit more effort. We're just a bunch of Oliver Twists, an unappreciative lot, never bloody satisfied.

★★★★

PALACE PIER stayed at a mile, won the Group 1 Queen Anne Stakes at Royal Ascot, a champion winning a championship race. Yet he lost top billing on the day to the admittedly brilliant performance of St James's Palace Stakes winner Poetic Flare. And even the Devil's advocate might

suggest that vanquishing Bless Him at Sandown, Lady Bowthorpe and Top Rank at Newbury, and Lope Y Fernandez and Sir Busker at Royal Ascot is hardly on a par with smacking down Mill Reef and My Swallow on the Rowley Mile (ask your dad, or possibly his dad). Gosden, that wise old head, looked squarely at the subject.

"He's exactly like his father [Kingman], as soon as he gets there he's done enough, and if I worked him at home with a very ordinary horse he would just stay with him – that's his game," Gosden said.

The Queen Anne was Palace Pier's fourth Group 1 victory, and none of them had come by more than the length and a half at Royal Ascot. Palace Pier gets the job done, and would no more garnish the outcome than his human equivalent would tie up his report with a red ribbon and deliver it with a blueberry muffin and a saucy wink. You wanted it done, didn't you? There you are then. Let's hear no more about it.

A blood disorder kept Palace Pier

▲ Pier shows: Frankie Dettori celebrates Lockinge victory on Palace Pier; previous page, an easy start to the season at Sandown and (inset) Royal Ascot success in the Queen Anne Stakes
▼ The front page of the Racing Post the day after the Lockinge

out of the Sussex Stakes at Glorious Goodwood, won in his absence by the filly Alcohol Free, and thus the road similarly travelled led to Deauville in August, where the twin attractions of Palace Pier's bid to retain his Jacques le Marois crown and his clash with the aforementioned Poetic Flare, as hard and as brilliant as a diamond and the pro tem leader of the three-year-old mile division, was a compelling prospect.

Not, though, as compelling as the race itself, which evolved into the type of titanic struggle that pushes the observer first to the edge of the seat and thence to a standing position, eyes fixed upon the spectacle unfolding. Palace Pier was driven hard to hit the front inside the final furlong, but Poetic Flare wouldn't let it lie. The Irish colt fought hard to narrow the advantage and was doing so all the way to the line, but if Palace Pier thought he'd done enough, as usual, he was right, holding on with perhaps a degree of nonchalance to score by a neck.

▶ *Continues page 56*

BRONCHIX PULMO

> **FOR PULMONARY SUPPORT AND ELASTICITY**

Richard Hughes; "I have used Bronchix Pulmo syrup and Bronchix Pulmo syringes on two individual horses who have unfortunately been categorised as "bleeders". The product is simple and easy to use and we have had great success with it. We now would not do without it."

PALACE PIER

This is where Dettori christened him the best miler he'd ridden, where Gosden confessed that Palace Pier had only just made the parade after his recovery from illness. "I've run a horse who is only on 80 per cent, he's come here on the complete minimum of work," he said. "His class got us through but full marks to him."

That's what the bosses say. They love him. He gets it done. The ratings boys sniffed, praised his victory faintly with a mark of 122, pointed at the flaws of the horses in fourth and fifth. Others saw the victory merely in the light of the merits of the up-and-coming unbeaten Baaeed, and made a moue at Palace Pier's latest narrowly gained, efficiently achieved tour de force.

★★★★

PERHAPS that was prescience in action. The big end-of-year showdown came in the Queen Elizabeth II Stakes at Ascot on Champions Day, Palace Pier v Baaeed, the first two in the betting and the rest nowhere. Palace Pier was favourite, but there was a frisson of change in the autumn air, as though Palace Pier had glanced across the office and seen the new recruit at work and known – as we will all know – with an eerie inevitability that here was the heir to his ergonomic chair, that we are all replaceable.

He put everything into his last shift, but in a slowly run contest, with Dettori spending too long looking over his shoulder for the shadow of his rival and not long enough reading the race, he was swamped by Baaeed a furlong out. Palace Pier did everything he knew, fought gamely, gallantly, it not being in his nature to clock off five minutes early, but Baaeed had his measure and beat him by a neck. The baton passes hand to hand.

Now Palace Pier's work here is done. He has been headhunted for another role and you won't see him in the office again. The smokers have already forgotten him; the woman at the next desk is busy flirting with his replacement; his bosses are mourning his departure, wondering where they'll find another like him.

Eleven races, nine wins, five Group 1s. What a horse. Yet for all he won, he never quite won our hearts. It wasn't you, it was us. Palace Pier, we hardly knew you.

▾ Number one: Frankie Dettori signals victory in the Lockinge

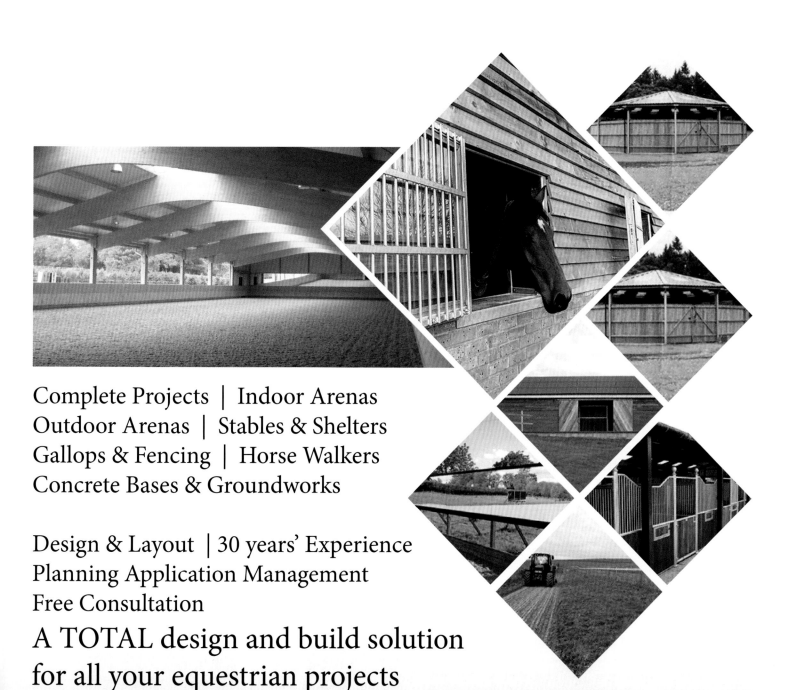

Poetic Flare combined hard graft with magical moments in an exceptionally busy season masterminded by Jim Bolger

IRON HORSE II

By Steve Dennis

DOGS resemble their owners, they say, so why not horses? Poetic Flare is the image of his trainer Jim Bolger: durable, indomitable, single-minded, a proper hard case with a tendency towards moments of genius. Oh, he's a real chocolate-coloured chip off the old tough cookie.

If Bolger were to design his own avatar, he couldn't do better than Poetic Flare, and in essence that is exactly what he did. Not only did Bolger train the son of Dawn Approach, he also bred him. He also bred and trained his sire and dam Maria Lee, trained his grandsire New Approach and both granddams Hymn Of The Dawn and Elida. Poetic Flare was officially owned, as were most of his family, by Bolger's wife Jackie. He was raised at Bolger's Redmondstown Stud, run by his nephew Ken. The colt is the epitome of Bolger Incorporated, and one of its finest products.

About the only thing Bolger didn't do was ride Poetic Flare, and even there it was an inside job, for the man in the saddle was Bolger's son-in-law Kevin Manning. It would be unjust to call Bolger Incorporated a one-man band, but the patriarch is the one calling the tune, and never has that tune swelled into such a song in his heart than the day Poetic Flare showed every facet of his class and determination to win the 2,000 Guineas at Newmarket.

It was a Classic without a standout two-year-old champion bidding to parlay juvenile promise into something more substantial, and the top of the market showed two colts from Ballydoyle and another from Joseph O'Brien vying for market share with the Godolphin contingent. Poetic Flare, despite a winning reappearance under his belt, was largely ignored, a dangerous course of action with one so rugged, so dogged.

The Guineas promised a tight, close-run affair and that is what played out. Poetic Flare had to fight hard to beat Master Of The Seas by a short head, with Lucky Vega a neck away third, but there was something inevitable about the outcome once he had taken the lead a furlong out. It was swiftly noted that Bolger was 79, Manning was 54. A day later, 50-year-old Frankie Dettori rode Mother Earth to win the 1,000 Guineas. At a time of year associated with green shoots and new blooms, it was uplifting to find the old growth still bearing fruit.

"I think the 2,000 Guineas at Newmarket is the best race in the world, and to be able to win it really means a lot," said the master trainer. "Poetic Flare is the most complete racehorse I've ever had.

▶ *Continues page 60*

▲ Royal procession: Poetic Flare and Kevin Manning win the St James's Palace Stakes at Royal Ascot by four and a quarter lengths

POETIC FLARE

He's the complete package, you couldn't find a fault with him."

★★★★

SOME statement, given the alumni from Bolger's Coolcullen yard: New Approach, Dawn Approach, St Jovite, Teofilo, Finsceal Beo, Give Thanks. Bolger's doctrine of hard work and discipline has left a lasting impression on the likes of former apprentice Sir Anthony McCoy and former assistant Aidan O'Brien as well as on a legion of high-class horses, and few have thrived on it quite so obviously as Poetic Flare.

Once upon a time they called Giant's Causeway the 'Iron Horse' for running in eight Group 1 races between May and September, and Poetic Flare was forged in the same crucible of competition. Bolger doesn't drink, doesn't smoke, doesn't miss a Mass. Idleness, judging by the workload shouldered by Poetic Flare, is also a sin.

Thus the 2,000 Guineas winner would embark on a fearsome schedule comprising three Classics within the month, and four Group 1s in less than seven weeks. Two weeks after Newmarket he was at Longchamp for the Poule d'Essai des Poulains, where he ran disappointingly to be sixth behind St Mark's Basilica. Undaunted – a word that applies to both horse and trainer – he was back in action just six days later in the Irish 2,000 Guineas at the Curragh, where he ran his stout heart out only to be beaten by a short head.

Bolger wasn't too downhearted, for he also trained the winner Mac Swiney. And bred him, naturally. And bred and trained his dam, his damsire and both granddams. For all that, the mudlark Mac Swiney was not of the same make as his fellow employee at Bolger Incorporated, and after running fourth in the Derby his form dropped away until a late revival to finish third in the Champion Stakes.

Poetic Flare, on the other hand, was just getting started. A little over three weeks later, he won the Group 1 St James's Palace Stakes at Royal Ascot with a bewitching display of brilliance, unleashing an unanswerable change of gear on the fast ground that

▶ Continues page 62

Keep on running . . .

Poetic Flare ran in eight races from April to September, seven of them Group 1s, winning three and going close in four more. On average those runs, spread across three countries, came at intervals of less than three weeks

April 11 *Listed 2,000 Guineas Trial, Leopardstown*
Wins by a length and a half from Ace Aussie

 20-day break

May 1 *Group 1 2,000 Guineas, Newmarket*
Wins by a short head from Master Of The Seas

15-day break

May 16 *Group 1 Poule d'Essai des Poulains, Longchamp*
Sixth to St Mark's Basilica, beaten two and a quarter lengths

Six-day break

May 22 *Group 1 Irish 2,000 Guineas, Curragh*
Second to Mac Swiney, beaten a short head

 24-day break

June 15 *Group 1 St James's Palace Stakes, Royal Ascot*
Wins by four and a quarter lengths from Lucky Vega

 43-day break

July 28 *Group 1 Sussex Stakes, Goodwood*
Second to Alcohol Free, beaten a length and three-quarters

 18-day break

August 15 *Group 1 Prix Jacques le Marois, Deauville*
Second to Palace Pier, beaten a neck

 27-day break

September 11 *Group 1 Irish Champion Stakes*
Third to St Mark's Basilica, beaten three-quarters of a length

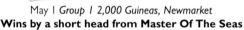
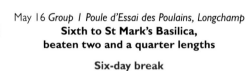

'The 2,000 Guineas winner embarked on a fearsome schedule comprising three Classics within the month and four Group 1s in less than seven weeks'

showed him to best effect. He thrashed them, simple as that, beating Lucky Vega by four and a quarter lengths. The performance drew the highest praise from his trainer.

"He's the best horse I've bred," said Bolger, weighing up the work of half a lifetime. "He's exceptional. I haven't had one that can take everything he's taken. I've never had a colt of his quality who needed as much work as he does."

★★★★

BUT even our Lord took a rest on the seventh day, and Poetic Flare's whistle-stop tour of Europe's Group 1 races was over. Bolger gave his iron horse a breather, sort of – "He's only had a break in as much as he hasn't been racing, but he's a horse who I have to keep moving, so it hasn't exactly been a holiday," he said - and brought him back for the Sussex Stakes in July, in which he found only the filly Alcohol Free too good on tacky ground that sapped even his superhuman strength.

That was the commencement of a run of narrow defeats, but the way Bolger campaigned Poetic Flare, the way he campaigns the majority of his good horses, is in the certain knowledge that defeat is neither a tragedy nor a crime but simply a by-product of fierce competition, an occupational hazard.

In the Prix Jacques le Marois at Deauville, only champion miler Palace Pier could get the better of him, and only by a neck. Poetic Flare was closing all the way to the line even though defeat seemed beyond question. Sometimes the struggle naught availeth, although for Poetic Flare the struggle was its own reward.

After that he moved up in trip for the Irish Champion Stakes at Leopardstown, a mile and a quarter for the first time, and it wasn't the extra distance that beat him but two high-class rivals in St Mark's Basilica

▲ Bolger Incorporated: Kevin Manning, the son-in-law of trainer and breeder Jim Bolger (left), celebrates Poetic Flare's victory in the St James's Palace Stakes at Royal Ascot

and Tarnawa, and even then by just three-quarters of a length and a nose in a performance rated the equal of his Royal Ascot victory.

That was his last shift at the coalface, as a month later Poetic Flare was retired. He is to stand at Shadai Stallion Station in Japan, and will hopefully produce horses who share his ferocious attitude to the job, an iron horse bequeathing the bloodstock world a multitude of little nuts and bolts. Perhaps Bolger may train a few of them, another generation of horses in his own image, more hard workers on the payroll at Bolger Incorporated.

'A Lance Armstrong in Irish racing'

JIM BOLGER has always possessed the courage of his convictions, whether that manifests itself in taking out a training licence at the relatively late age of 35, putting all his chips on a young stallion named Galileo, or speaking out against perceived injustices within the governance and operation of racing.

It is perhaps not correct to say that Bolger courts controversy, but when he believes he is right about a subject he does not shrink from any furore that may ensue, as occurred in 2008 when he announced that New Approach would not be running in the Derby. Punters were left high and dry at the subsequent volte-face, with New Approach taking his place at Epsom and winning the Derby to boot.

In 2020 Bolger unpinned the conversational grenade that the number one problem in Irish racing was drug cheats, and demanded that the Irish Horseracing Regulatory Board introduce more rigorous testing and take appropriate action when required.

He reaffirmed this stance in a Sunday-paper interview with journalist Paul Kimmage, suggesting that "there will be a Lance Armstrong in Irish racing", although he mentioned no names and later declined to attend parliamentary hearings convened to examine his allegations. Until Bolger adds substance to the bare bones of his claim "I know who they are" the issue will linger, to the division of the sport and the detriment of its reputation.

NATURE'S LIGHT

Delivered using smart Stable Lights and award-winning Light Masks.

Health. Breeding. Performance.

www.equilume.com   info@equilume.com

B AAEED was on the prowl all year, waiting for his moment to strike. While others hunted big game over the summer, he picked off easy prey in the shadows but was strengthening all the time, an ominous and threatening presence. Finally, he made his move and it was devastating. The Beast had arrived.

The moment came in the Queen Elizabeth II Stakes on Champions Day at Ascot, where Baaeed took on top dog Palace Pier in a showdown that would determine whether he had the speed and strength to be the leader of the pack. The challenger was ready for the fight and he won it, albeit only just.

Baaeed struck out for victory a furlong and a half from home and built a vital lead over Palace Pier, who battled back hard in the closing stages but fell short by a neck for his first defeat of the season.

It was a powerful statement by the William Haggas-trained winner even on ground that was softer than ideal, taking him to a perfect six out of six in a career that had started barely four months earlier.

The plaudits rained down on Shadwell Estate's new star, who had emerged in the year founder Sheikh Hamdan Al Maktoum died and ace sprinter Battaash was retired.

"I think Baaeed could be a world champion," said jockey Jim Crowley. "He's just a beast, he keeps getting better. It was magical. I think people forget he's come such a long way in a short space of time. It's a great buzz to ride a horse that good."

Haggas, having nurtured Baaeed with great care and skill, was equally excited. "Now he's fulfilled all our dreams and ambitions. What can you say? I'm still shaking a bit," he said. "I was watching the race and walking around a good bit. I've been trying to get up to 10,000 steps, but I've far exceeded that today. Jim said he coped with the ground rather than loved it and he's beaten the best miler in Europe."

▶ Battle for supremacy: Baaeed (blue and white striped cap) takes the Queen Elizabeth II Stakes from Palace Pier (left)

THE BEAST

★★★★

WITH just over a week to go until Royal Ascot, where Palace Pier and Poetic Flare would stake their claims to the miling crown with Group 1 triumphs, Baaeed was only just starting out. The Shadwell homebred, unraced at two, made a winning debut in a Leicester maiden worth just under £5,000 to the winner, a far cry from the riches and prestige on offer at the royal meeting.

Already there were hints that he could be a cut or two above the average. "William likes him and his work had been good," said Dane O'Neill, the winning jockey. "He's from a family that has done Shadwell proud in the past and has a nice way about him." The obvious reference point was his year-older brother Hukum, a four-time Group 3 winner from a mile and a half to a mile and three-quarters. It soon became clear Baaeed was something different.

Twelve days later, on the final afternoon of Royal Ascot, Baaeed won a mile novice at Newmarket by seven and a half lengths, and he was back there at the July meeting, stepping up to Listed company with Crowley taking over from O'Neill for the first time. The winning margin was four lengths and Haggas said: "He's got plenty of speed and showed a great turn of foot. His brother is a mile-and-a-half horse but there's no hurry to step him up in trip right now. I'm not sure where we could go next with him but I won't miss a good entry."

Haggas toyed with the idea of supplementing him for the Group 1 Sussex Stakes at Goodwood but instead kept him in the calmer waters of the Group 3 Thoroughbred Stakes two days later. This time Baaeed scored by six and a half lengths. He was

Baaeed ate up the opposition as he went from unraced to unbeaten QEII winner in the space of four months

already up to a Racing Post Rating of 124, just over seven weeks after his debut.

His first Group 1 opportunity came in the Prix du Moulin at Longchamp in early September and it was a relatively easy task for the grade, although Baaeed was at his least impressive as he won by a length and a quarter from Order Of Australia, who had been beaten further by Palace Pier in the Prix Jacques le Marois a few weeks earlier.

If that raised some questions about whether Baaeed really was a Group 1 miler, he gave an emphatic answer in the QEII. As

well as Palace Pier, his victims included Sussex heroine Alcohol Free, 1,000 Guineas winner Mother Earth, 2,000 Guineas runner-up Master Of The Seas, Nassau Stakes winner Lady Bowthorpe and The Revenant, who was trying to land the QEII for the second year running. Baaeed's performance merited an RPR of 127, equalling Palace Pier's career-best.

★★★★

WITH Palace Pier and Poetic Flare heading to stud, and notwithstanding the star three-year-olds who might appear next

season, the way seems clear for Baaeed to stamp his authority on the miling division in 2022. The Shadwell operation, now headed by the late founder's daughter Sheikha Hissa bint Hamdan Al Maktoum, will be slimmed down, but Baaeed looks set to keep the famous blue and white in the spotlight.

"The plan always was to [see him run again next year]," said Angus Gold, Shadwell's longstanding racing manager. "He hasn't had a hard life so far. He has done what has been asked of him the whole way through and I can't see why he wouldn't go on next year. We'll

hope to keep the best ones and we'll have some yearlings to come into training next year. Compared to most owners, it would be fairly sizeable."

As Baaeed raced to QEII glory, there was poignancy along with the excitement. "You know me, I tend to get a bit emotional," Gold said. "In the last 50 yards I thought how much Sheikh Hamdan would have loved this. It's a huge day for the team, for his family and for his legacy in the year he died."

Baaeed might prove to be even more of a legacy horse next year. He is quite a beast.

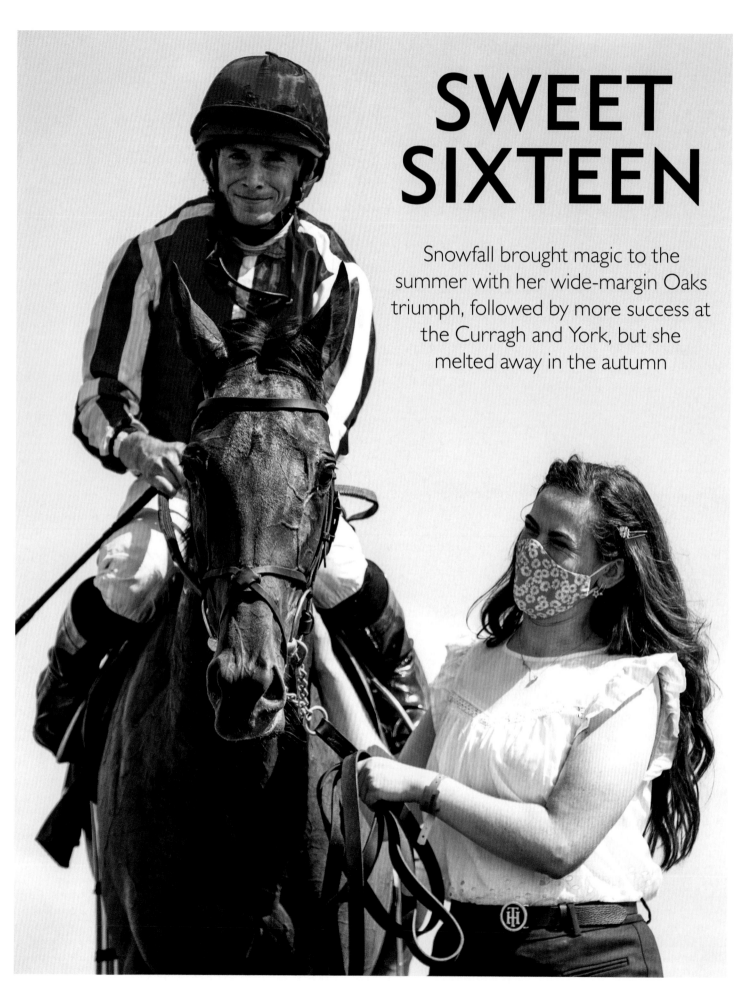

SWEET SIXTEEN

Snowfall brought magic to the summer with her wide-margin Oaks triumph, followed by more success at the Curragh and York, but she melted away in the autumn

By Steve Dennis

SNOWFALL is normally measured in inches, not in lengths, but for an exceptional filly exception must be made. Snowfall in June is rare enough, even with the climate in growing crisis, but rarer still is the setting of a record that is almost without equal in British racing history.

Sixteen was the magic number, 16 lengths the winning margin for Snowfall in the Oaks, a scarcely credible rout of the opposition that had historians blowing dust off their ancient archives as they sought its like. Longer than Shergar's ten-length Derby in 1981, longer than Never Say Die's 12-length St Leger in 1954, longer than the 12 lengths Sun Princess managed in the 1983 Oaks, longer than Tudor Minstrel's eight-length 2,000 Guineas in 1947.

Snowfall outdid them all, apart from the 20 lengths by which Mayonaise is reckoned to have won the 1859 1,000 Guineas, although as in those days there was no photo-finish strip, no sectional timing, no microchips in saddlecloths, just one judge standing at the winning post and squinting balefully down the Rowley Mile, that filly's winning margin could have been anything

from 12 lengths to 25. Snowfall's sweet sixteen might, then, be the widest margin of victory in any British Classic.

On a gloomy, drizzly day at Epsom, it was suddenly as though a shaft of sunlight had slanted in through a stained-glass window. Snowfall lit up the turf and dazzled us, everyone rubbing their eyes. She cruised through the pack to lead two furlongs out, was six lengths clear at the furlong pole, and simply drew further and further away without any sign of encouragement from jockey Frankie Dettori, in the saddle after Ryan Moore preferred her stablemate Santa Barbara, the favourite.

"I was like a hot knife through butter," said Dettori, like any good Italian reaching for the terminology of the kitchen to describe events. "She was unbelievable. Four out I had everything beat, they were all gone. The only horse I hadn't seen was Santa Barbara, so I had a glance back and there was daylight – it was like an Arazi moment."

Arazi, Secretariat, Frankel, they all came to mind. It was a time not to dwell too heavily on the absolute merit of the performance but simply to marvel at the visual impression, a once-in-a-lifetime thrill. This was not a bad Oaks in

any case; three fillies – Santa Barbara, Saffron Beach and Teona, of whom more later – emerged from the broken pieces of this Classic field to win at the highest level during the season, and Divinely and Zeyaadah would one day be Group 1 runners-up. But rarely has a big race been so much, so conclusively about the winner.

So dramatic was Snowfall that she relegated another mighty milestone to the small print – her victory meant that Aidan O'Brien had trained 40 British Classic winners, a record he shares with Victorian-era titan John Scott and a record O'Brien is almost guaranteed to have for his own next year. Other choice titbits swept up in the aftermath like so much confetti in a churchyard were a first Epsom Classic success for the late, great Japanese sire Deep Impact, and Dettori's own record-book moment in drawing level with Fred Archer on 21 British Classic wins.

★★★★

THIS was not the first time in the headlines for Snowfall, who had played a part in the 'wrong horse' fiasco in the previous year's Fillies' Mile at Newmarket, when she and stablemate Mother Earth carried each other's numbercloth and jockey and earned O'Brien a

£4,000 fine for the mix-up. That was the last act of a two-year-old campaign that certainly didn't suggest Snowfall could win a Classic, with just one maiden win to her name from seven outings as the nights drew in.

Even on her reappearance as a three-year-old, in the Musidora Stakes at York, Snowfall was allowed to go off at 14-1 and surprised all and sundry when staying in front after being granted an easy lead. She was only the Ballydoyle second-string at Epsom, but that empire rarely entertains an angel unaware. "We thought she was a proper Group 1 filly last year but she had a few races that didn't work out for her," O'Brien said at Epsom, as the 16 lengths began to sink in. "She got a lot of experience, raced a lot and did very well over the winter physically. Maybe she got stronger. Usually if they show that kind of Group 1 class, it will come through."

It came through loud and clear, nothing lost in translation. After that tour de force, all the conversation moved ahead a few jumps and Snowfall's campaign began to be all about working backwards from the Prix de l'Arc de Triomphe. The Irish Oaks was the obvious next step and Snowfall performed equally as brilliantly at
▸ *Continues page 68*

▲ Home and dry: Snowfall storms to victory by 16 lengths in the Oaks at Epsom, prompting an astonished reaction from Frankie Dettori
◂ Ryan Moore and Snowfall with groom Aimee Murphy after the Irish Oaks

SNOWFALL

the Curragh when winning by half her Epsom margin, with Moore back in the saddle.

A month later she emulated the magnificent Enable when adding the Group 1 Yorkshire Oaks to her haul, as easy as one-two-three, although the winning margin was again cut in half to a mere four lengths. The performance was rated the equal of her Epsom blitz, the high-water mark of a sizzling summer. "She got me there very easily and the race was over two and a half furlongs out," Moore said. "Today the performance was as good as anything I've felt. She definitely felt better than she did at the Curragh and hopefully she will continue to do that into the autumn."

★★★★

YET as every excited six-year-old knows, the snowfall doesn't stay around forever. Its otherworldly glow and its bewitching novelty come and then quickly go, and so it was for Snowfall. The Prix Vermeille at Longchamp was supposed to be a straightforward stepping-stone to the Arc, but in an eerie echo of O'Brien's words, it was a race that didn't work out for her.

Hamstrung by the languid pace set by stablemate La Joconde, left further back in the field than Dettori – Moore was riding at the Curragh – wanted, Snowfall stayed on adequately but could never lay a glove on Teona, who benefited from the tactical astuteness of Olivier Peslier where Snowfall missed it from Dettori, who confessed his temporary failing.

The Arc was still the target, but Snowfall's air of invincibility had been lost, and even though she still held a prominent position in the betting market there were doubts surrounding her for the first time since that Musidora victory. Justifiably so; as Torquator Tasso galloped to an unexpected success, Snowfall stayed on from mid-division to finish an undisgraced but undistinguished sixth, hardly ordinary but no longer extraordinary.

The magic had melted away. Less than a fortnight later, at Ascot on Champions Day, Snowfall was a tired-looking third in a weak renewal of the Group 1 Fillies & Mares Stakes behind Eshaada, who had been cast

▲ Snowfall lands the Yorkshire Oaks under Ryan Moore, the final victory of her glorious summer run

37 lengths adrift in the Yorkshire Oaks. As the villainous poet once wondered, where were the snows of yesteryear? Or even four months earlier?

We were beguiled by those 16 lengths, borne away on the back of that record-breaking display. Snowfall had maximised her talent into one breathtaking performance that will be dragged into the light every time some new star strolls home by a huge margin of victory. Given the evidence of history, though, we'll never see anything like that again.

Sometimes people keep a snowball in the freezer to remind them of some long-melted wintry wonderland. So then we'll keep that sweet 16 lengths, preserved incorruptible within memory's frosty vault, and this particular Snowfall will stay with us forever.

Classics master

SNOWFALL'S annihilation of her rivals in the Oaks put Aidan O'Brien level on 40 wins in British Classics history with John Scott, who had held the record on his own for 158 years.

Snowfall was O'Brien's ninth Oaks winner – five of which have been in the last seven years – to go alongside a record-breaking haul of ten 2,000 Guineas successes, seven in the 1,000 Guineas, six in the St Leger and eight in the Derby, which is also a record.

O'Brien's dominance in the British Classics has been achieved in a 23-year timespan since 1998, when King Of Kings landed the 2,000 Guineas. By contrast, Scott's 40 Classics came in 36 years between 1827 and 1863 with his stars including the first Triple Crown winner, West Australian, who landed the 2,000 Guineas, Derby and St Leger in 1853.

Now it is only a matter of waiting for O'Brien to take the record outright. He has landed at least one British Classic in each of the last ten years.

Top trainers in British Classics

Wins	Trainer	2,000	1,000	Derby	Oaks	Leger
40	John Scott	7	4	5	8	16*
40	**AIDAN O'BRIEN**	10*	7	8*	9	6
34	Robert Robson	6	9*	7	12*	-
28	Mat Dawson	5	6	6	5	6
25	Sir Henry Cecil	3	6	4	8	4
23	John Porter	5	2	7	3	6
21	Alec Taylor jr	4	1	3	8	5
19	Fred Darling	5	2	7	2	3
19	Sir Noel Murless	2	6	3	5	3
17	Dixon Boyce	5	3	5	4	-

* Record for the race

RoR
Retraining of Racehorses

Racing to a new career at ror.org.uk

RoR Source a Horse
Retraining of Racehorses

sourceahorse.ror.org.uk

A new website for selling or loaning a horse directly out of a trainer's yard and for all former racehorses.

Owner/Trainer Helpline

A dedicated helpline to assist in the placement of horses coming out of training.

Rehoming Direct

RoR has compiled a checklist to safeguard your horse's future when moved directly into the sport horse market.

Retrainers

RoR has a list of retrainers recommended by trainers who can start the retraining process and assess each horse.

Visit
ror.org.uk
for rehoming options and advice

Equine Charities

Retrain former racehorses for a donation, as well as care for vulnerable horses with the help of RoR funding.

RoR is British horseracing's official charity for the welfare of horses retired from racing.

T: 01488 648998

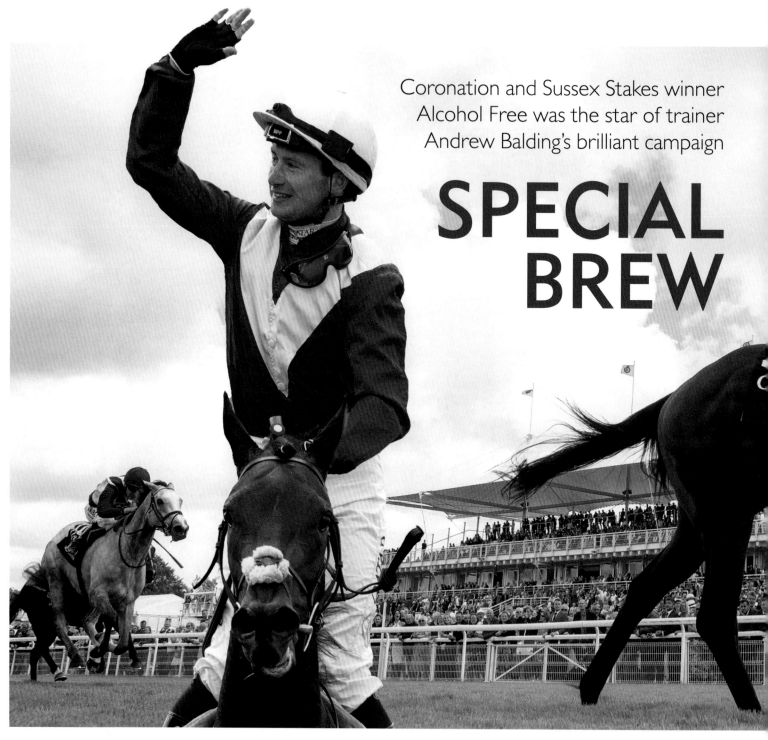

Coronation and Sussex Stakes winner
Alcohol Free was the star of trainer
Andrew Balding's brilliant campaign

SPECIAL BREW

By David Carr

ALCOHOL FREE? What an inappropriate name for a top-class standard bearer who inspired some of the many celebrations in the season of seasons for her trainer.

While neighbouring villages struggled with shortages of fuel, food and hospitality staff in a troubled year, it was the stocks of champagne that a wily shopkeeper in the Hampshire hamlet of Kingsclere would have been desperate to ensure were kept topped up.

The residents of a locale once owned by Alfred the Great had every excuse to party like it was 1971 – the year that Ian the Great reigned over the entire country. Ian Balding, that is, the man who masterminded the three-year-old career of the brilliant Mill Reef and earned the trainers' championship in the process.

Exactly 50 years on, his son Andrew made a determined effort to reclaim it for the family, to wrestle back a crown that had become the personal plaything of John Gosden and Aidan O'Brien in recent seasons. Unexpected though such a bold bid seemingly was in some quarters, this was no Leicester City-style transformation from relegation battlers into title chasers.

The numbers tell the tale of a trainer who has been growing more powerful by the year and is now among the strongest in Britain. After a dream start when he took over the licence in 2003 and won the Oaks with Casual Look almost immediately, Balding had settled into the head of the second division of trainers, in or around the top 20 in the table. As he expanded, he began to flirt with the top ten from 2011 onwards – and that flirtation has become a positive consummation of late.

He breached the top five in 2019, thanks largely to the high-class trio Donjuan Triumphant, Beat The Bank and Shine So Bright, whose owners King Power know plenty about title winning thanks to their association with Leicester City. Balding made it into fourth in

2020's Covid-shortened campaign, when Kameko gave him a second British Classic success and was much the yard's highest earner.

Surely the trainer could not finish fourth again in 2021, after the 2,000 Guineas winner had been retired to stud? Of course not. Why settle for fourth when the top three beckons?

When Ian Balding was champion it was something of a one-horse effort. Mill Reef's huge prizes in the Derby, Eclipse and King George VI and Queen Elizabeth Stakes were always going to make his trainer mighty hard to beat in the title race.

Fifty years on, it was more of a team effort that thrust Kingsclere into the battle for the crown with Charlie Appleby and John and Thady Gosden from the off and kept the yard there through the whole season. Training is all about getting the best from every horse and by Champions Day Balding had won with more than half of the 175 different horses he had run. Ten horses had contributed £100,000 or more to the British prize-money tally and he had ten individual Group winners through the season.

★★★★

EVERY division pulled their weight. Berkshire Shadow and Sandrine each won two-year-old races at Royal Ascot, a meeting that underlined how far the yard has come in recent seasons. Between 2003 and 2018, Balding had a total of three winners at the world's greatest festival of Flat racing; he had four in 2021 alone and would have been crowned top trainer had he matched the Gosdens' one second place over the five days.

Harrow (who won the Weatherbys Scientific £200,000 2-Y-O Stakes at Doncaster) and Majestic Glory (Sweet Solera Stakes) were other notable contributors among a juvenile team so strong that eight of them were put in the Irish 1,000 Guineas or 2,000 Guineas when they closed in September.

Coaxing improvement out of older horses is always a sign that you are doing something very right

▶ *Continues page 72*

ALCOHOL FREE

and Balding's efforts with a couple of King Power five-year-olds deserves recognition. Chil Chil, a useful handicapper at the start of the season, won the Chipchase Stakes and finished a close third in the Betfair Sprint Cup, while persevering with the perennial Lingfield winner Bangkok back on turf paid off when he upset the odds in the York Stakes.

And no son of Ian Balding, especially one who spent part of his early career with Yorkshire alchemists Jack and Lynda Ramsden, is ever a man to oppose lightly in handicaps. Johnny Drama gave the yard its second John Smith's Cup in three years, while Valley Forge (Melrose), Foxes Tales (Golden Gates Handicap) and Alounak (Old Newton Cup) also showed he has not lost his touch.

Yet it is the three-year-olds that a Flat trainer's season really hangs on. Becoming champion without a Classic horse is like winning Love Island without a suntan: decidedly unlikely.

Step forward Alcohol Free, the €40,000 foal who had put herself firmly into the reckoning for the Qipco 1,000 Guineas with a game victory in the Cheveley Park Stakes at Newmarket in the autumn of 2020. That said, further success was far from guaranteed. Only one of the ten previous winners of that supposed championship event had gone on to score again at Group 1 level – and six of them had failed to win again in any grade.

There was no doubting Alcohol Free's ability. Balding marvelled at her efforts on the gallops and said: "Watching her work is demoralising for the other horses: we have to keep swapping the lead horse because she is just so, so good."

Yet she can be highly strung and is best when able to get cover in a race, which makes her vulnerable to circumstance, to draw and to luck in running. That much was evident on her reappearance in the Dubai Duty Free Stakes – the Fred Darling as was – at Newbury, where she was stuck on the outside of the group, raced freely, hung left and only just held on by a short head from Statement, who was 26lb her inferior on BHA ratings.

While she got away with it there, her luck ran out in the 1,000 Guineas. Drawn away from her main rivals,

finding little cover and tending to hang once more, the joint-favourite could finish only fifth. Victory went to Mother Earth, making Aidan O'Brien the first trainer to win the 1,000 Guineas in three straight years since George Lambton did it from 1916 to 1918.

★★★★

ALCOHOL FREE ducked another Classic bid at the Curragh as Balding deliberately targeted her at Royal Ascot's Coronation Stakes – a plan that paid off spectacularly. Safely covered up this time by Oisin Murphy, she showed her true colours as she burst clear in the final furlong for a length-and-a-half victory that had the taste of redemption about it, especially when her trainer admitted afterwards that he had gone to the Guineas expecting to win.

A messy Falmouth Stakes at Newmarket muddied the waters among the three-year-old miling fillies as Alcohol Free broke too well, found herself in front much too soon and was beaten by her Ascot victims Snow Lantern and Mother Earth.

But she left no doubt as to who was the best around when she was turned out again just 19 days later at Goodwood and became the first filly

▲ Flying filly: Alcohol Free wins the Dubai Duty Free Stakes at Newbury; below, Group 1 success in the Coronation Stakes (top) and narrow defeat in the Falmouth Stakes; previous page, Group 1 victory against the colts in the Sussex Stakes and Oisin Murphy salutes the Goodwood crowd

to beat the colts in the Sussex Stakes for 17 years. Her ready length-and-three-quarters defeat of 2,000 Guineas and St James's Palace Stakes winner Poetic Flare brooked no argument and gave Murphy his own measure of redemption, 12 months after he had blamed himself for getting Kameko beaten in the same race.

Owner Jeff Smith was delighted to land a second Sussex Stakes, 37 years after Chief Singer gave him his first. And he took the sporting decision to aim the winner at the Juddmonte International. Although his filly could never challenge Mishriff on her step up to a mile and a quarter at York, anyone who rejects the safety-first, reputation-protecting approach of most folk involved with top-class horses has to be applauded.

In similar fashion, Alcohol Free bypassed the easier pickings of the Sun Chariot Stakes at Newmarket, where 1,000 Guineas runner-up Saffron Beach reversed the form with Mother Earth to give Jane Chapple-Hyam her first Group 1 win. Instead, she waited for the Queen Elizabeth II Stakes at Ascot and, even if her keenness ultimately counted against her once more, no-one can say she had not earned the chance to mix it with the best.

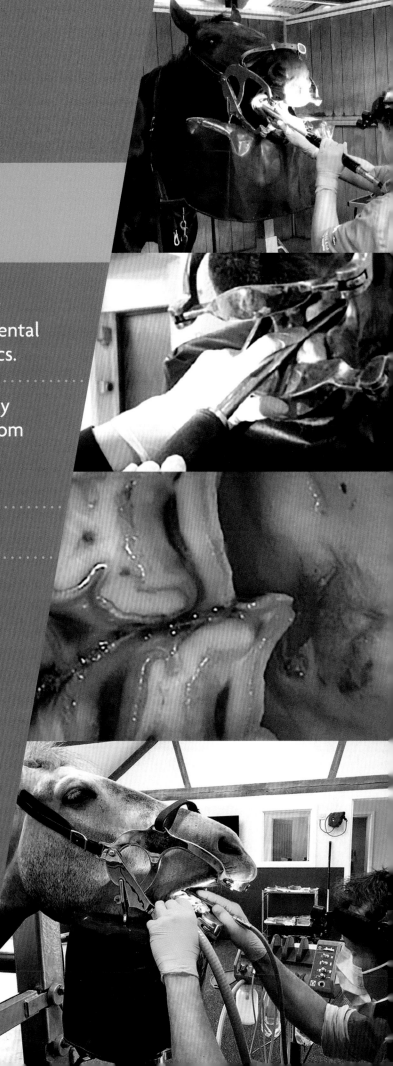

IN THE PICTURE

Murphy holds on to trophy after late challenge by Buick

OISIN MURPHY lifted the British Flat jockeys' championship trophy for the third time at Ascot on Champions Day after seeing off a determined challenge from William Buick in a fraught final week.

Murphy, champion for the previous two years, looked well on course for the hat-trick when he led by nine with a week to go but Buick whittled away at the deficit day after day, and the Godolphin rider got within one of Murphy with a winner midway through the Friday card at Haydock.

With 24 hours to go until the Ascot finale and just 11 races left in the title race, that promised to set up a grandstand finish but Murphy quickly pulled clear again with a double later on the Haydock card. He led by three before racing at Ascot and, while Buick scored with Creative Force in the British Champions Sprint, the trophy was back in Murphy's hands before the day was out. The final score was 153 to 151.

After the presentation, Murphy said: "It's fantastic to win this trophy again – it's a dream come true. William is one of the best riders in the world and it's been very tough. He's a tremendous competitor with a fantastic job. Thanks to all my trainers and owners for putting me on winners, this is what it's all about."

The celebrations seemed muted, however, after the morning papers had brought lurid headlines in two tabloids that revealed details of a drunken altercation involving Murphy in a Newmarket bar the week before. He attempted to play a straight bat when asked for his reaction to the stories, admitting "I need to do better", but it was an unwelcome distraction on the tenth anniversary of Champions Day. The card is sponsored by Qipco, the private investment company of the family of Sheikh Fahad Al Thani, who is Murphy's main backer through Qatar Racing.

Asked about the reports involving Murphy, Qatar's racing and bloodstock adviser David Redvers said: "Clearly there are things that have happened over recent times that he has regrets about and will work hard to put right. I have no doubt that when the pressure of Champions Day is out of the way and he can breathe and regroup, there will be changes made to his lifestyle and he's going to look very hard at that."

As for runner-up Buick, he enjoyed a tremendous year with Godolphin stars Adayar and Hurricane Lane and was proud of his efforts in the title race. "I gave it everything I had, I left nothing on the table and I didn't quite make it," he said.

Picture: EDWARD WHITAKER (RACINGPOST.COM/PHOTOS)

RISING & FALLING

A novice chase season of rich promise saw Shishkin enhance his reputation while Envoi Allen and Monkfish ran into difficulties

By Steve Dennis

HONESTLY, you wait the best part of six decades for the new Arkle to arrive and then three come along at once, like the proverbial London bus. But what in the distance is a red blur, full of promise, exactly what is needed, is by the time it finally reaches the earnest traveller often a disappointment, going the wrong way, its number the wrong number, all that hope now turned into just another slow-moving vehicle clogging up the traffic.

Novice chasers are like London buses. Plenty of potential, but hardly ever 'The One'. At the beginning of the 2020-21 season, though, we were really going places. All the bases were covered – Shishkin would rule at two miles, Monkfish was the new three-mile king, Envoi Allen would fill in between. All these stars would align to cast a bewitching light over the campaign, with the real possibility of some of that Arkle sparkle finally reaching us from across the light years. How did that turn out?

Pre-Cheltenham, of course, everything went absolutely to plan, because pre-Cheltenham is all about minimising risk, eliminating the negative. Pre-Cheltenham is about tiny field sizes, prohibitive odds, uncompetitive contests that err to the mundane, slipping unmemorably down the gullet and leaving no taste on the tongue, satisfying no hunger.

Pre-Cheltenham, Shishkin ran three times, beat nine horses, with his longest odds 1-3. Monkfish ran three times, beat 22 horses (Ireland does things slightly differently), with his longest odds 1-2. Envoi Allen ran three times, beat 11 horses, with his longest odds 1-2. Perfect records, perfectly efficient, perfectly perfunctory.

Yet the promise was intact, which was, after all, the point. Only a fool gets his embryo superstar beaten on the way to Cheltenham; given the manifold opportunities to keep the best horses apart, it's almost harder to lose than win. All three of our seven-year-old novices had joined the dots like little Rembrandts. The Cheltenham Festival would provide the colouring in, so we could at last see the picture for what it really was.

Also, from out of the long grass, had come new faces. Energumene, a stablemate of Monkfish at Willie Mullins' yard, ran three times pre-Cheltenham, beat 20 horses, longest odds 10-11, and was expected to give Shishkin a thorough test in the Arkle Chase, only for the yearned-for opportunity to see Shishkin taken out of his colossal comfort zone to expire when

▶ *Continues page 78*

NOVICE CHASERS

Energumene went lame the week before. Then there was Royale Pagaille, a proper outlier, who improved unrecognisably through midwinter and absolutely marmalised experienced handicappers at Haydock in January. He shares an owner – Rich Ricci – with Monkfish, and because good horses are kept apart he was sent for the Gold Cup itself.

✳✳✳✳

SHISHKIN was first up, and produced a flawless performance at odds of 4-9 against only four rivals in the Arkle, succeeding where Sprinter Sacre and Altior had struck gold for trainer Nicky Henderson and looking as good as those two superstars, although he has some way to go to assure us of that. He won by 12 lengths and his resultant Racing Post Rating of 174 was 6lb higher than any of the Queen Mother Champion Chase runners could manage on the day, suggesting Shishkin would have won that if he had been given the opportunity.

One real deal certified, two to go. Monkfish was next, a 1-4 chance to beat five rivals in the Brown Advisory Novices' Chase, which he did, but not in the manner expected of such an overwhelming favourite against underwhelming opposition. He was not flawless, making several jumping errors, notably at the last with the race in the bag, but nevertheless won going away by six and a half lengths, job done efficiently if not brilliantly.

The following day Envoi Allen put his unbeaten streak (11 races) on the line in the Marsh Novices' Chase, having recently joined Henry de Bromhead following the suspension of Gordon Elliott. He was 4-9 to beat seven rivals, but the wheels came off the juggernaut with a fall at the fourth fence. It was enough to stun; Envoi Allen was mortal after all.

The race was won by Chantry House, a stablemate of Shishkin, elbowing his way into the discussion with no little panache. A day later, the gutsy Royale Pagaille left this debate when 'only' sixth in the Gold Cup, although he came back lame after losing shoes and will still be a force when the midwinter mud is deep.

Cheltenham, as ever, given its

▶▶ *Continues page 80*

▲ Chasing glory: Monkfish jumps the second-last with the riderless Eklat De Rire on his way to victory in the Brown Advisory Novices' Chase at Cheltenham
▼ Emerging forces Energumene (top) and Royale Pagaille

Previous page: Shishkin and Nico de Boinville fly high in the Maghull Novices' Chase at Aintree

Punter wins big on £5 accumulator

One punter had good reason to follow a couple of the 'big three' novice chasers on their way to the Cheltenham Festival after including them in the bet of a lifetime.

Paul Dean, from Stockton-on-Tees, struck a £5 five-fold accumulator when the sport returned from lockdown in June 2020 and got off to a flyer that month when Golden Horde (12-1) and Hello Youmzain (10-1) won the Commonwealth Cup and Diamond Jubilee Stakes at Royal Ascot.

The other three legs were at Cheltenham nine months later and the first two, Shishkin (4-1) and Bob Olinger (25-1), won the Arkle Chase and Ballymore Novices' Hurdle, leaving the bet resting on Envoi Allen (9-2) in the Marsh Novices' Chase.

Dean, 40, stood to win £511,225 if Envoi Allen kept his unbeaten record intact, but on the day he decided to accept a partial cashout offer from Betfair – and it proved a wise decision as the 4-9 favourite fell at the fourth fence.

At first Dean was offered a £275,000 cashout on the bet, but following discussions with the bookmaker he accepted a partial cashout of £300,000 if Envoi Allen won and £250,000 if he was beaten.

"It would have been better if he'd won but I can't complain," Dean said. "I wanted him to win as a racing fan and looked away when he fell. I'm not annoyed I didn't take the original cashout option of £275,000. It's Cheltenham and everybody knows how competitive the racing is and how easily things like this can happen."

His selections were far from stabs in the dark and Dean added: "I study form all the time and the festival is my big target every year. I always try to land a big one and I fancied the pair at Royal Ascot.

"It's not so much the races that make me nervous, it's the months leading up to the festival when my selections shortened. You've seen how many drop out and you just hope yours doesn't get injured."

With shrewd selections, and a cool head at the end, Dean made himself £250,000 richer.

monolithic stature in the jumping calendar, elevated its winners and downgraded its losers. Practically every race of the season is regarded as a step on the road to the Cotswolds, so we are slowly being encouraged to take every event there as gospel, while rendering all else secondary.

★★★★

SHISHKIN and Chantry House embellished their newly earned status with victory at Aintree. Shishkin was not at his best but did not need to be to add another Grade 1 to his record, while Chantry House took a wrecking ball to the Grade 1 Mildmay Novices' Chase, taking the step up past three miles in his capacious stride. He beat Fiddlerontheroof by 58 lengths; Monkfish had beaten him by six and a half at Cheltenham.

Then, finally, we were treated to an encounter between two neo-Arkles when Monkfish and Envoi Allen met at Punchestown over a little more than three miles. The plans of mice and men; Monkfish ran flat in second, Envoi Allen ran poorly and was pulled up, although vindication later emerged with the news of a chipped joint in a hind leg, and the admirable mare Colreevy waltzed off into the sunset of retirement with a convincing win.

A novice chase season that had initially seemed to be of the most exquisite vintage was thus a little flat to the aftertaste, and the verdict of the end-of-year Anglo-Irish Jumps Classification confirmed this. In the two-mile division, Shishkin and Energumene – who had won very easily at Punchestown – shared top spot among the novices with a rating of 169, overall behind only Chacun Pour Soi (176) in this division.

That is the same rating allotted to Sprinter Sacre and Douvan after their novice campaigns and 1lb below Altior after his, which suggests this was an exceptional crop of two-mile novices and hints at an enthralling power struggle in the senior division in the coming months.

The assessment of the staying novices was less complimentary. Monkfish, Royale Pagaille and Envoi Allen were all rated 163, with Chantry House and Asterion Forlonge (third to Chantry House at Cheltenham, and a

winner at Punchestown) next on 162 – Cheltenham Gold Cup winner Minella Indo was rated 175, basically a stone superior. Good staying novices and plenty of them but nothing outstanding. Improvement can be expected in certain cases but it is also required if any of these are to reach Gold Cup level, and Monkfish's attempt to get there is on hold after he was ruled out for the season with a tendon injury.

So we got half of what we hoped for, which is not a bad ratio for life in general. There is a lot to look forward to in the two-mile division, our

Top novice chasers in Britain and Ireland in 2020-21

169 Energumene
169 Shishkin
163 Envoi Allen
163 Monkfish
163 Royale Pagaille
162 Asterion Forlonge
162 Chantry House

Official ratings

▲ Unhappy endings: Envoi Allen with Rachael Blackmore after being pulled up at Punchestown; inset, Jack Kennedy walks back alone and Envoi Allen gallops loose after their fall at Cheltenham

embryo stars having begun to dazzle most satisfactorily.

Among the stayers, though, the neo-Arkles are now not-Arkles, something to which we have grown accustomed. "There'll be another one along in a minute," calls the driver with careless cheer, as we squint hopefully into the distance at the next splash of red, waiting for the right one to come around the corner.

PACESETTER

All-the-way Stayers' Hurdle winner Flooring Porter led a Grade 1 double for trainer Gavin Cromwell at the Cheltenham Festival

By Steve Dennis

CROMWELL was once a name to inspire dread in the Irish, but now the British have good cause to shiver at its mention. This time it isn't Oliver's army on the march but Gavin's brigade, and its infinitely more benevolent order of battle deals with prize-money and prestige at the annual, amiable engagement at Cheltenham in the spring.

Trainer Cromwell has always had plenty of irons in racing's fire, initially through his role as Gordon Elliott's farrier, a position that steadily turned part-time and then vanished entirely as the numbers and quality in his own string of horses increased. The quietly spoken man from Meath, who uses his words as carefully as he once placed those horseshoe nails, has blossomed into one of the big names of Irish racing, perhaps not up there with Elliott, Willie Mullins and Henry de Bromhead, not yet, but it is a blossoming that nevertheless bore the sweetest fruit at the latest Cheltenham Festival, primarily through the exploits of crack staying hurdler Flooring Porter.

Flooring Porter is an unusual sort of name for an unusual sort of horse, a horse who wasn't even a household name in his own household at the beginning of the 2020-21 season. He got his name

from the occupations of his enthusiastic syndicate owners – Ned Hogarty owns a flooring business in Galway, while Alan Sweeney and Kerril Creaven once owned a Galway pub that sold plenty of, well, you join the dots – and, although that convention wouldn't be very suitable for a lot of owners, it has made for something memorable here.

The syndicate, which also includes Alan's father Tommy, acquired the six-year-old by the thoroughly modern method of responding to an advert on Facebook. Click and collect, you'd say, but it took a while for the goods to start arriving.

★★★★

THE key to Flooring Porter's heady rise was the change of tactics first employed at Navan last December, when he led all the way to make matchwood of a competitive handicap hurdle. The official handicapper raised him a stone for that, putting him out of handicaps, but no bother, next time out Flooring Porter did the same to the opposition in the Grade 1 Christmas Hurdle at Leopardstown.

"It wasn't the plan to make the running with him, but he barged his way to the front and won very well on the day. He decided on his tactics, so we went along with that, and it has proved to be the way to

▸ *Continues page 84*

ride him," said Cromwell matter of factly.

Such a dramatic reinvention, from makeweight to heavyweight, could mean only one thing. Flooring Porter was a Cheltenham horse now, and Cromwell knew what that meant. After all, he had overseen the ascent of Espoir D'Allen all the way to the top of the tree and Champion Hurdle glory in 2019. That most lofty peak for trainer and horse was followed, before that summer was out, by the heartrending trough of despair at the death of Espoir D'Allen in a freak accident at the yard, but Cromwell has a gift for both finding and making good horses, as his record illustrates.

His first good one was dual Grade 1-winning hurdler Jer's Girl, and she was succeeded by Welsh Grand National winner Raz De Maree, who handed on the baton to Espoir D'Allen. Without ever voicing the sentiment, Cromwell would have known that more were on the way, given his alchemist's talent for turning base metal into gold. That's no use for a farrier – unless you had the job of seeing to Vaguely Noble way back when – but it is the lifeblood for an ambitious trainer. Flooring Porter had been led out of the Goffs ring unsold at €5,500 in June 2018, and just look at him now.

★★★★

NOT everyone was so convinced of Flooring Porter's credentials for the Paddy Power Stayers' Hurdle, notably the bookmakers, who had half a dozen ahead of him in the market, with hot favourite Paisley Park looking as though he might just be back to the form that had seen him win the race two years earlier. Flooring Porter was fifth choice even of the Irish contingent, his recent and rapid improvement given less credit than was due. Cromwell had more to contend with than a lack of faith from the layers, though.

Four days before the big race, Jonathan Moore, Flooring Porter's almost constant partner and the only jockey to win on him, had taken a heavy fall at Naas and was a doubt for the ride. The usual jockey's approach of gritting the teeth and grinning through the pain in order to ride must have tempted Moore, but this

Cracking the other code

It is unremarkable for a jumps trainer to win a race at Royal Ascot, on Flat racing's most glittering stage, but such success generally comes in one of the long-distance handicaps with some old hearty, hardened campaigner. What Gavin Cromwell did in June with his first Royal Ascot runner was, then, remarkable.

He targeted the Queen Mary Stakes – a Group 2 affair for two-year-old fillies over five furlongs – with Quick Suzy, who sprinted home to win by a length and a quarter from the US-trained speed demon Twilight Gleaming. The daughter of first-crop sire Profitable was named after a champion greyhound, so clearly inherited the speed at the same time as the name.

Cromwell had previously left his mark on the Flat Pattern when saddling Princess Yaiza to win the Group 2 Prix de Royallieu at Longchamp in 2018, but this was something quite different and underlined his increasing versatility and ambition as a trainer.

"Fair play to Gavin – from three-mile staying hurdlers to five furlongs at Ascot, he can do it on both ends of the Richter scale," said jockey Gary Carroll, who was also winning for the first time at the big meeting. "He's invested a lot of money into his set-up and it's great to see it paying dividends."

Cromwell had 15 Flat horses in addition to his jumping string in 2021 and may yet embark on the type of dual-purpose assault on the record books made familiar by the remarkable Jessica Harrington.

"I'm not known as a trainer of two-year-olds or sprinters," he said in the aftermath of Quick Suzy's show of speed. Give it time, Gavin.

honourable man knew he was too sore to do his mount justice and recommended that Danny Mullins take his place. He told Mullins how to ride him, wished him luck, cursed his own, and climbed up into the grandstands to watch.

What he saw made him forget his physical soreness, although being only human it would have caused Moore more than a twinge of spiritual discomfort. Flooring Porter, who had been the one to decide on tactics, now utilised them in barnstorming style. It is not easy to make all the running in a championship race at the Cheltenham Festival, but Flooring Porter made it look as though it was.

▼ Vanillier wins the Albert Bartlett under Mark Walsh to add to a superb festival for Gavin Cromwell

The uninitiated may consider there is something one-dimensional about leading all the way, something simple, but the tightrope strung between doing too much on the lead and not doing enough has prompted many a jockey to take the fall. Mullins trod it nervelessly, as though he was walking across one of Ned Hogarty's flattest and finest, never putting a foot wrong.

Catch me if you can. They couldn't. Mullins sent him to win the race after the second-last and, despite a little deviation from the straight and narrow on the run-in, Flooring Porter was too strong, too good for his rivals. He won by three and a quarter lengths from Sire Du Berlais, with Paisley Park third. Spare a thought for Moore; Mullins did.

"Johnny was the first man to come and congratulate me, and that was a real bittersweet moment for him and a real mark of a solid man. I had my feet in the irons but he had done all the work," Mullins said.

★★★★

CROMWELL had also done a fair day's work and would do another the day after, when he sent out Vanillier to win the Grade 1 Albert Bartlett Novices' Hurdle by 11 lengths. Mark Walsh was in the irons on that occasion instead of the hapless Moore, who was back in the saddle at Punchestown but out of luck on both horses, their exertions at Cheltenham having proved too much to overcome so soon, as is often the case.

Flooring Porter's Cheltenham exploits had the ratings compilers whistling, with Dave Edwards (Topspeed) reckoning his performance was bettered in the last decade by only Thistlecrack and Big Buck's, which is sound company to keep. Trainers are not subject to the stark realities of ratings, but Cromwell's stock has risen without respite since he stopped knocking nails into horses and started winning with them instead, and can be expected to continue on the upward trend.

Now he has two of the four championship jewels of Cheltenham on his record, and at the age of 47 has plenty of time to add the others. Oh, Cromwell will be a name for the British – and Irish – to fear for years to come.

Shamrock
Thoroughbreds

WE PROVIDE THE BEST OWNERSHIP EXPERIENCE TO OUR SHAREHOLDERS

Shamrock Thoroughbreds is one of Ireland's leading racehorse syndicators. We aim to bring small groups of like-minded people together to share in the fun and enjoyment of racehorse ownership. Shareholders receive all the benefits of racehorse ownership and equity shares can be purchased from 5% and upwards.

Our Shamrock Thoroughbreds syndicate horses are trained by Group 1 winning trainer Ado McGuinness.

To share in the fun of owning your own Racehorse, visit our website, call Stephen on Mob: +353857163850, email stephen@shamrockthoroughbreds.com or follow us on Twitter with @ShamrockTBS.

www.shamrockthoroughbreds.com

FESTIVAL HEAVEN

In a jumps season dominated by Irish trainers, a succession of stables big and small enjoyed memorable days at the major spring meetings

HEAVEN HELP US 33-1
Coral Cup, Cheltenham

"I think I'm dreaming. We needed a miracle. Heaven Help Us, that's her name and heaven has helped us." The words of trainer Paul Hennessy, better known as a top greyhound handler, summed up his remarkable part in Ireland's tidal wave of success at the Cheltenham Festival.

Most of the prizes in the first day and a half of the festival had been shared among the big yards, but the 33-1 success of Heaven Help Us in the Coral Cup came from the fairytale storybook.

Hennessy won the English Greyhound Derby with Jaytee Jet in 2016 and Priceless Blake three years later, but this victory was on a different scale. He has only three horses in training, compared with 40 greyhounds, and yet he conquered jump racing's highest peak with his unfancied homebred mare, who carries the colours of Jaytee Jet's owner John Turner.

"She's just amazing, I can't describe her. We bred her, she was born at home and I've raised her," Hennessy said. "The places she has brought us are just ridiculous. It's amazing, just one animal and there she goes. She's my Enable."

Hennessy was unfazed by taking on jump racing's biggest names and made a bold plan to seize the ultra-competitive 26-runner handicap hurdle by the scruff of the neck. "It looked a little bit questionable, I suppose, coming up the first time, to make the running in a race of this calibre, and looked a bit cheeky, but that's what we wanted to do and we thought she'd stay. There were probably 26 Plan As in the race, but at least we got to use ours. What can I say? It's quite incredible."

What made it even more incredible was that Hennessy handed the task to inexperienced 7lb conditional Richie Condon against a field of seasoned professionals, but the 24-year-old rose to the occasion with a brilliant ride. "I must say Richie was absolutely incredible on her," Hennessy said. "I don't think anyone could have ridden her better than that. You wouldn't think he was a 7lb claimer out there, would you?"

Condon had taken valuable advice from Paul Townend and David Mullins on how to ride his race and he refused to be thrown off course by a false start. "With all the commotion at the start I thought it was going to be a mad gallop and it might be a bit more difficult than it was [to make the running]," he said. "But when I landed over the first I had an easy lead and from there I was in a gorgeous rhythm the whole way."

Heaven Help Us had all her rivals on the stretch coming down the hill to the second-last and from there she drew away for a nine-length success. At 33-1 she became the joint-longest-priced winner of the race, but it was an immensely popular success and Irish colleagues emerged from the weighing room to applaud Condon back to the winner's enclosure.

"For the Irish jockeys to give me a guard of honour on the way in was really special. We're like a family back in Ireland and all great sportsmen," Condon said. "It's my first experience over here and I'm absolutely delighted. You dream about these things and it hasn't sunk it in yet. That's it now, one ride, one winner. I can go home to Ireland a happy boy."

There were many more successes to come for Ireland, but few were welcomed as warmly as this one. "If someone said to you, you could have a wish in life – anyone would wish a winner at Cheltenham, wouldn't they?" Hennessy said. The remarkable Heaven Help Us made the wish come true.

BELFAST BANTER 33-1 / 9-1
County Handicap Hurdle, Cheltenham / Top Novices' Hurdle, Aintree

Kevin Sexton thought his chance of a Cheltenham Festival winner had gone when Royal Kahala was beaten favourite in the Mares' Novices' Hurdle on the Thursday, finishing a disappointing ninth, but less than 24 hours later he was on the scoreboard for the first time with 33-1 shot Belfast Banter in the County Handicap Hurdle.

Having scraped into the 25-runner field on bottom weight, the Peter Fahey-trained six-year-old overcame his lengthy bout of seconditis to take the competitive contest by a length and a quarter from Petit Mouchoir, who as a dual Grade 1 winner was at the opposite end of the weights. It was only the second win in 15 hurdles runs for Belfast Banter, who had found one too good on six occasions.

Not this time, though, much to Sexton's relief as well as joy. "I have a bit of a love-hate relationship with this horse," he said. "He tends to finish second a lot and he's obviously been minding his mark for today. We gave him a big chance first time in a handicap with a light weight, but I thought if he finished in the first five I'd be delighted, and that's kind of the way Peter told me to ride him. I was lucky enough that I never got stopped coming down the hill and he stuck to it really well."

It was a Cheltenham Festival first for Fahey as well as the rider, who added: "I finished second here a couple of years ago, beaten in a photo-finish, and I never thought I'd get a chance like that again. I had very high hopes of Royal Kahala and she ran disappointingly, and I thought it was never going to happen for me. I got quite emotional pulling up."

There was good reason for that, as the 26-year-old, who had been Ireland's champion conditional in 2014, explained. "I actually stopped riding two years ago because it just wasn't happening for me," he said. "I had a couple of injuries and I got kind of into a low place, and if it wasn't for my family, my girlfriend, friends and Peter, I wouldn't be back riding. In my head I had given up. I was persuaded to give it one last go and I haven't looked back since. Although I had given up, no-one had given up on me, luckily enough."

Just how low Sexton had been was revealed in a Racing Post interview at the end of the season. "I was done with everything," he told David Jennings. "I'd say every day for over a year or more I thought about doing away with

myself. I used to sleep all day and stay awake all night because I didn't want to be around people. I felt like there was no fixing what was going on. So for me to get the help I needed was massive."

Invaluable help came from Ciara Losty at the Racing Academy and Centre of Education. "When I went to Ciara she was just unbelievable," Sexton said. "I can still remember the relief I felt coming out of the very first session. A weight was lifted off my shoulders. I'm happy now, much happier than I was two years ago, that's for sure."

Belfast Banter played his part on the track. Three weeks after his County success, he stepped up to Grade 1 company in the Top Novices' Hurdle at Aintree and once again came out the winner by a length and a quarter. It was a first top-level triumph for Fahey and Sexton, who revealed he had made a pact with his mount before the race.

"I told the horse going down to the start that if he could pull this one off I would forgive him if he never won again," Sexton said. "I suppose now he has done it, I can't give out to him if he really doesn't win another race. Something has clicked with him in the last month. He has found a will to win. What he did at Cheltenham he had never done before. He put his head down, galloped to the line and wanted to win. I believe he has got such a lot of confidence from that day."

In an altogether different way, Sexton's confidence was restored too. "Life is good again," was how he summed up in that end-of-season interview. It was good to hear.

THE SHUNTER 9-4
Paddy Power Plate Handicap Chase, Cheltenham

The Shunter, who proved himself equally adept and well handicapped over hurdles and fences in the latest season, opened up so many options for his connections that choosing the right one could be a headache in itself. His shrewd trainer Emmet Mullins, though, made a series of

▲ Kevin Sexton celebrates on Belfast Banter at Aintree; below, The Shunter wins at Cheltenham; opposite page, Heaven Help Us lands her festival victory

»» Continues page 88

▶ No fluke: Jeff Kidder (leading, centre) springs an 80-1 Cheltenham surprise and, below, strikes in Grade 1 company at Punchestown

right decisions and the ultimate reward was victory at the Cheltenham Festival and a £100,000 bonus.

Mullins kept switching between hurdles and fences with The Shunter, who won a beginners' chase and finished fourth in a Grade 3 novice chase before landing his first big win of the season in the Grade 3 Greatwood Handicap Hurdle at Cheltenham in November. After The Shunter returned from a break to take third in a handicap chase at the Dublin Racing Festival, Mullins changed tack again to land the Morebattle Handicap Hurdle at Kelso, just ten days before the start of the Cheltenham Festival.

It was Kelso that offered the £100,000 bonus if the Morebattle Hurdle winner could also be successful at Cheltenham and Mullins was now faced with the hardest decision of all. In the end, from the five options open to him, he plumped for a return to fences in the Paddy Power Plate and, once again, The Shunter delivered the goods.

Partnered by 7lb conditional Jordan Gainford, Mullins' 9-4 favourite was in the front rank all the way before powering clear up the straight to score by three lengths.

Asked about winning the bonus, Mullins said: "It's unbelievable. It's great from Kelso. Win, lose or draw we always felt going to Kelso was the right move. It's a huge pot in its own right and [we decided] to go there and take on 13 others, rather than come here for the County Hurdle off the same mark against 24. That was first and

foremost and we were delighted to get that one right. Everything has fallen into place since then."

Going back further, it was testament to Mullins' talent how it had all come right. An unremarkable maiden after 18 starts up to the end of 2019, The Shunter was sourced by the keen eye of bloodstock whiz Paul Byrne, Mullins' comrade in arms. Their new project got off to an infamous start at Tipperary in July 2020 when the stewards hit Mullins with a record €6,000 fine under the non-triers' rule and banned the horse from racing for 60 days, but then The Shunter reeled off five wins in seven starts culminating in his Cheltenham Festival success. No wonder Mullins described it as "an unbelievable journey".

If the 20-year-old Gainford felt the pressure of going for the £100,000 bonus at the festival, it didn't show. "Jordan is catching everyone's eye in Ireland at the moment," said Mullins, who rode a festival winner himself as a 3lb claimer on Sir Des Champs in the 2011 Martin Pipe Handicap Hurdle. "He's very talented and the owner was fairly insistent on claiming 7lb. He's very good and he showed that here."

Subsequently bought by JP McManus, The Shunter continued to run well at the big festivals, finishing second in a Grade 1 novice chase at Aintree, third in a handicap hurdle at Punchestown and fourth in the Galway Plate. In less than 12 months the horse plucked from obscurity had compiled a singularly impressive CV.

JEFF KIDDER 80-1 / 22-1
Boodles Juvenile Handicap Hurdle, Cheltenham / Ballymore Champion 4YO Hurdle, Punchestown

Most people were surprised when Jeff Kidder became the longest-priced winner at the Cheltenham Festival since 100-1 shot Norton's Coin turned over Desert Orchid in the 1990 Gold Cup, but Noel Meade wasn't. Only three of the 22 runners in the Boodles Juvenile Handicap Hurdle were sent off at longer odds than Meade's 80-1 shot, but the veteran trainer expected a decent showing.

"I'm not a punter and the prices don't make any difference. But he wasn't entitled to be 80-1, he was entitled to be shorter," he said. "We thought we had a fighting chance. He just sneaked in at the bottom of the weights and his runs weren't too bad."

Jeff Kidder proved Meade right with a two-length win over Willie Mullins' 9-2 favourite Saint Sam, giving jockey Sean Flanagan his first festival winner. "I was talking yesterday with a few lads who have ridden winners here, and they said it's a feeling you can't really explain, and even though there are no crowds here, I can only imagine what it would be like if there were," Flanagan said.

"To be fair to Noel, he maintained the horse had a right chance, and generally when he says something like that you have to stand up and take note."

If it seemed like a fluke by a juvenile who had finished last of seven at Leopardstown's Christmas meeting on his previous outing before the festival, Jeff Kidder was

about to prove any doubters wrong in the most emphatic fashion.

Three weeks later he won a Grade 2 at Fairyhouse by three lengths, setting up a tilt in the highest grade at the Punchestown festival. Sent off at 22-1 for the Ballymore Champion 4YO Hurdle, Jeff Kidder defied the odds again to score by three-quarters of a length from Zanahiyr, who had won the Christmas race at Leopardstown and finished fourth in the Triumph Hurdle at Cheltenham.

"Fortune favours the brave," Meade said. "He's just never stopped improving and since he came back from Cheltenham he's like a film star in the yard – everyone wants to see him. I think he's liking every minute of it and improving all the time."

That improvement was measured in a hurdles rating of 147 after this win, up 22lb from the mark he ran off at Cheltenham, and Flanagan confirmed the difference he felt in the saddle. "He's an amazing little horse. The amount of improvement he's found since winning his maiden is unreal," he said. "He winged his hurdles and was properly fluent. He was very long at the last and I just kept the boot down, hoping for the best. He duly delivered."

Named after a famous lawman in the closing days of the American Old West, Jeff Kidder had taken some time to find his range but ultimately he was the one calling the shots.

Reporting by Scott Burton, Brian Sheerin, Lee Mottershead, Richard Forristal, David Carr, David Jennings and Mark Boylan

IN THE PICTURE

Miracle of Navan as ironless Morgan defies the odds

CONDITIONAL jockey Hugh Morgan made an early pitch for ride of the year with a jaw-dropping victory on Young Dev at Navan on February 21.

It proved to be a case of 'no irons, no problem' as the 5lb claimer somehow managed to keep going despite breaking his right stirrup after the first of 17 fences in the three-mile handicap chase and riding without his irons for the remainder of the 11-runner contest.

Staying on board was a feat in itself but miraculously Morgan managed to bring Young Dev home in front at the end of a gruelling race run on heavy ground. The 17-2 shot hit an in-running high of 499-1 on Betfair, but there was a dawning realisation that the impossible was turning into the possible up the home straight as Young Dev began to stay on under Morgan's fearless handling.

A close fifth at the third last, Young Dev jumped the next in third before Morgan bravely took him between the two leaders going to the final fence, gaining a crucial advantage before the run-in. Se Mo Laoch was closing in second as the line approached but Morgan held on by three-quarters of a length.

Among the many plaudits for Morgan's ride was this glowing tribute from Ruby Walsh on Racing TV: "That was brilliant to watch. That is horsemanship at its absolute best. Take a bow."

Reliving the experience, the 24-year-old rider said: "My right stirrup broke after the first and I kicked it out. He had run plenty of times and I thought I might as well keep going. It took a bit of getting used to going down to the fences without the irons, but I just left him to sort himself out and gave him a squeeze."

Asked if he had thought of pulling up at any stage on the Denis Hogan-trained seven-year-old, he replied: "No, I didn't really. I felt comfortable. He's a safe old jumper and I was happy enough to keep going. Denis had said to take my time and let him warm up. I also spoke to Damien Skehan [assistant trainer], who filled me with a bit of confidence and told me exactly what the horse was like."

And when did it cross his mind that he might win? "At the third-last I'd say. Going up the hill I thought they had got away from me a bit and I just gave him a chance. Going to the third-last I felt I had them covered. He doesn't like to hit the front too soon, so it worked out ideal."

Pictures: PATRICK McCANN (RACINGPOST.COM/PHOTOS)

'All the people came to see him – listen to the noise!'

CROWD PLEASER

Stradivarius lost his Gold Cup crown but still added to his legend in a York thriller and a Doncaster record-breaker

By Lee Mottershead

IN THE latest movement of a particularly long and glorious symphony, there was one decidedly duff note, although it was possibly more the fault of the player than his instrument. It's not what should linger longest in the mind anyway. The defining sound of Stradivarius's seven-year-old season was an ovation.

It came at York in August, although there was also nothing wrong with the one heard a month later at Doncaster. The reason what happened after the York race stands out is it took place following a wonderfully thrilling duel that resulted in one of the sport's most popular and enduring stars receiving the sort of adulation he deserved.

The wave of delight that swept across those present on the Ebor festival's third afternoon was perhaps linked to the fact Stradivarius had just revived, perhaps even rescued, his career.

Sure, he was the horse who had won three Gold Cups, four Goodwood Cups and a hell of a lot more, but that was in the past. His attempt to join Yeats as a four-time winner of Royal Ascot's centrepiece ended in deflating defeat. Many lengths separated him from Subjectivist at the line, although many lengths had separated the two horses through most of the marathon journey. Even if rider error in part explained what occurred, and other factors might have excused the reverses of the previous autumn, it was hard to escape the feeling Stradivarius had gone from being invincible to vulnerable.

He had lost his final three starts of 2020. There was nothing wrong with his narrow second to a former Derby winner in the Prix Foy but we expected more from him in the Arc and then again on Qipco British Champions Day. At Longchamp on October's first Sunday he was undone by an inadequate gallop over an inadequate trip on unsuitable ground. The underfoot conditions were then similarly swampy at Ascot 13 days later, but to see that famous white face finish 62 lengths adrift of the winner, only one horse behind him at the line, was troubling.

Crucially, they still believed in him. Towards the end of October, the staff at Clarehaven Stables applauded Enable as she paraded around the main yard before leaving for pastures new. Stradivarius had also wanted to say goodbye, in his own way. "The Strad started shouting at her as she went by," said John Gosden when interviewed by the Racing Post in May. "I had to tell him: 'No, old boy, that won't be allowed.' At least we still have him here, a great old character and a seven-year-old stallion."

★★★★

BY THEN he was also the winner of the 2021 Sagaro Stakes. Stradivarius started his new season where the old one had finished, and where he himself had looked finished. Strangely, given his age, this was his first time contesting the Sagaro. In 2018 and 2019 the Yorkshire Cup was chosen to commence a campaign that in both years took him back to York, where in consecutive seasons he landed a £1 million bonus offered by insurers Weatherbys Hamilton. In 2020, there was no Yorkshire Cup, nor indeed any racing at the time it ought to have taken place, so Stradivarius began the Covid-complicated year in a Coronation Cup transferred to Newmarket. Up against Ghaiyyath over a mile and a half, it was hard to see him winning that one. Had he not won the Sagaro there would have been genuine cause for concern.

He not only won, he won well. The trademark turn of foot, not so potent against elite middle-distance performers, was too much for the slightly slower opponents taking him on at Ascot in April. Having swept into the lead halfway up the home straight, he coasted to victory. "The dream is still alive," said Dettori, blissfully unaware their return visit would be a nightmare.

➤ *Continues page 94*

◀ Victory salute: Frankie Dettori waves to the crowd after the Lonsdale Cup at York in August

STRADIVARIUS

Having twice failed to break a record aboard Enable, Dettori was still fixated on equalling a record aboard Stradivarius. Yeats was in Dettori's mind. Gosden was thinking not of a past staying star but an up-and-coming force. "The Gold Cup will be tough because there's a certain horse of Mark Johnston's who has come on to the scene who will give us plenty to race against." Gosden was right about that. He was also wrong, in that there was never really a race.

Stradivarius had been 4-7 favourite for the Sagaro. He was not a massively bigger price when returning two months later for the Gold Cup, a race he had won by ten lengths in 2020. There was also that day a personal-best Racing Post Rating of 125, one recorded on the sort of soft terrain that then and subsequently frightened Gosden. On the Thursday of the 2021 royal meeting, the ground was good to firm. Stradivarius had the racing surface his connections were confident he wanted. He did not get the ride he needed.

It all went wrong so quickly. On the climb out of Swinley Bottom, Stradivarius was eight to ten lengths behind the Johnston-trained Subjectivist. As the northern raider kicked clear around the home bend, Dettori found his way hopelessly blocked by equine traffic. As Subjectivist was going forwards, Stradivarius was going backwards. Headway was made up the home straight but the 5-6 favourite could manage only fourth, seven and a half lengths behind the enormously impressive winner.

★★★★

THAT was in mid-June. It was only in early September, as Gosden stood close to Stradivarius in happier times, that a confession of sorts was delivered. Dettori had erred and he was prepared to admit it, albeit through the mouth of his boss.

"The Gold Cup went wrong, but Lanfranco Dettori finally admitted, exactly 12 minutes ago, that he messed the race up," Gosden said. "I'm not saying we would have beaten Subjectivist – he was exceptional – but we were never in the race."

Nor, quite literally, was he in what

▸ *Continues page 96*

'He's a great little horse to have around the place'

Lee Mottershead spent a morning with Stradivarius at Clarehaven Stables in September

At 5am Andy Laird, head lad in Clarehaven's main yard, begins his shift – and that shift normally kicks off with Stradivarius. His legs are checked, temperature taken and general wellbeing assessed. With those jobs done, Stradivarius gets his first meal of the day, half a bowl of racing mix, a feed whose contents vary according to the proximity of a race.

"This fella is a character," Laird says. "He's a great horse to be around. He's more like a friend really. Flat horses are normally in and out, but when you're with this lad it feels like you're in a jumps yard. He has been with us for so long that if there was something wrong with him you would know immediately."

Garry Rothwell is one of the assistants to John and Thady Gosden, a part of the team for 15 years. He stands looking out over the members of the first lot as they walk around the outdoor ring, their morning manoeuvres on Warren Hill completed. "I've got two children aged five and six, but I've probably spent more time with Stradivarius than I have with them," Rothwell says. "He's definitely a character and a great little horse to have around the place. Some mornings he can be a handful when he's being tacked up, but that's just to let us know he's the boss. He is only ever playful, never nasty. There's not a bad bone in him."

This is already the horse's second stint in the ring. Having been left alone to enjoy his breakfast, he had been greeted by Bradley Bosley at 6am. As Stradivarius's regular morning rider, Bradley's role requires him to brush the horse, check his shoes, pick out his feet, apply bandages and tack him up, prior to 15 minutes of walking in the ring and then five laps of trotting.

"It's great to ride him every day," Bosley says. "He's such a good horse and he loves doing what he's doing. When the other horses come towards him he gives a little whinny. He has plenty of character."

From the great horses down to the not so great horses, the animal husbandry is the same. The horses, however, are very much not.

"The top horses are more assertive," Gosden snr says. "All the great horses can take it to another level mentally. People just think it's about one horse being able to run faster than the others. It's actually about much more than that. When a great horse gets into a battle, when it becomes tight and tough, they have that extra bit to give, just like Federer, Nadal or Djokovic in a fifth set.

"Stradivarius has certainly proven to be both mentally and physically very strong indeed. He's an amazing character but he has the mental strength to go with it."

▼ Home stretch: Stradivarius and work-rider Bradley Bosley

International Racing Club

was supposed to be his next race. Stradivarius was taken to the Sussex Downs in pursuit of a fifth Goodwood Cup. When he won it for the fourth time, it was behind closed doors. Following the government's lifting of Covid restrictions, Goodwood was able to open its doors to all who wanted to be there. The spectators duly came. Unfortunately, so did the rain.

"It's bottomless," said Gosden, placing his hands far apart to indicate how deep his stick had sunk into the Sussex soil. The withdrawal of Stradivarius was quickly announced to the public, although friends Sue Styles and Julie Newman only heard of the key defection when informed by the Racing Post.

Asked how much the absence of Stradivarius would detract from their day, they offered differing perspectives. "It will bother me, definitely," said Sue. Julie looked likely to cope better. "It will bother my husband," she said. "He'll be devastated. It doesn't really bother me, but because it will bother him it's going to end up bothering me as well."

It is not possible to say how Julie's hubby coped with the news. We can only hope he got himself to York 24 days later, for it was then that something marvellous happened. There was no £1 million giveaway connected to this latest Lonsdale Cup, but racegoers at York were treated to a bonus of which Brucie would have been proud.

Two furlongs out The Grand Visir was headed – but who was he headed by first? Stradivarius and Spanish Mission (one place in front of him in the Gold Cup) were inseparable. They pretty much stayed that way for the remainder of a duel that transfixed those fortunate to be on the Knavesmire. Entering the final furlong it looked as though Dettori had got his mount's head in front, yet it was for just a fleeting second. Spanish Mission went past him and looked set to score until the old warrior at his side spied the winning post, scented triumph and duly brought the house down. For the runner-up – matched at 1.07 to exchange punters – it had proved to be mission impossible.

"That was a horserace, wasn't it!" declared a beaming Dettori. "He

passed me once, then I passed him back, then he passed me and then on the line my horse went, 'Boom, I won!'

"When I crossed the line there was a five-second delay and then an explosion from the crowd. I love the horse so much. He's loved by everyone. All the people came to see him – listen to the noise!"

★★★★

THERE was noise as Dettori spoke because Stradivarius was by then conducting his second lap of honour. Such was the level of love being directed his way, the star of the show might have felt he was at home, where two weeks later he graciously consented to be visited by the Racing Post. It became apparent he is a character. We learned the Strad becomes vocal on Warren Hill when seeing riders wearing the Godolphin blue. He likes seeing them and people like seeing him.

"People stop and take photos," said his regular morning rider Bradley Bosley. "The Heath is a public place so people can always come and see the horses. Everybody knows him. When

▲ Duel in the sun: Stradivarius outbattles Spanish Mission to win the Lonsdale Cup at York by a head; below, the tight finish and post-race celebrations

I'm out on him I can see people saying: 'Look, there's Stradivarius!'"

They see him. Bosley experiences him. "When you gallop him, he basically does it all himself," he said. "You only have to point him up there. He gets to the five pole, changes his legs and quickens. He knows what he has to do. He's pretty clued up."

That's what Stradivarius is like in a gallop. It's also what he was like in the Doncaster Cup. He won without turning a hair. It was his 17th Group-race success, breaking a European record he had previously shared with Cirrus Des Aigles. He was denied an 18th three weeks later when well beaten into second by Trueshan in the Prix du Cadran. It was a race staged in the sort of very soft ground Gosden had warned us about at Doncaster. "When it gets autumn deep he can't take it," he said. "He's got a beautiful action and small feet, so he sinks in."

After that latest sinking, owner Bjorn Nielsen dropped strong hints he felt the time had come to pull the plug. "I don't want to race him on like an old boxer who still thinks he's got

◀ Frankie Dettori and Stradivarius after the Doncaster Cup

it when everyone can see he doesn't," Nielsen said. "I'm not saying we're at that point but at some stage you have to pull up stumps and say he isn't what he was. For as much as I want to see him stay in training, the worst thing would be for him to go downhill."

It sounded as though an announcement was imminent. When one came it was unexpected. Stradivarius was going back to Ascot on Champions Day. He ran well but could manage only third. Trueshan was once again the winner and Dettori was once more in the spotlight, although this time he claimed blame should be attributed not to him but to young Irish jockey Dylan Browne McMonagle, who he alleged kept him wide around the bends. "The kid in front did everything he could to get me beat," Dettori fumed. "It was a disgrace."

Gosden was not happy either. "He has run a great race after a horrible trip," he rued. "They seemed to ride to beat him. One day they box him in, the next they push him out."

It was an anticlimactic end to the season – but on that day at Ascot, as on so many other days, Stradivarius showed a fire still burned in his belly.

"He's a wonderful horse," said Gosden at Doncaster. "He's a phenomenon, really. I've always enjoyed Cup horses, so being able to train him has been a dream come true for me."

For the rest of us, it has been an absolute joy.

Record holder

Stradivarius failed to join Yeats on four Gold Cup wins but later in the season he equalled and then broke the European record for most Group-race successes.

MOST WINS IN EUROPEAN GROUP RACES

17 STRADIVARIUS (2017-21), 16 Cirrus Des Aigles (2009-15), 13 Brigadier Gerard (1971-72), 13 Ardross (1979-82), 13 Acatenango (1985-87), 13 Persian Punch (1997-2003), 13 Famous Name (2008-12), 12 Double Trigger (1994-98), 12 Goldikova (2008-11), 12 Frankel (2010-12), 12 Enable (2017-20)

(In addition, Cirrus Des Aigles won 1 in UAE, Goldikova 3 in USA, Enable 1 in USA)

Compiled by John Randall

GOLD RUSH

Subjectivist made rapid progress to take the Gold Cup crown from Stradivarius but then injury stopped him in his tracks

By Nick Pulford

SUBJECTIVIST went to the races twice in 2021 and struck gold both times. More riches appeared to lie ahead for the new star of the staying division but then he was robbed of the opportunity to add to his big-race haul. Cruel injury intervened to end his season and leave an inevitable sense of what might have been.

What there was in those two races was pretty special. No challenger got within five lengths of him in the Dubai Gold Cup and then, in the biggest statement of all, in the Gold Cup at Royal Ascot where he took the crown from Stradivarius. He was utterly dominant in both races and a bullishly confident Mark Johnston marked the map with the battles to come at Goodwood, Longchamp and Ascot that would confirm this was the new king.

"He's one of these horses that don't come along very often where you're not going to look at who's in the Goodwood Cup, we're just going to look if the horse is right. If he can run up to his best, we don't mind who comes," Johnston said after Royal Ascot.

Unfortunately, the next time Johnston made a statement about Subjectivist, just a fortnight later, there was bad news. "He had filling in his right foreleg at the start of the week," the trainer revealed at Newmarket's July festival. "We left him in the Goodwood Cup in the hope it would come to nothing. But it's not proved to be the case and you certainly won't be seeing him again this year. It's devastating because he's the most exciting horse I've had for some time."

★★★★

IN HIS first two seasons Subjectivist had shown the talent to be a staying contender, even if it tended to come in fits and starts. As a juvenile he had finished nearly last in the Zetland Stakes, one of Johnston's favourite targets for a staying prospect, and the following year he did the same in the Great Voltigeur Stakes at York before coming home seventh of the 11 runners in the St Leger. He was a Group 3 and Listed winner in the summer of 2020, however, and the autumn brought the clearest sign yet of his ability.

For his final run as a three-year-old, Subjectivist was sent to Longchamp for the Group 1 Prix Royal-Oak, the French equivalent of the St Leger that came six weeks after the Doncaster Classic. It had been the longest break of a busy season for Subjectivist and, even on stamina-sapping heavy ground, Johnston's refreshed challenger claimed a two-length victory. With a career-best Racing Post Rating under his belt, he could be put away for the winter with high ambitions in the staying division for 2021.

That was certainly Johnston's thinking after the Royal-Oak. "Staying has always been the plan for him and he's just done it a little bit sooner than we had originally planned," he said. "The idea was that he would be a Cup horse for next year and he's proved himself a Cup horse already."

Further proof came in the Dubai Gold Cup at the end of March when Subjectivist routed a decent Group 2 field by five and three-quarter lengths with a dazzling display, this time on good ground. Johnston wasn't surprised. "I kept looking at the form and he wasn't being mentioned before the race, which didn't make any sense. He was a Group 1 winner last time and he had all the credentials for this," he said. "The whole way through the race I was very happy and I thought we were going best. When he hit the front it was clear the others had a lot of ground to make up."

Royal Ascot was almost 12 weeks away but that was now the aim. Shortly after Subjectivist returned to his box at Kingsley Park in Middleham, Charlie Johnston, assistant to his father, said: "We're generally accepting his next run will be in the Ascot Gold Cup. We showed we can have the horse in the form of his life off the back of a long layoff, so the time off between Dubai and Ascot isn't a concern."

▸ *Continues page 100*

SUBJECTIVIST

Subjectivist may have been out of sight as the other leading stayers limbered up in trial races for Royal Ascot, but he wasn't out of John Gosden's mind. After Stradivarius returned to action with a comfortable victory in the Sagaro Stakes at Ascot in late April, his trainer noted Subjectivist's progress. "The Gold Cup will be tough because there's a certain horse of Mark Johnston's who has come on to the scene who will give us plenty to race against," said Gosden, although that did not mean he lacked confidence in his three-time Gold Cup winner. "As long as Stradivarius trains well between now and the Gold Cup," he added, "there's no reason why he won't put up one of his vintage performances."

★★★★

ON THE day Stradivarius was hot favourite for the Gold Cup at 5-6 with Subjectivist next in the betting at 13-2. The only other runner not priced in double figures was 7-1 shot Spanish Mission, who had been almost ten lengths behind Subjectivist in Dubai but had come back to form with a clear-cut win in the Yorkshire Cup. The going was good to firm but it didn't worry Johnston. "Until he went to Dubai the doubt was whether he could handle fast ground. You'd have to say he was even better on it," the trainer said. As for the step up to two and a half miles, he added: "He's not been beyond two miles but we're pretty confident he'll stay."

The stage was set for a vintage performance but it came from Subjectivist, not Stradivarius. Having tracked the pacesetting Amhran Na Bhfiann from the off, Joe Fanning pressed the button on Subjectivist around the home turn and there was an immediate injection of pace. As Fanning powered into a clear lead with the line in sight, Frankie Dettori was caught in heavy traffic on Stradivarius and unable to go in pursuit at a crucial point in the race.

It was debatable whether Stradivarius could have beaten Subjectivist even with a clear run. Relishing the conditions and the trip, Fanning's mount glided away to score by five lengths from Princess Zoe, the 2020 Prix du Cadran winner, with Spanish Mission third and

Stradivarius fourth. The performance merited a Racing Post Rating of 122, better than Stradivarius managed in his first two Gold Cups but behind the 125 that had sealed the hat-trick 12 months earlier.

Reflecting later, Johnston hailed Subjectivist's performance. "It was a proper race and he's won it by five lengths in the fastest time of the day – the only time below standard on the day – and he's done the fastest final furlong. To beat him, anything would have had to have been in front of him going into that final furlong. Nothing was going to change the result. It was probably the best Gold Cup there's been in a long, long time."

While Stradivarius had failed to match the record held by Yeats, Johnston enjoyed a fourth Gold Cup triumph of his own having taken the prize in 1995 with Double Trigger and then in 2001 and 2002 with Royal Rebel. "There are much bigger races and more valuable races, even at Royal Ascot, but I say every year I come here the one race I want to win is the Gold Cup. This is what Royal Ascot is all about," he said in the winner's circle.

▲ Gold top: Subjectivist is five lengths clear as he lands the Gold Cup
▼ Joe Fanning celebrates his impressive success

There had been issues along the way with Subjectivist. "We had a scare straight after the Dubai race and thought that was going to be really serious and he missed quite a bit of time," Johnston said. "Then, to cap it all, last week he fell on the road at Middleham – you can see his knees and hocks are skinned."

The Johnston team had done a fantastic job to get Subjectivist to Royal Ascot at the top of his game, but he would go no further. No sooner had the prospect of a rematch with Stradivarius been touted as something akin to the great rivalry between Le Moss and Ardross more than 40 years ago than the devastating news broke of Subjectivist's injury. "It's absolutely heartbreaking," Johnston said as the new staying star departed the stage at the end of act two.

Even with a resurgent Stradivarius and the redoubtable Trueshan on the scene, no other staying performance all year bettered Subjectivist's Gold Cup. His rivals could not improve on that, but he might have done. It was such a pity that opportunity was snatched away from him.

Horseboxes – Uprating and Downplating

Uprating Horseboxes

As you may be aware, the DVSA is paying close attention to the horsebox industry and in particular, to lightweight horseboxes which they suspect may be operating overweight.

We have seen cases of horseboxes being stopped, checked and impounded on the roadside, owing to running overweight. The horses in transit have to be loaded into a different box and taken away, and the resultant fines are ever increasing in size. Yet, there is an alternative.

SvTech is keen to promote its uprating service for lightweight horseboxes (3500kg), whereby the horsebox can gain an extra 200-300kg in payload. This provides vital payload capability when carrying an extra horse and/or tack and offers peace of mind for the owner.

SvTech has carried out extensive work and testing on lightweight models and has covered uprates for most lightweight vehicles.

It is worth noting that some uprates require modifications or changes to the vehicle's braking, tyres and/or suspension, for which SvTech provides a simple

purpose-built suspension assister kit. This will take between 1-2 hours for you to fit. Your horsebox will then go for a formal inspection to bring it into the 'Goods' category, and, depending on the vehicle's age, may also require fitment of a speed limiter, for which there are one or two options. Most importantly, vehicles registered after May 2002 must be fitted with manufacturer's ABS, if going above 3500kg.

If you're unsure, or don't believe that you need to uprate your lightweight horsebox, try taking it to a public weighbridge when you're fully loaded with your horse, tack, passenger, hay, etc. and weigh off each axle individually and the vehicle as a whole. There could be a distinct chance that you've overloaded one of the axles, even if you're within the GVW. If there is a problem, we can help. Call us to discuss your options.

Due to recent changes at DVSA, we are no longer required to make a mechanical change to the vehicle and, once downrated, we will be supplying you with a revised set of Ministry plating certificates, or if exempt, plating and testing, a converter's plate and certificate at the lower weight.

Depending upon vehicle usage, it is at the discretion of DVSA as to whether they will require a formal inspection of your vehicle.

DOWNLOAD AND FILL IN THE ENQUIRY FORM AND RETURN IT ALONG WITH THE INFO REQUESTED

Downplating Horseboxes

Do you own a 10 - 12.5 tonnes horsebox and do you want non-HGV licence holder to drive it? Your horsebox could b downplated to 7.5 tonnes so that any driver with a licence issued prior to 1st Jan 1997 could drive it.

● You are paying too much Vehicle Excise Duty.

● You want to escape the need for a tachograph.

The most important aspect when downplating is to leave yourself suitable payload to carry your goods. The Ministry requires that for horseboxes of 7500kg there is a minimum payload of 2000kg. Hence, when downplating to 7500kg, the unladen weight must not exceed 5500kg. For 3500kg horseboxes, you must ensure that you have a payload of at least 1000kg, thus, when empty it cannot weigh more than 2500kg.

SvTech
Special Vehicle Technology

T +44 (0)1772 621800
E webenquiries@svtech.co.uk

TRUE STAYER

By Jonathan Harding

WHEN the going gets soft, Trueshan gets going. His connections had to be patient in waiting for the right conditions throughout a long and sometimes frustrating season, but there was no better stayer in deep ground and the reward was a pair of runaway Group 1 triumphs as well as a second Long Distance Cup on Champions Day. "Lethal" was how trainer Alan King described him, and that's exactly what he was on the sodden battlefields of Goodwood, Longchamp and Ascot.

That pronounced preference for soft ground was crystal clear on Champions Day 2020 when Trueshan left his rivals for dead in the Long Distance Cup, bringing his season to a close with a seven-and-a-half-length victory, and the whole of his 2021 campaign revolved around holding out for his preferred conditions. Four turf runs was all he managed, but they were enough.

The first outing came at Chester's May meeting in the Ormonde Stakes, which was an unusual venue and race as prep for the Gold Cup at Royal Ascot, but already the weather had reduced King's options. The trade-off for good to soft going was that Trueshan had to concede 5lb to dual Group 1 winner Japan over an inadequate trip, but he ran the Aidan O'Brien-trained favourite to three-quarters of a length with subsequent Irish St Leger winner Sonnyboyliston well back in third.

King was pleased Trueshan's season was up and running. "It's been worrying me that he's been ready to run for the last three or four weeks," he said. "I wasn't sure I could hang on to him for much longer. I'm thrilled with the way he's run."

So was Hollie Doyle, renewing her partnership with Trueshan from their Long Distance Cup success the previous autumn. "He probably wasn't at home 100 per cent on this track. There are big things to come from him," she said.

Those big things would not come in the Gold Cup, which was the first tempting prize that had to be spurned by Trueshan's team when the going on day three of Royal Ascot came up good to firm. If the rain that turned the ground heavy on the Friday had arrived 24 hours earlier, Trueshan would have been allowed to take his chance – and it would have been a very good chance at that. Instead, as Subjectivist took the crown from Stradivarius, Trueshan's connections had to rue their luck and bide their time.

"You couldn't believe we didn't get any rain on Thursday but it wasn't to be and I've no doubt it was the right decision not to run him," King said as he redirected Trueshan to the Northumberland Plate, which came nine days after the Gold Cup. It was an entirely different test in a handicap under top weight of 9st 13lb on Newcastle's all-weather surface, but a necessary one according to his trainer.

"It was always the plan that if Ascot wasn't right for him we had this to fall back on. If we back off him and then prepare him for the Goodwood Cup, that's a long time to wait and the ground might not be right there either."

Trueshan ran with credit at Newcastle, beaten just under four lengths in sixth place, and King was confident he would have him ready for Glorious Goodwood if conditions were right.

★★★★

THIS time the weather gods heard the prayers. More than 30mm of rain hit the Sussex track on the Sunday, two days before the

▶ *Continues page 104*

Trueshan relished gruelling conditions at Goodwood, Longchamp and Ascot and gave trainer Alan King his first Group 1 honours on the Flat

meeting opened, and an unexpected thunderstorm on Monday night left the ground described as heavy, soft in places for day one, which had the Goodwood Cup as its centrepiece. "I thought the rain they had already would make it safe to run, but to see Trueshan at his best it's a case of the more rain the better," said a happy King.

When things went right for Trueshan, they usually went wrong for Stradivarius and that was the case again. After walking the track following the first race of the meeting, John and Thady Gosden decided their star stayer would not bid for a fifth consecutive Goodwood Cup. "We made the mistake of running him on the wrong ground at Longchamp and Ascot. There's no point making that mistake again," Gosden snr said. "The ground is bottomless. This is going to be a slog."

A slog, you say? That was just what Trueshan wanted and, having finally got his ideal conditions, he produced a commanding performance. After racing freely, Trueshan, who took over as favourite in Stradivarius's absence, was switched to the rail by Doyle and amid cries of "Go on Hollie" he stretched three and three-quarter lengths clear of Away He Goes.

It was a huge moment for King, whose gradual shift in focus towards the Flat at his Barbury Castle yard in Wiltshire was rewarded with his first Group 1 success. He has registered 31 wins at the highest level over jumps since his first in 1999, including the Queen Mother Champion Chase with Voy Por Ustedes in 2007 and the Champion Hurdle with Katchit the following year.

"It's right up there with the Champion Hurdle and races like that, of course it is," he said. "All I want to do is train proper horses – I don't mind if they're jumpers or not."

Training proper horses comes with its pressures and expectations, and they doubled in size following the late withdrawal of Stradivarius. "I was okay until about 1.30pm – maybe it was too many glasses of red wine – but the nerves kicked in when John [Gosden] took him out," King said. "We got shorter and shorter in the market and I've not felt that nervous for a long time."

King, who also won the Group 2 Richmond Stakes with two-year-old Asymmetric in a landmark week, has formed a strong working relationship with Doyle, whose decision to switch Trueshan to the rail proved pivotal to their Goodwood Cup success.

"I was confident but I've not had many top-level experiences, especially not on a short-priced favourite, but he's exceptionally talented on this ground," said Doyle, who perhaps received the warmest reception during Glorious Goodwood. "I got some buzz," she said after her second Group 1 victory. "I try not to get too high or low but you have to make the most of experiences like that."

★★★★

DOYLE was set to partner Trueshan in the Group 2 Lonsdale Cup and Doncaster Cup, which were run on quick ground and won by Stradivarius, but he was twice ruled out and instead redirected to the Group 1 Prix du Cadran at Longchamp, where the damp October weather turned the going very soft.

Unfortunately, while Trueshan made that date, Doyle did not. She failed to overturn a six-day whip ban and King had to turn to another Doyle, James, to do the steering.

Stradivarius turned up, even though the ground seemed against him. In the only previous encounter between the top stayers with very different going preferences, Trueshan had finished 62 lengths clear of his rival on Champions Day 2020 and, while the margin was much reduced at Longchamp, the outcome was the same.

Trueshan once again relished the testing ground and, after taking the lead with a furlong to travel, forged clear to beat Stradivarius by four and a half lengths. Speaking after the race, Doyle spared a thought for the jockey he had replaced. "Hollie has been a big part of this horse's career and to miss out through suspension is pretty tough," he said. "I'm thinking of her but it's not the first time it's happened in racing. She has a lot to look forward to with him."

The winning Racing Post Rating of 122 took Trueshan alongside Subjectivist at the top of the 2021

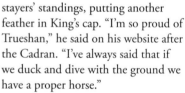

▲ Long game: Trueshan and Hollie Doyle win the Long Distance Cup for the second year running; below, a jubilant Doyle and Alan King after their Group 1 success in the Goodwood Cup; previous page, another Group 1 victory in the Prix du Cadran, this time with James Doyle on board

stayers' standings, putting another feather in King's cap. "I'm so proud of Trueshan," he said on his website after the Cadran. "I've always said that if we duck and dive with the ground we have a proper horse."

The autumn ground was good to soft for Champions Day and King sent Trueshan back to the Long Distance Cup a fortnight later, with Hollie Doyle back on board. Sent off even-money favourite, he came out on top in a messy race by a length and a half from 50-1 shot Tashkhan, with Stradivarius third.

Doyle, taking a lead role on Champions Day for the second year running, was delighted. "He's so brave and the further he goes the better," she said. "He's a horse you dream of finding in your career and thankfully I did."

Trueshan is a dream horse for King too, although relief appeared to be the overriding emotion on this occasion. "The pressure was huge," he said. "I was more nervous today because of the fact it had only been two weeks since Longchamp. I don't think he was at his best but we got away with it."

There is still unfinished business. "Let's hope we get a wet Royal Ascot next year as it would be lovely to run him in the Gold Cup," King added.

The ducking and diving goes on.

THE
BIGGER
PICTURE

David Redvers, owner and manager of Tweenhills Stud in Gloucestershire, with the 2020 2,000 Guineas winner Kameko, who is now one of the resident stallions

EDWARD WHITAKER (RACINGPOST.COM/PHOTOS)

TORQUATOR WHO?

Germany's Arc hero Torquator Tasso made a name for himself with a stunning upset in Europe's greatest race

By Steve Dennis

THERE were many questions to be answered as the runners for the 100th Prix de l'Arc de Triomphe, Europe's greatest race, went one by one into the stalls at Longchamp. Could Adayar become only the third horse ever to win the Derby, the King George and the Arc? Could Hurricane Lane be the first St Leger winner to triumph on the Bois de Boulogne? What about that great pioneering trainer Dermot Weld, could he win his first Arc? Was this to be Japan's year at last? Would the record-breaking filly Snowfall bounce back from her recent defeat? Two and a half minutes later, only one question remained. And it was "Who?"

It was a question that did a great disservice to the answer. Torquator Tasso won the Arc fair and square, this archetype of the stamina-rich German bloodstock industry splashing swiftly through the mud to beat rivals who on the day were not better horses but only better fancied. Torquator Tasso was a 72-1 chance, blithely dismissed by the vast majority of pundits, but that was our fault, not his.

It has been this way for decades. German horses have been widely ignored by the wider world since before Niederlander finished fourth in the inaugural Washington International in 1952. The victories of Star Appeal in the Eclipse and the Arc in 1975 didn't change a thing. He was 119-1 at Longchamp; what were we thinking? Perhaps Torquator Tasso, whose name once heard is impossible to forget, might be the one to make the difference, the latest in a long line of German-trained stars who have been underestimated and underappreciated, and have overachieved.

. . . Star Appeal . . . Acatenango . . . Mondrian . . . Lomitas . . .

There were 14 runners in the Arc, eight of them Group 1 winners, not quite a ratio to rival the incomparable year of Dancing Brave but a field brimming with

▸ *Continues page 110*

Have saddle . . .

FOR Rene Piechulek, the Munich-based jockey who delivered Torquator Tasso to the winner's enclosure with such assurance, the Arc was only the third Group 1 success of his career. As he returned to weigh in, Piechulek held up his saddle to show the name Minarik inscribed underneath.

Filip Minarik, four-time champion jockey of Germany, had his career cut short by a fall at Mannheim in July 2020, in which he sustained head injuries that left him in a coma, from which he is steadily recovering. Minarik never rode in an Arc but his saddle did the job very nicely for him, to the delight of the Czech-born rider.

"When I was forced to end my career, of course my home was full of riding equipment," he told Czech racing writer Michaela Moricova. "When jockeys came to visit, to see how I was doing, to say hello, I was very glad when they took away various items to use and then put some money into my daughter's bank account. It was important for me that my things were still being used, even though I couldn't use them any more. Rene took lots of stuff, including the saddle.

"I wouldn't have dreamed of the saddle being in the Arc; it just didn't cross my mind at all. I won the Grosser Preis von Baden in 2014 and he went on to run in the Arc, but I was replaced by another jockey [William Buick]. That's just the way it is."

Piechulek had won both his previous Group 1s when using Minarik's saddle, and Minarik backed Torquator Tasso for the Arc through sentiment rather than confidence. "Did I think he could win? No, not at all," he told Moricova. "I had no hopes even in the final straight, but when Torquator Tasso charged forward I shouted and screamed like crazy, we all did. I still can't believe he really won."

brilliance nevertheless. Torquator Tasso was one of those Group 1 winners, having won the Grosser Preis von Berlin and the GP von Baden; also on his resume was the runner-up spot in the 2020 Deutsches Derby, in which he was beaten by subsequent Arc runner-up In Swoop. And still the little alarm bells didn't ring.

It was a stellar line-up, though. Derby and King George winner Adayar; Irish Derby and St Leger winner Hurricane Lane, backed down to favouritism as the going deteriorated; Breeders' Cup Turf and Prix Vermeille winner Tarnawa; triple Oaks winner Snowfall; Sheema Classic runner-up and multiple Grade 1 winner Chrono Genesis; Grand Prix de Saint-Cloud winner Broome; Juddmonte International runner-up Alenquer.

It is understandable that Torquator Tasso was somewhat lost in the mix, but there was no reason for him to be drowned out entirely. After all, before the race Torquator Tasso, with his two Group 1s, had a higher Racing Post Rating than Alenquer – with whom

he shares Adlerflug as a sire – with no Group 1s. Alenquer was 22-1 and finished ninth. Torquator Tasso was 72-1. Hello hindsight, our old friend, we've come to talk with you again.

In the aftermath, some sought to call it a fairytale, but Torquator Tasso was hardly a Cinderella horse, although his trainer Marcel Weiss and jockey Rene Piechulek were relatively unknown outside Germany. He was a Group 1 winner who stayed well and relished testing conditions, and as Weiss noted: "I thought this was the strongest Arc of the last few years but I still thought he deserved to go to the start. We would have been very happy if he had finished sixth."

Happy days.

★★★★

BROOME made the running with no real intent until Adayar came swinging by to take it up and press on. Piechulek had Torquator Tasso in

mid-division, on the outside of Hurricane Lane and Tarnawa, his white face showing clearly as the mud flew around him. As the field emerged from the false straight, William Buick kicked Adayar clear, and for a moment looked as though he had gained a crucial advantage, but that moment didn't last.

Behind, his pursuers fanned out, gaps for all who could go through them, and Tarnawa and Hurricane Lane soon drove through and caught Adayar. On the right of camera-shot, the distinctive yellow, red and black silks worn by Piechulek went left and then right as Torquator Tasso was unable to match the push-button acceleration around him. He needed more time, and there was enough of that. A hundred yards out he came for Tarnawa and Hurricane Lane, 50 yards out he had them. Piechulek put his whip down. A million watching worldwide picked up their racecards. Who? For German horses, it's always "who?"

... Lando ... Silvano ... Monsun ... Shirocco ... Borgia ...

It was a very good Arc and Torquator Tasso won it like a very good horse by three-quarters of a length from Tarnawa, with Hurricane Lane a short-head third, with Adayar fourth. Take out the winner, and people would have called it an Arc for all the ages. Put him in, and perhaps, for other reasons, it still was.

"You cannot go higher than the Prix de l'Arc de Triomphe. Every trainer dreams of it. That I have won it is absolutely unreal," said Weiss, who had been an assistant trainer for 20 years, his own man for just two.

"During the race I was very quiet. When we won I screamed but nobody saw me." How refreshing for one of the world's greatest races to be won by a man experiencing such elation for the first time. The heart warmed to Weiss, to Piechulek, to 88-year-old Helga Endres, who with her husband Peter-Michael are the people behind Gestut Auenquelle, who bought Torquator Tasso for the modern-day loose change of €24,000 at the yearling sales.

After so many big races, won by the same big owners, the response is a

Shock winner up to standard

TORQUATOR TASSO produced a performance largely on a par with other recent winners of the Prix de l'Arc de Triomphe having earned a Racing Post Rating of 126, *writes Matt Gardner.*

It looked a bang up-to-scratch running beforehand and, with Tarnawa (RPR 122) and Hurricane Lane (125) running right up to their previous best, the form looked solid, giving a firm foundation for the winner's mark.

That figure represented a significant improvement for Torquator Tasso and placed him right at the mid-point of recent winners, ahead of the likes of Sottsass and Found but behind Golden Horn and the better of both Enable and Treve's Arc wins.

Last ten Arc winners

Year	Horse	RPR
2013	Treve	131
2017	Enable	129
2019	Waldgeist	128
2015	Golden Horn	127
2021	TORQUATOR TASSO	126
2014	Treve	126
2016	Found	124
2012	Solemia	124
2020	Sottsass	123
2018	Enable	122

Longest-priced Arc winners

Odds*	Horse	Year
119-1	Star Appeal	1975
82-1	Topyo	1967
72-1	TORQUATOR TASSO	2021
53-1	Gold River	1981
52-1	Oroso	1957
52-1	Levmoss	1969
40-1	Soltikoff	1962
797-20	Priori	1925
37-1	Urban Sea	1993
33-1	Solemia	2012

*Pari-mutuel odds

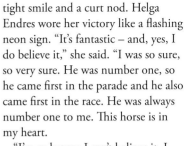

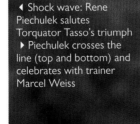

◀ Shock wave: Rene Piechulek salutes Torquator Tasso's triumph ▶ Piechulek crosses the line (top and bottom) and celebrates with trainer Marcel Weiss

tight smile and a curt nod. Helga Endres wore her victory like a flashing neon sign. "It's fantastic – and, yes, I do believe it," she said. "I was so sure, so very sure. He was number one, so he came first in the parade and he also came first in the race. He was always number one to me. This horse is in my heart.

"I'm so happy, I can't believe it. I have a broken leg, so I can't do much at the moment. I am a skier and I have never broken anything but I fell over in the garden. The leg was already feeling better. Now, thanks to this horse, it feels very much better."

★★★★

THE horse in Helga's heart is now in the record books alongside Star Appeal and Danedream as German-trained winners of the Arc. As Dermot Weld, Tarnawa's trainer, said without a hint of the disappointment he must have felt: "This is not a surprise. I have the highest regard for German racing. Every so often they've come up with a good horse."

... Tiger Hill ... Danedream ... Novellist ... Protectionist ...

The cornerstone of German breeding is stamina. German breeders continue to concentrate on producing horses who reach their peak at four or five, and who stay very well. Because the rest of the world tends to neglect this ancient art, it is always surprised when it flourishes, more so because Germany is widely regarded as a second-tier racing nation. "German racing is always hanging on a thread," said bloodstock consultant Jocelyn de Moubray, who has years of experience of the German model. "It is, in many ways, a mystery that it continues. It's not a national sport. People will go to their local track and not even look at what's happening at the track on the other side of the country."

They will all have looked at what happened at the track on the other side of the border. Torquator Tasso, who will stay in training next year, will not rescue German racing single-handedly, his victory will not transform its nature. But he has reinforced the notion that when Germany produces a good horse it is often a really good one.

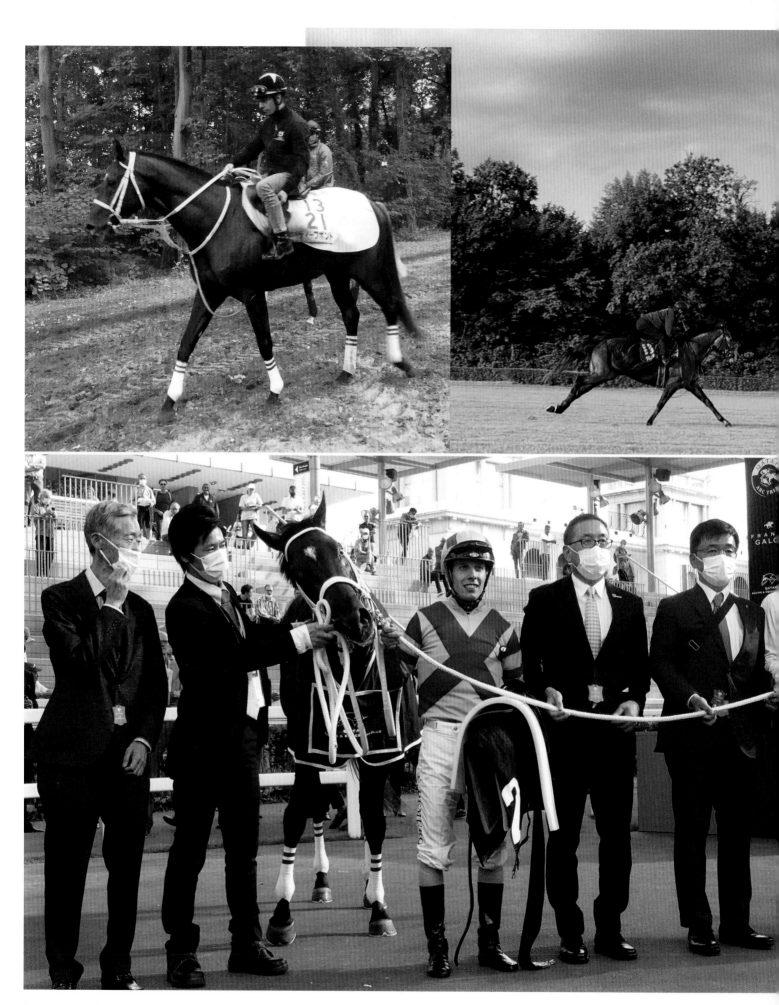

The weather favoured Germany in the Arc but scuppered Japan's hopes for Chrono Genesis and Deep Bond

WAITING GAME

By Scott Burton

WHILE Germany had another Arc moment, Japan was left waiting and longing for the embrace that is desired above all others. Once again they brought strong contenders to Paris – Chrono Genesis had been a neck runner-up to Mishriff in the Dubai Sheema Classic and Deep Bond won the Prix Foy on Arc trials day – but once again there was heartache. This time it was the weather that scuppered their chances.

The ability of Japanese trainers to win on the biggest stages has become an ever greater part of global Flat racing in the last 25 years, while the country's breeders now produce arguably the deepest crops of middle-distance talent anywhere in the world, but still that elusive Arc triumph won't come.

There was El Condor Pasa's heroic attempt to make all in 1999, which forced a career-best effort from the mighty Montjeu to deny him by half a length. Deep Impact, another of Japan's best, was a close third in 2006, albeit later disqualified for a post-race positive test, while the underrated Nakayama Festa went down by a head to a Ryan Moore-inspired Workforce in 2010. Most heartbreakingly of all, Orfevre looked set to land the 2012 Arc, only to fade inside the last furlong and lose by a neck as Solemia swooped late.

This time the presence of Chrono Genesis, a four-time Grade 1 winner at home and a proven traveller, once again sparked hope in Japanese hearts. With Oisin Murphy booked to ride and a daring plan to arrive only a week before the race, many were drawn to the daughter of 2004 Arc hero Bago.

While trainer Takashi Saito was putting the finishing touches to Chrono Genesis's preparation at the JRA's western training centre in Ritto, Deep Bond's connections took a more conventional approach in sending him to Chantilly in late August.

Four days out from the Prix Foy, a tiny smattering of media were on hand to see 2020 Arc-winning jockey Cristian Demuro wind up the near-black colt on Chantilly's most famed testing grounds, Les Aigles. The work confirmed what Deep Bond's record already suggested: a powerful galloper who may not be blessed with quite the same instant change of gear as his sire Kizuna – who trod the same path eight years before him – but whose raking stride might make him dangerous to underestimate if he could successfully adapt to the Longchamp turf.

On trials day he showed he could. With Demuro injecting a burst of pace in the false straight, Deep Bond posted a powerful statement of intent with a length-and-a-half victory over Broome, the Grand Prix de Saint-Cloud winner. In Arc week he put in another powerful gallop on Les Aigles – this time under Mickael Barzalona and in front of considerably more journalists – while the freshly arrived Chrono Genesis went through the gears under Murphy. Everything appeared set for two major efforts.

But one thing that no amount of advance planning can affect is the Paris weather as September turns to October. After a near-tropical early autumn, Longchamp was still at its slickest three days before the Arc, but the forecast was for heavy rain through the weekend.

Connections attempted to convince themselves and the media that Deep Bond and Chrono Genesis were equipped to deal with whatever conditions threw at them. Saito even referred to "the eternal debate" as to whether Japanese horses raised, trained and raced on fast ground would be able to cope if conditions got really deep on Arc day.

And deep they would become, as for a third consecutive year the Longchamp turf took a late lashing, turning the official going description to holding, potentially the worst of all worlds. It all proved too much, with Chrono Genesis burning plenty of petrol early before failing to show her trademark turn of foot in the straight. An honourable seventh was so much less than the dreamers had visualised.

Deep Bond fared even worse. After making short-lived progress in the false straight, he back-pedalled to finish last of the 14 runners. For plans hatched months before, it came down to a final unravelling amid the onset of a Paris autumn. One which, had it happened 24 hours later, might not have washed away their dreams.

THE
BIGGER
PICTURE

Hollie Doyle on Forbearance (right) beats
fiance Tom Marquand on Domino Darling by
a nose in the Listed Sir Henry Cecil Galtres
Stakes at York in August

EDWARD WHITAKER (RACINGPOST.COM/PHOTOS)

Ireland's champion jockey Colin Keane smashed a seemingly unbreakable barrier with an astonishing record haul on the Flat

WINCREDIBLE

WHEN Joseph O'Brien rode a record 126 winners in the 2013 Irish Flat season, backed by his father Aidan's powerful Ballydoyle operation, it looked like a monument built to last. The previous record of 115 held by Mick Kinane had stood for almost two decades and O'Brien's mark seemed as if it would be unassailable for even longer. Nobody could have imagined it would be smashed just eight years later.

What would turn out to be the first steps towards breaking that record were already in motion soon after O'Brien had raised the bar. The following year, 2014, the ambitious and increasingly successful Ger Lyons took on a fresh-faced apprentice as his number one jockey. The teenager's name was Colin Keane and, like Keanu Reeves' character Neo in The Matrix, he was The One. Just after 2pm on October 10, 2021, Keane overtook O'Brien's record.

The name that went into the record books alongside Keane's was Power Under Me, whose Listed win was the rider's 127th of the season. Fittingly, the record-breaking mount was saddled by Lyons, whose support for his stable jockey has been instrumental in his rise to the pinnacle, and the trainer was quick to pay tribute.

"Colin is a credit to himself, his family and the whole racing industry. He's a fine example of

what a champion jockey should be," Lyons said. "The industry is full of people trying to make heroes out of x, y and z, but Colin has done it his way, the old-fashioned way, and let his riding do the talking."

Keane, 27, had to do some talking on this occasion but admitted the scale of his achievement, which came with three weeks of the season to go, was hard to put into words. "It hasn't sunk in and probably won't until we start on zero next year and we're looking back on it all," he said. "We try to beat the previous season's tally every year but we might not have a year like this again for a while, so we'll appreciate it while it's here."

★★★★

THE winners started at a trickle for Keane, with just 12 in May, but quickly became a flood as he surged towards a third title in five years. There were 26 winners in June, 17 in July, 29 in August and 18 in September. On August 28 he became the quickest ever to reach a century when he won on the Lyons-trained Barretta at Navan, putting him well ahead of schedule compared with O'Brien, who did not get to three figures until September 7 in his record year.

Keane was taking note, and he did not hide behind the old cliche of taking it one race at a time as he readjusted his sights. "There's only

one target! I won't be too greedy – 127 winners will do me just fine," he joked. A few days later he said: "It's very doable if things keep going the way they are."

Things kept getting better. On the first day of Irish Champions Weekend, the autumn's showpiece occasion, Keane rode a treble at Leopardstown, all part of a four-timer for Lyons, who made a spectacular return to the races having been away for more than a year. "We're just riding the wave with him and we're lucky to have him," was the trainer's succinct comment on his stable jockey's remarkable form.

The SPs of Keane's winners that afternoon were 11-1, 10-1 and 11-2 – an 857-1 treble. He was not riding good things, he was getting the very best out of horses with small chances. As young trainer Jack Davison said: "He gets every inch out of every horse. He's world class."

When Keane was asked for his highlight of the record-breaking campaign, that was the day he picked. "The whole season in general has been a highlight, but I'd say Champions Weekend at Leopardstown is the one that stands out," he said. "It was the first time the boss [Lyons] was back racing and he wanted to have as many runners as possible that weekend. None of them were favourite, but they were all going there with good chances if things fell right, which they did."

★★★★

IN 2013, as O'Brien rode 126 winners, Keane had 35. That was already a big jump from nine the previous year and he was getting noticed. His biggest win that season came in the glare of the Galway festival spotlight aboard Brendan Brackan in the Topaz Mile and he credits that success as the launchpad for his career. "Brendan was the horse who put me on the map," he said in a Racing Post interview. "I was only 17 and had just finished school. I had crashed my car the week before, so I needed the money too!"

Brendan Brackan was trained by Lyons, who was keen to have Keane on his side every time. The following summer he signed him up as stable jockey and their link-up was instrumental in catapulting Keane to the apprentice title. Lyons' career had been more of a slow burner but he was getting noticed too and the combination of a hungry trainer and jockey working with a common goal was a winning one.

In 2014, the year Keane was champion apprentice, he rode 54 winners and the Lyons stable had 48. The next season rider and trainer increased their numbers to 65 and 60 respectively, and when Keane won his first senior title in 2017 those numbers were 100 and 72. In 2019, as he claimed his

▸ Continues page 118

▲ All this and more: just some of Colin Keane's wins on the road to his record with (left to right from facing page) Search For A Song, Atomic Jones, Acanella, Haparanda, Maker Of Kings, Amhran Na Bhfiann, Helvic Dream (right) and Straight Answer

second title, Keane had 103 winners and Lyons 69. When Power Under Me carried Keane to his record-breaking 127th success of 2021, the three-year-old was Lyons' 78th winner in another personal-best campaign.

One of the most significant moments for Lyons came at Roscommon on August 30 when Offiah took him to 1,000 career winners, nearly 27 years after his first with Maelalong at Navan. Inevitably, Keane was on board.

As much as Lyons has been the foundation stone for Keane's success, having provided 71 winners in 2021 by the time he beat O'Brien's mark, a jockey of such talent will always be in big demand and his record-breaking figure included winners for 26 different trainers.

One of the most significant links is with Dermot Weld, who provided Keane with his biggest career success on Tarnawa in the 2020 Breeders' Cup Turf. That followed hard on the heels of breakthrough Classic triumphs that year for both Keane and Lyons with Siskin in the Irish 2,000 Guineas and Even So in the Irish Oaks.

In 2021 Keane had Group 1 success for another Irish giant with the Aidan O'Brien-trained Broome in the Grand Prix de Saint-Cloud, as well as for Noel Meade on Helvic Dream in the Tattersalls Gold Cup.

Whenever he goes to Britain, Keane is much in demand for spare rides from big stables, and it is clear he is widely regarded as being in the top bracket.

Major wins are sure to keep flowing and that is what he wants, as he made clear just before he rode Tarnawa to a narrow and unfortunate defeat against St Mark's Basilica in the Irish Champion Stakes. "These are the races you want to ride in as a jockey, you get the biggest buzz out of riding in them," he said. "Riding the best horses in the best races and against the best jockeys, that's why you do it and I'm looking forward to it."

In time that might mean Keane pares back the quantity to concentrate more on quality, as many of the elite jockeys do. If that happens, he might not get near his record total again. Nor might anyone else. This monument could last a long time.

▼ Keane hits the fastest-ever century with Barretta at Navan on August 28, putting him ten days ahead of Joseph O'Brien's schedule in his record chase

THE
BIGGER
PICTURE

The 28-1 winner Never Mistabeat, ridden by
Wayne Lordan and trained by Jarlath Fahey,
is in second place as the runners head away
from the stands under a dramatic sky in a
1m2f handicap at Dundalk in January
PATRICK McCANN (RACINGPOST.COM/PHOTOS)

HOME OF CHAMPIONS

Willie Mullins' Closutton stable had a host of table toppers, both human and equine, as he claimed a 15th Irish jumps trainers' title

PERHAPS the most telling observation on Willie Mullins' dominant position in Irish jump racing came towards the end of the season-closing Punchestown festival. "He was the easiest man to find all week – he's spent the week in the winner's enclosure," said rival trainer Noel Meade. "All you had to do was look down and there he was. After nearly every race." It was a comment that could have applied to almost any week of another remarkable campaign for Mullins.

Punchestown was just the final demonstration of his power in the 2020-21 season, but it was a stunning one. Mullins set the seal on his 15th trainers' title – and the 14th in a row – with a remarkable 19 winners from 34 runners, including nine Grade 1 triumphs. He had eclipsed his previous Punchestown record of 18 and put his rivals in the shade again.

"We've had a fantastic festival," Mullins said when it was all over. "I said I'd throw the whole lot at it, which we did, and it seems to have paid off." The master trainer is also a master of the understatement.

The numbers everywhere were staggering. He was champion with prize-money of almost €5.5m and 182 winners, on both measures well up with his career-bests even in a pandemic-hit season, and his strike-rate was 28 per cent. He was leading trainer at the Dublin Racing Festival with nine of the 15 winners and at Leopardstown's four-day Christmas meeting with 13 winners. Even at the Cheltenham Festival, despite Henry de Bromhead's headline-grabbing exploits, Mullins could not be deposed and he took the leading trainer award for the eighth time. He matched De Bromhead's six winners – which of course included the unique Champion Hurdle-Champion Chase-Gold Cup treble – and beat him on the number of placed horses.

Mullins' six victories came with Appreciate It (Supreme Novices' Hurdle), Monkfish (Brown Advisory Novices' Chase), Sir Gerhard (Champion Bumper), Allaho (Ryanair Chase), Colreevy (Mares' Chase) and Galopin Des Champs (Martin Pipe Handicap Hurdle). Yet there was some disappointment with what he described as an "in and out sort of week", which in itself gives an insight into his ceaseless quest for the highest standards. "I was so disappointed with how a lot of the horses ran at Cheltenham and we changed a few things coming here," Mullins said at Punchestown. The results there spoke for themselves.

There was the usual quality to match the quantity at Mullins' Closutton yard. He claimed 23 of the 37 Grade 1 prizes on offer in Ireland and produced the overall champion in the Anglo-Irish Jumps Classification in Chacun Pour Soi, along with a host of division toppers – Chacun Pour Soi (two-mile chaser), Allaho (two-and-a-half-mile chaser), Energumene (two-mile novice chaser), Monkfish (two-and-a-half-mile novice chaser), Appreciate It (two-mile novice hurdler), Klassical Dream (three-mile hurdler) and Galopin Des Champs (three-mile novice hurdler). Although bumper horses are not officially recognised in the end-of-season rankings, Mullins also had the top performer in that division on Racing Post Ratings with Kilcruit.

And once again Mullins was the kingmaker in the jockeys' championship, providing the bulk of Paul Townend's winners as the Closutton number one took his fourth title, having assumed the top job when 12-time champion Ruby Walsh retired in 2019.

▸ *Continues page 124*

★★★★

CHACUN POUR SOI was the biggest disappointment at Cheltenham, trailing in a limp third in the Queen Mother Champion Chase, but he led the charge for Mullins on other major occasions, winning at Leopardstown's Christmas meeting, the Dublin Racing Festival and most impressively of all in Punchestown's Champion Chase. "Chacun was in full flow at Punchestown and that was him doing what he does best," Mullins reflected. "We'll probably keep him to two miles next season, but I wouldn't rule out trying him over two and a half miles at some stage."

If Chacun Pour Soi was 'out' at Cheltenham, two who were 'in' and really enhanced their reputations were Appreciate It and Allaho, scoring by 24 lengths and 12 lengths respectively. Allaho was the highest-rated chaser of the week outside the Gold Cup, while Appreciate It produced the best performance by a novice hurdler, joining the likes of Vautour and Douvan in becoming Mullins' record seventh winner of the Supreme.

Energumene did not confirm himself a divisional leader until Punchestown, having been forced to miss Cheltenham after going lame days before his hotly anticipated Arkle clash with Shishkin. The wait was worthwhile as Energumene powered 16 lengths clear of stablemate Janidil, a recent Grade 1 winner, to put himself alongside Shishkin in the official ratings on a mark of 169.

"It was a great performance to finish up the season," Mullins said. "I thought when we had to scratch him from Cheltenham he'd miss Punchestown, but he made a quick recovery. He's going to go down the Champion Chase route. If Chacun Pour Soi and himself, and obviously Shishkin, get there, it's going to be a hell of a race."

★★★★

GETTING Energumene ready for Punchestown was simple compared with the problems Mullins had faced with Klassical Dream, who took the Grade 1 Stayers Hurdle on the same day.

A three-time Grade 1 winner as a novice hurdler, including the 2019 Supreme, Klassical Dream had not been seen since the days when barely anyone had heard of Covid-19. He had been sore after finishing last at Leopardstown's Christmas meeting that year and had twice missed comeback engagements in 2020 with lameness, being scratched late from the Irish Champion Hurdle in February and a beginners' chase in December. By the time he lined up at Punchestown, he had been absent for 487 days.

Mullins, however, is a past master at bringing back horses from long layoffs at the top of their game even in Grade 1 contests, and he did it again with Klassical Dream. Flooring Porter, the Stayers' Hurdle winner at Cheltenham, was 100-30 favourite but there was plenty of market confidence in Klassical Dream, who was 20-1 the evening before but down to 5-1 at the off.

Patrick Mullins matched that confidence in the saddle and Klassical Dream could be called the winner a long way out, coming home nine lengths clear of stablemate James Du Berlais to earn a Racing Post Rating of 171. Flooring Porter, pulled up here, had been 3lb below that mark in his Cheltenham victory, although he shared top spot with Klassical Dream in the Anglo-Irish Jumps Classification.

It was yet another demonstration of Mullins' powers, and the continual thought processes at work were evident again after Klassical Dream's win. "This horse has missed a year and to come back with a performance like that, he could stay hurdling or go novice chasing," he said. "Staying hurdling is very hard on horses. I'd rather go chasing and, if it doesn't work out, you can always come back."

Mullins is blessed to have such choices with his string of all the talents and he will face difficult decisions again as he juggles his options this season. One thing's for sure, though: he will plot a winning course more often than not.

▶ Leading players: Chacun Pour Soi (main); inset from top, Energumene, Klassical Dream and Patrick Mullins

Championship treble

Three of the 2020-21 Irish champion jumps riders had the backing of Willie Mullins, including stable jockey Paul Townend, who held off the challenge of Rachael Blackmore to land his fourth title.

Townend, whose first championship came in 2010-11, made it three in a row with 100 winners, eight clear of Blackmore. The 30-year-old rode through the pain of a fractured foot at the Punchestown festival to seal his success with five winners from nine rides in the final week.

"It feels brilliant," he said. "I'm riding for the champion trainer so I'm probably supposed to be champion jockey. I'm lucky to have the support of Willie and his team."

It was a memorable campaign for the Townend family, with Paul's sister Jody becoming champion female amateur for the first time. "To do it in the same year as Paul won the jockeys' championship is a lovely thing," said the 23-year-old, who shared in the stable's Punchestown success with victory on Adamantly Chosen in the Goffs Land Rover Bumper.

The third title winner was Patrick Mullins, who held off Jamie Codd after a season-long tussle to take his 13th amateur riders' championship. The 31-year-old, who had Grade 1 victories on his father's Echoes In Rain and Klassical Dream at the Punchestown festival, said: "I needed all the wins in the professional races to see off Jamie. It's very hard for him coming to Punchestown. When I'm riding for Willie at this meeting it's like being at the Battle of Hastings with a machine gun – it's a bit of an unfair advantage."

BDR
SYNDICATES

Putting the fun into Racehorse Ownership

Small partnerships. Winning syndicate with proven success on the track. Three superb trainers, Fergal O Brien, Caroline Bailey and Stuart Edmunds. Stable days and communications integral to what we offer. New members Welcome.

TO BE PART OF OUR JOURNEY

| 07780 607976 | colin@bdrsyndicates.com | BDRsyndicates.com |

TOP RANK

Glory days: Paul Townend celebrates on Chacun Pour Soi after the Dublin Chase at Leopardstown; inset top, scenes from a brilliant finale at Punchestown

Last season's four victories at Cork, Leopardstown (twice) and Punchestown

Chacun Pour Soi was the champion chaser of 2020-21 with a brilliant campaign marred only by huge disappointment at the Cheltenham Festival

By Nick Pulford

CHAMPIONS are not forged only in the white heat of the Cheltenham Festival, even if it is so often where their qualities are weighed and measured. Chacun Pour Soi bore the championship hallmark at the end of the 2020-21 season, deservedly so after a campaign stamped with the highest quality, and yet there was still a sense of disappointment that he failed to withstand the heat of Cheltenham's unforgiving furnace.

Willie Mullins' exciting two-mile chaser dominated his division at every turn except when, in many people's eyes, it mattered most. In his long-awaited first appearance at the festival, he ran half a stone or more below his usual level and was a well-beaten third behind Put The Kettle On in the Queen Mother Champion Chase. It was a devastating low point among a series of highs.

Chacun Pour Soi was better than ever after Cheltenham, recording a career-best Racing Post Rating of 179 in a stupendous performance at Punchestown, and that only

heightened the lingering bewilderment over his failure to perform at the biggest festival of all. "That was the real Chacun," said jockey Paul Townend at Punchestown, while Mullins admitted: "Cheltenham was very disappointing, knowing what he can do. I just felt it wasn't the Chacun Pour Soi we know. I don't know why he did what he did at Cheltenham – maybe we just weren't positive enough on him."

Everything else about Chacun Pour Soi's campaign was positive. In a season when only five chasers recorded an RPR above 175, he exceeded that mark three times in a string of wide-margin Grade 1 wins on home soil. Having started off with a 19-length victory in the Grade 2 Hilly Way Chase at Cork in early December, he took his RPR to a new high of 176 in his Grade 1 victory at Leopardstown's Christmas meeting, with Put The Kettle On more than eight lengths back in third.

At that point credible challengers seemed thin on the ground, with Altior turned over by Nube Negra at Kempton on the same day, and Chacun Pour Soi was already

11-10 favourite for the Queen Mother Champion Chase. His position seemed even more secure after another emphatic display in the Dublin Chase back at Leopardstown in early February, taking his RPR up another notch to 177.

Physically and tactically he seemed to be improving, with Townend biding his time behind Fakir D'Oudairies and Notebook until easing between them going to the final fence. From there Chacun Pour Soi cruised away to win by eight lengths from Fakir D'Oudairies and 15 lengths from Notebook, who had been a closer second to him at Christmas.

"He's special," Townend said. "What's rare is beautiful. I thought we were going as hard as the rest of them could and I was comfortable at all stages that I could pick them up. When I got the gap in the straight, he took it."

The hardest part now appeared to be getting Chacun Pour Soi to the start line at Cheltenham. The previous year, when he was a 7-4 shot, he had been withdrawn on race morning owing to a foot abscess, and Mullins was hoping

for a clear run this time. "Hopefully there won't be any last-minute hiccups and he'll get the chance to prove himself in Britain," said the trainer, who remarkably had something to prove in the Champion Chase too.

Chacun Pour Soi did make it to the start, along with stablemate Cilaos Emery, and they became the 12th and 13th runners in the race for Mullins. The previous 11 had all failed, including Un De Sceaux at odds of 4-6 in 2016 and Douvan at 2-9 the following year, and that left the Champion Chase as the most glaring omission from the Mullins roll of honour.

Just under four minutes after the starter lowered the flag, it was still missing. With Cilaos Emery always struggling near the back, it was up to Chacun Pour Soi to claim the victory his season appeared to have been building towards, but the 8-13 favourite could not deliver. He led over the last and hit a low of 1.15 in running, but his effort flattened out up the hill as Put The Kettle On and Nube Negra came past him. An RPR of 167 told how Chacun Pour Soi had been reduced to the realm of the very good,

▶ *Continues page 128*

Top five chasers in Britain and Ireland in 2020-21

176 **Chacun Pour Soi**
175 **Minella Indo**
174 **Allaho**
172 **A Plus Tard**
172 **Clan Des Obeaux**

Official ratings

'Altior was something special. We've been blessed'

ALTIOR, one of the best chasers of the modern era and second only to the great Sprinter Sacre on Racing Post Ratings in the past decade, was retired in September at the age of 11 after an outstanding career for Nicky Henderson.

The brilliant two-mile chaser followed Sprinter Sacre as the kingpin at Henderson's Seven Barrows yard in Lambourn and set a world record of 19 consecutive wins over jumps, including back-to-back Queen Mother Champion Chase triumphs in 2018 and 2019.

He reached his peak in ratings terms in the first of those Champion Chases with a seven-length victory over Min, recording an RPR of 183 that is bettered in the past ten years only by the 190 achieved on two occasions in 2013 by Sprinter Sacre. Since Racing Post Ratings began in 1988, just six chasers – Kauto Star (191), Sprinter Sacre, Desert Orchid (189), Carvill's Hill (187), Master Minded (186) and Denman (184) – have had a higher mark than Altior.

Paying tribute, Henderson said: "He was something special. You can go back to See You Then and Remittance Man and all the other wonderful horses we've had but Sprinter and Altior would be the best two. We've been blessed."

Altior's winning run started in his first season over hurdles, which culminated in Supreme Novices' Hurdle success at the 2016 Cheltenham Festival, and continued over fences, with his initial campaign including Grade 1 victories in the Arkle Chase at the festival and the Henry VIII Novices' Chase and Celebration Chase at Sandown.

Following wind surgery, he did not reappear until the February of the following campaign but an easy win in Newbury's Game Spirit was the perfect platform to his first Champion Chase triumph, which was followed by another Celebration Chase success.

The 2018-19 season was his most prolific in terms of Grade 1 wins as he collected the Tingle Creek Chase, Clarence House Chase and repeat victories in the Champion Chase and Celebration Chase. The last of those races took him past Big Buck's to his 19-win world record.

He was finally beaten at the start of the following season when he stepped up to 2m5f to take on Cyrname at Ascot, finishing a lacklustre second on soft ground. He won only once more in three outings after that, becoming plagued by injury and untimely ailments such as the bacterial infection that caused him to miss last season's Champion Chase. He was second to Greaneteen in the Celebration Chase in April in what turned out to be the final outing of his 26-race career, which brought 21 wins and earnings of £1,320,795.

Altior's retirement home is in Lambourn with Mick Fitzgerald, the ITV Racing pundit who was Henderson's long-serving jockey. "To have him around the place is going to be special and a privilege," Fitzgerald said. "The one thing I'll guarantee you is that he'll enjoy his retirement."

rather than the great he had promised to be.

Mullins said the writing was on the wall before the run-in. "Paul says usually in the middle of the race he gives the feel that he's got plenty in the tank but he didn't get that feel at all today, from early on. I don't know why. I'm not sure the hill was a big problem for him, I think it was more of him on the day."

Chacun Pour Soi was back to his imperious best at Punchestown with another runaway success from stablemate Allaho, the Ryanair Chase winner, and Nube Negra. Allaho tested the 6-5 favourite's mettle over the first few fences but Townend gradually turned up the power on Chacun Pour Soi and the others could not live with them. The winning margin was five and a half lengths over Allaho with Nube Negra almost 25 lengths back in third.

"That was the proper performance we were hoping for," said Townend, breathless with excitement at this emphatic return to form. "Jesus, he was electric. At every fence he galloped away from the back of it. He was a joy to ride, a serious thrill."

A few weeks later came confirmation of Chacun Pour Soi's championship honours in the Anglo-Irish Jumps Classification when he was awarded an official rating of 176, 1lb ahead of Cheltenham Gold Cup winner Minella Indo in the end-of-season standings. During the season he had registered conclusive victories over Put The Kettle On and Nube Negra, the two rivals who had finished ahead of him at Cheltenham, and there was no disputing his overall quality.

That ultimate festival success was the only thing missing, and it still rankled, but he was a deserving champion.

Top chasers of the past decade

190 **Sprinter Sacre**	181 **Cyrname**
183 **Altior**	181 **Long Run**
182 **Bristol De Mai**	180 **Cue Card**
182 **Don Cossack**	180 **Vautour**
182 **Kauto Star**	

Racing Post Ratings in Britain and Ireland since 2011-12

THE
BIGGER
PICTURE

Nicky Henderson's champion two-mile chasers Sprinter Sacre (left) and Altior at Seven Barrows in Lambourn on the trainer's owners' day in September
EDWARD WHITAKER (RACINGPOST.COM/PHOTOS)

SERIAL NUMBERS

By Nick Pulford

FOR more than a decade at the start of his training career, Paul Nicholls was denied a coveted championship as arch-rival Martin Pipe racked up title after title. Pipe's retirement in 2006 opened the door for Nicholls to take over as serial winner and in the latest season he claimed his 12th title, putting him ever closer to matching and even beating Pipe's record of 15.

That has become a big ambition for Nicholls, whose latest championship came in his 30th year with a licence. Having built up his Ditcheat yard to challenge Pipe and eventually take the title in his fellow Somerset trainer's final season, Nicholls has enjoyed periods of dominance but has also had to readjust his gameplan at various points in the face of fierce competition at home from Nicky Henderson and from the Irish powerhouses of Willie Mullins and Gordon Elliott. Staying at the top has been far from easy.

Nicholls opened up on just how tough it had been at times in a major Racing Post interview during the latest season, revealing that the period after Kauto Star's acrimonious departure from the yard was a particular low point. "It felt as though after an incredible period we had taken a step back," he told Lee Mottershead. "I started to hear little sniping things and people saying we had gone, questioning us. A lot of things weren't going well. It all took a toll and I had a little spell when I may have suffered from a bit of depression.

"For a year or two it was quite tough, and I did struggle, but I always tried to keep it to myself. I probably bottled it up too much instead of talking about it. I thought I had to be strong and positive. I did think about stopping training, but that lasted for about five minutes. We got over it and we're in a good place now."

Just how good a place was emphasised in the latest season, which brought a personal-best tally of winners for Nicholls just before the end of his title-winning campaign. He ended on 176, beating his previous high of 171 set in 2016-17, which was all the more remarkable as the season did not start until July 1 after the lockdown imposed shortly after the 2020 Cheltenham Festival. Nicholls made sure he was ready for the resumption, winning the first race back at Southwell with novice chaser Nineohtwooneoh, and fittingly he also won the season's final race at Sandown on April 24 with handicap hurdler Scaramanga.

Speaking just before Sandown,

Paul Nicholls took his 12th British jumps trainers' title in a season highlighted by big-race success for Frodon and Clan Des Obeaux

with the title long since won, Nicholls said: "It's been a fantastic season and when you consider we missed May and June, it makes it all the more incredible. It reflects well on the whole team, from everybody who has been riding so well to all the owners and staff. Everyone has worked hard during some difficult times and the owners have stuck with us. Everyone's enthusiasm has been rewarded and the horses have been fit and healthy and kept on running well and winning the right races."

★★★★

THE most high-profile of those races was the King George VI Chase when Frodon gave Nicholls a record 12th success in the Christmas showpiece under a brilliantly controlled front-running ride from Bryony Frost. In one giant bound, Frost became the first woman to ride a King George winner and the winningmost female jump jockey of all time with this 175th career victory.

Nicholls saddled the two market leaders, two-time winner Clan Des Obeaux and Cyrname, then the highest-rated chaser in training, but they could not match their effervescent stablemate, a 20-1 shot. Rounding the home bend, it was clear Frodon had them all in trouble. "That was the moment I thought 'God, they're going to have to be really something special to come past us today," Frost said. "I still can't believe me and 'Frode' are classed as a King George-winning pair. But when you have a horse that gains as many lengths as he does at his obstacles, who is as athletic and determined as he is, anything is possible."

Frost and Frodon were eclipsed in the Cheltenham Gold Cup – at a festival where Nicholls, like so many British trainers, drew a blank – but they were in the thick of the action again on the final day of the season at Sandown, winning the Grade 2 Oaksey Chase in a thriller by a neck from Mister Fisher. Frost quickly followed that with another landmark success in the Grade 1 Celebration Chase on the Nicholls-trained Greaneteen, beating Altior in what turned out to be that great chaser's final race.

Greaneteen was the sixth Grade 1 winner of Nicholls' latest championship season, joining Frodon, Politologue (Tingle Creek Chase), Bravemansgame (Challow Novices' Hurdle), Monmiral (Anniversary Juvenile Hurdle) and Clan Des Obeaux (Betway Bowl).

▶ Continues page 134

Nicholls' final total was £2,470,877, more than £600,000 clear of nearest challenger Dan Skelton, his former assistant.

★★★★

THE most valuable win was still to come, however, and it was significant not just in monetary terms. Four days after the end of the British season, Clan Des Obeaux landed the big prize of the Punchestown Gold Cup, which was worth more than the King George, with one of the performances of the season. After the incessant bombardment suffered by British trainers at the Cheltenham Festival, it also felt valuable in striking an important blow against the Irish on their own territory.

Clan Des Obeaux had stepped outside his adopted country only once before since arriving at Nicholls' yard from France, and that journey had ended in defeat in the Down Royal Champion Chase in November 2019. This time he was at his brilliant best, recording a Racing Post Rating of 177 that bettered his two King George-winning marks and was only 1lb below the high he had reached with his power-packed 26-length triumph at Aintree three weeks earlier.

Nicholls' bullish approach in going from Aintree to Punchestown was matched by the boldness in the saddle of Sam Twiston-Davies, his former stable jockey who was called up as Harry Cobden was recovering from a facial injury sustained at Aintree. Renewing his 2019 King George-winning partnership with Clan Des Obeaux, Twiston-Davies seized the initiative early on and gradually turned the screw on his five Irish rivals, who included multiple Grade 1 winners Al Boum Photo, Fakir D'Oudairies and Kemboy.

One by one, they wilted under the pressure and the last to falter was Al Boum Photo, whose untidy jump two out left a decisive advantage for Clan Des Obeaux to take the prize by a length and a half. Only Chacun Pour Soi, in the previous day's Champion Chase, produced a better chasing performance on RPRs on Irish soil in the entire season.

For Nicholls it was a third Punchestown Gold Cup, to go with his Grand National, four Cheltenham

Gold Cups, six Champion Chases, four Stayers' Hurdles, a Champion Hurdle, 12 King Georges and 11 Tingle Creeks. Reflecting on that Punchestown triumph, he said: "That was the icing on the cake for the season – it was a proper job. To go and win the big race over there was brilliant. There's a lot being talked about the Irish and English thing, but as Ruby [Walsh] said England needs Ireland and Ireland needs England to make competitive racing."

There is nobody more competitive than Nicholls, who has relished every battle in his 30 years as a trainer and is still finding new ways to win them. He started the 2021-22 season with a dozen titles in the bag, having won 3,277 races over jumps in Britain and 27 in Ireland, and his twin targets of 15 championships and 4,000 winners, while still some way distant, are looming into view.

He will turn 60 next April, just before the season's end, but there is no sign that the fire is dimming. At the end of that mid-season interview with Lee Mottershead, Nicholls said: "For me, aside from my three daughters, training winners comes first. In a lot of respects that's a sad thing to say, and it has cost me dear in so many ways, but it's how my life has gone. I don't regret it. I still love it now as much as ever."

The juices are still flowing and so are the winners, in greater numbers and at a faster rate than ever before. Nicholls is far from finished yet.

▲ Star quality: Clan Des Obeaux takes the Punchestown Gold Cup under Sam Twiston-Davies; left from top, Frodon wins the King George VI Chase and Clan Des Obeaux scoots home in the Betway Bowl at Aintree; previous page, on the gallops at Ditcheat and Paul Nicholls with the championship trophy

'A brilliant friend'

ANDY STEWART, one of the leading owners in Paul Nicholls' yard and whose famous red, white and black silks will be forever associated with four-time Stayers' Hurdle hero Big Buck's, died in September at the age of 70.

Stewart, who was a stockbroker and international businessman, also owned Grade 1 stars including Celestial Halo, Cenkos and Saphir Du Rheu as well as two-time Foxhunter Chase winner Pacha Du Polder. He died peacefully in hospital in Guernsey following complications from a fall at his Barbados holiday home.

"I've been blessed to have trained for him," Nicholls said. "His loyalty was second to none and it'll be awfully sad without Andy. I spoke to him nearly every day for the best part of 20 years and he was a brilliant friend and supporter.

"He had a heart of gold and for all the money he put into racing, he deserved a superstar like Big Buck's. The fourth win in the Stayers' was an amazing day, but it was just one of plenty of brilliant days."

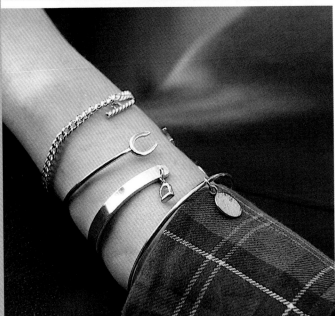

TITLE CHARGE

Harry Skelton became British
champion jump jockey for the
first time with a strong late run

By Lewis Porteous

AT THE end of January, Harry Skelton's ambition of winning a first jump jockeys' title in Britain was fading. He trailed leader Brian Hughes by 21 winners and there seemed little hope of clawing back the deficit, yet less than three weeks later he started to believe his dream might still be alive.

"Shannon Bridge winning at Ascot was the turning point where I knew we had some fresh ammunition to go at," said Skelton, pinpointing February 20 as the day that changed his mindset. "That was a big plus, having horses who hadn't been racing over the winter. Once I had a sniff of something, I'm a competitor and I was willing to give it my all."

Having scored just six winners from 38 rides in January, the 32-year-old jockey swiftly added a further 23 to his tally from 76 mounts in February and the "fresh ammunition" did not stop there. March became his most prolific month in terms of both winners and rides, and he drew level with Hughes for the first time on 129 victories on the last day of the month thanks to a treble at Southwell.

The reigning champ had edged back in front by the end of that day, but Skelton had clocked up 31 winners from 129 rides in March, not to mention more miles than an Eddie Stobart trucker, and the momentum was with him. "It's brilliant and it's down to a good team," he said at the time. "Dan's horses are flying and I'm picking up a few outside rides. I'm in a very privileged position with a lot of good people around me."

Dan is, of course, the rider's older brother and the linchpin in Harry's title bid. A fierce competitor just like his younger brother, he became only the second jumps trainer in history to record more than 200 winners in a season in 2018-19, yet even with his brother riding the majority of them, Harry still wasn't crowned champion jockey, and it took some serious planning to make up the difference last season.

Rather than blast out from the start, the Skeltons treated the campaign like a staying chase, gradually building up the tempo as the race progressed. Whereas Dan had brought forward some horses to run in the summer when he broke the 200-winner mark, this time he held some back to run in the spring, handing his brother an advantage when he needed it most.

Their timing was impeccable, yet Hughes was not about to relinquish his title without a fight and still held a marginal advantage over the challenger until April 13, which started with Hughes leading by one but ended with Skelton ahead by two, thanks to three more winners at Southwell.

That set up a grandstand finish but, with Skelton outscoring Hughes 23 to 12 in the final month of the season, the gap became insurmountable for the reigning title-holder and two days before the seasonal finale at Sandown on April 24, Skelton was crowned champion for the first time.

★★★★

AS A son of Nick Skelton, a dual showjumping Olympic gold medallist, Harry was bred for competition, although it was always race-riding rather than showjumping that captured his imagination. He had his first ride on the Flat with Richard Hannon, but after a year with the Classic-winning trainer his weight had started to climb and he moved to champion jumps trainer Paul Nicholls, where his career took flight.

He had his first ride for Nicholls in 2006 and, while his first winner did not come until the 2007-08 season, doors opened for him. In 2009 he became the youngest rider to win the Irish Grand National when successful on the Bob Buckler-trained Niche Market and he was already being spoken about as a potential champion.

However, there was a period when the outlook was not so rosy. With his riding claim whittled away, the 2012-13 campaign was perhaps the biggest challenge of his career. He rode only eight winners that season, two fewer than he managed during the final week of his championship-winning season. His back was firmly to the wall.

The turning point came shortly afterwards when Dan left his job as assistant to Nicholls to start his own training operation at Lodge Hill Stables, developed near Alcester in Warwickshire by father Nick, and Harry went to work alongside him.

The rider topped 50 winners in a season for the first time in 2014-15 and five of the last six campaigns have ended with a three-figure tally, including 178 in 2018-2019 and 152 to secure the title in a truncated season. It is not all about quantity, with the brothers combining to win at the Cheltenham Festival with Superb Story, Ch'tibello and Roksana, while Harry teamed up with Nicholls to win the 2020 Queen Mother Champion Chase on Politologue.

Yet one look at the rider's big-race wins on racingpost.com reveals succinctly that last season was on a different level altogether. Not only did Skelton realise his dream of becoming champion jockey, he rode more high-level performers than ever before. He

▶ *Continues page 138*

might have been quiet in the summer but his autumn started with a bang when he partnered Roksana to Grade 2 success at Wetherby in October, and that achievement was soon eclipsed with a Grade 1 double at Sandown on December 5.

First came Allmankind, who had started his season over hurdles but ran out a convincing winner of the Henry VIII Novices' Chase, and Skelton struck again on old warrior Politologue in the Tingle Creek. "It means an awful lot," the rider said at Sandown. "I rode eight winners one season and thought the world was going to end. It's a tough game; Paul [Nicholls] has always told me to be patient and after the afternoon I've had now, every single hardship has been worthwhile.

"I spent a long time at Paul's, we learned the game from him, and now I've come here and ridden a Grade 1 winner for my brother and one for Paul. Everything I've put into my career has been worth it for this and I'm very lucky to be in the position I'm in now."

★★★★

DECEMBER in general was a month that left the two brothers full of goodwill, and if there were two days in particular that perhaps gave a glimpse of just how dominant team Skelton might become, it was December 26 and 27. The duo landed five of the 12 races on offer at Kempton's two-day Christmas meeting, including the Grade 1 Kauto Star Novices' Chase with Shan Blue and the Grade 2 Desert Orchid Chase with Altior's conqueror Nube Negra.

There was more Graded success in the new year for Roksana and Allmankind under Skelton and, while the rider drew a blank at Cheltenham in March, he was flying high at Aintree in April thanks to Grade 1 strikes with My Drogo and Protektorat, two talented individuals who look set to play a leading role for the jockey in seasons to come. In all there were five Grade 1 wins and seven Grade 2s for the jockey in his title-winning season, with Uttoxeter and Southwell his most prolific tracks in terms of winners.

His final push for the title involved 90 rides over the final 15 days of the

▲ Brothers in arms: Harry Skelton celebrates his championship success with older brother Dan, who trained 136 of his 152 winners; previous page: inset from left, big-race winners Shan Blue, Nube Negra and Allmankind

season and there was no underplaying the importance of his big brother to the winning run. In all, 136 of his 152 winners were trained by Dan and you have to go back to the days of trendsetter Martin Pipe to find an individual trainer having such a major influence on the jockeys' title race.

"I know Dan's planning and I know what he's capable of," said the new champion jockey. "When he's got something in his mind, you'd be doing well to get it out of his head. I've always dreamed of having my name on the trophy. Not everyone is fortunate enough to have their childhood dream become a reality. I've had a lot of people behind me and I have a lot of people to thank for getting me here. Holding that trophy is an amazing feeling."

From off the pace to out on his own in front, last season really was the stuff of dreams for Harry Skelton.

Clear focus on bigger targets

IT WAS only three seasons ago that Dan Skelton became just the second trainer to saddle more than 200 winners in a British jumps season, yet almost as soon as he reached that landmark he was adjusting his focus.

Whereas the majority would be looking to consolidate with another winner-laden season, Skelton had the courage to change tack, choosing to ease back over the summer to make sure the bigger prizes during the autumn, winter and spring were not forfeited.

Saddling five of the 12 winners at Kempton's prestigious two-day Christmas meeting last season, including a Grade 1 winner, is a pretty reliable indicator that the change has been a success.

Over the past four seasons no-one has saddled more runners or winners over jumps in Britain than Skelton. Yet it is the winners of the major races and big prize-money that ultimately decide the jumps trainers' title and, as he made clear from the moment he left Paul Nicholls to start his own training operation in 2013, being number one is his ultimate ambition.

With father Nick never far away, his brother Harry and sister-in-law Bridget Andrews relaying crucial feedback from the saddle and wife Grace, in her role as the business's finance director, controlling the purse strings, working with family for a common goal is a winning recipe for Skelton.

But make no mistake who the boss is. The 36-year-old trainer has unwavering conviction in his own judgement and, without exception, there is a plan for every horse in his five-star Warwickshire stable. For the first time last season, he took second place in the trainers' championship, becoming the only British-based trainer other than Nicholls or Nicky Henderson to occupy one of the top two spots in the past 13 years.

The final step to the top rung is the toughest of all but, if anyone can beat Nicholls and Henderson, Dan is surely the man.

Poochiful

Designed For Dogs That Live Life To The Full!

Poochiful
LOVE YOUR DOG

MUCKY PUP

DEEP CLEAN PUPPY & DOG SHAMPOO

GRAPEFRUIT & MINT

•Cruelty Free •Pro Vitamin B5
•PH balanced •Deodorising

300ML℮

Poochiful
LOVE YOUR DOG

FURFRESH

NO RINSE DOG SHAMPOO SPRAY

GRAPEFRUIT & MINT

BUILT IN CONDITIONER

300ML℮

poochiful.co.uk

A Curated Collection Of PH Balanced Shampoos, Conditioner & Coat Sprays

 MADE IN THE UK

Richard Johnson, four-time champion and second to Sir Anthony McCoy in the all-time list of winningmost jump jockeys, announced his retirement at the age of 43 on April 3. Racing Post writers paid tribute to a legend of the saddle

RICHARD
THE LIONHEART

By Lee Mottershead

GOD, he tried. With Richard Johnson, you knew what you were going to get – and it was never half-hearted. He faced the starter in more jumps races than anyone in history and rode more winners than all but one other individual, yet while Johnson

▸ *Continues page 142*

Weighing-room giant: Richard Johnson's career highlights

Full name Richard Evan Johnson

Born Hereford, July 21, 1977

Parents Keith and Sue Johnson (farmers & trainers)

Apprenticeship Amateur rider, conditional jockey with David Nicholson

First point-to-point winner Space Mariner, Brampton Bryan, April 9, 1994

First winner under rules Rusty Bridge, hunter chase, Hereford, April 30, 1994

First Grade 1 winner Billygoat Gruff (1996 Heineken Gold Cup Chase, Punchestown)

Cheltenham Gold Cup winners Looks Like Trouble (2000), Native River (2018)

Champion Hurdle winner Rooster Booster (2003)

Queen Mother Champion Chase winner Flagship Uberalles (2002)

Stayers' Hurdle winner Anzum (1999)

Triumph Hurdle winners Made In Japan (2004), Detroit City (2006), Defi Du Seuil (2017)

Other Grade 1 Cheltenham Festival winners One Knight (2003 Royal & SunAlliance Chase), Massini's Maguire (2007 Ballymore Novices' Hurdle), Menorah (2010 Supreme Novices' Hurdle), Captain Chris (2011 Arkle Chase), Cheltenian (2011 Champion Bumper)

Irish (Hennessy) Gold Cup winner (Leopardstown) Florida Pearl (2001, 2004)

Punchestown Gold Cup winner Planet Of Sound (2010)

BMW/Punchestown Champion Chase winner Flagship Uberalles (2003)

Tingle Creek Chase winner Flagship Uberalles (2000)

Martell Cup Chase winner (Aintree) Escartefigue (1998)

Hennessy Gold Cup winner (Newbury) Native River (2016)

Betfred/bet365 Gold Cup winners (Sandown) Lacdoudal (2006), Monkerhostin (2008)

Welsh Grand National winners Edmond (1999), Native River (2016)

Scottish Grand National winner Beshabar (2011)

Championship Hurdle winner (substitute Champion Hurdle at Sandown) Landing Light (2001)

Liverpool Hurdle winner Mighty Man (2006, 2007)

Champion Stayers Hurdle winner (Punchestown) Anzum (1999)

Other Cheltenham Festival winners Dark Stranger (2000 Mildmay of Flete Chase), Rooster Booster (2002 County Hurdle), Young Spartacus (2003 Mildmay of Flete Chase), La Landiere (2003 Cathcart Chase), Monkerhostin (2004 Coral Cup), Copper Bleu (2010 Jewson Novices' Chase), Balthazar King (2012 & 2014 Glenfarclas Cross Country Chase), Fingal Bay (2014 Pertemps Hurdle Final), Flying Tiger (2017 Fred Winter Juvenile Hurdle)

Grand National runners-up What's Up

Boys (2002), Balthazar King (2014) from 21 rides (record)

Last winner Camprond, Taunton, March 23, 2021

Last ride Brother Tedd, third at Newton Abbot, April 3, 2021

Overall champion steeplechasers (official ratings) Looks Like Trouble (1999-2000 joint), Native River (2017-18)

Overall champion hurdlers (official ratings) Rooster Booster (2002-03 joint), Mighty Man (2006-07)

Highest-rated steeplechasers Gloria Victis (RPR 177, 2000 Racing Post Chase), Native River (RPR 177, 2018 Cheltenham Gold Cup)

Highest-rated hurdler Anzum (RPR 174, 1999 Long Walk Hurdle)

Cheltenham Festival wins 23 (1999-2018) including two on Rooster Booster, Balthazar King; leading jockey 2002

Champion conditional jockey 1995-96

Champion jump jockey Four times (2015-16 to 2018-19); runner-up 17 times (record; 16 times to Sir Anthony McCoy, once to Brian Hughes)

Most wins in a season 236 in 2015-16 (235 Britain, 1 Ireland)

Total wins over jumps in Britain/Ireland combined 3,819 (3,800 Britain, 19 Ireland); second to Sir Anthony McCoy (4,348) in all-time list. Also two in France, four on Flat

Official honour OBE (2019) for services to horseracing

Compiled by John Randall

RICHARD JOHNSON was a statistical marvel, ranking second in the all-time list of winningmost jump jockeys with a total of 3,819 victories in Britain and Ireland, *writes John Randall*.

Champion four times and with nearly all the top prizes to his credit including Cheltenham's big four of the Gold Cup (two), Champion Hurdle, Champion Chase and Stayers' Hurdle, he had a career that a young rider can only dream of emulating.

When Peter Scudamore (1,692) and Richard Dunwoody (1,874) in turn retired as the winningmost jump jockey of all time, it would have been preposterous to suggest that their career totals would soon be more than doubled, but Sir Anthony McCoy and Johnson have done just that.

When discussing Johnson's statistics, McCoy is the elephant in the room. Johnson compiled awesome figures but is destined always to be overshadowed by a colleague and friend who rode his first jumps winner in the same month as him (April 1994) and, if numbers and records mean anything at all, was the greatest all-time jump jockey.

McCoy, with a jumps score of 4,348, was champion jockey 20 consecutive times, and in 16 of those seasons Johnson was runner-up, although justice was then served and he claimed four titles after McCoy's retirement in 2015. In other words, in McCoy's absence Johnson would have been champion 20 times and would now be hailed as the greatest of all time.

Not surprisingly he was the oldest-ever first-time British champion jump jockey. He was 38 when clinching his first title in April 2016 with his best seasonal score of 235, plus one in Ireland. He thus beat Bert Gordon, who was 36 when securing his only title in 1909; Joe Mercer set the Flat record when champion for the only time in 1979 at the age of 45.

Johnson also holds the unenviable record of being runner-up in the British jump jockeys' championship 17 times – 16 times to McCoy and once to Brian Hughes. The previous record was a mere six by Billy Speck, who suffered fatal injuries in a race-riding fall in 1935 without ever being champion. The Flat record is ten runner-up seasons by Willie Carson (plus five titles).

It must be admitted that Johnson, like McCoy, was notable more for the quantity than the quality of his winners, and if the title were decided on prize-money he would have been champion only three times.

At the Cheltenham Festival his career tally of 23 wins ranks him sixth behind Ruby Walsh (59) and he was the meeting's leading rider only once, in 2002, when his two winners included Flagship Uberalles in the Champion Chase.

It is possible to argue that he never rode a great champion. According to Racing Post Ratings his best mounts over fences were Gloria Victis and Native River (both 177). Neither of his Gold Cup winners, Looks Like Trouble and Native River, was that season's top-rated chaser, and his Champion Hurdle winner, Rooster Booster, was inferior to the stayers Baracouda and Limestone Lad.

Johnson owed his historic career statistics above all to talent and hard work, initial guidance by David Nicholson, Philip Hobbs's horses, the support of agent Dave Roberts (shared with McCoy) and the advent of a 12-month season.

He was a role model for all young jockeys to follow, and in achievement he was a giant.

crossed the line with second position in the all-time list, nobody could have ever bettered him in a different league table.

This most excellent of men was the finest ambassador this or any sport could hope to have. It is said a person reveals more of their true self in defeat than victory. In such times we learned plenty about the jockey who would go on to be crowned champion of his profession on four occasions.

For at the end of 16 battles, Johnson finished one place behind Sir Anthony McCoy in the standings. Judge him not simply on the fact he reacted to each defeat with good grace and a hunger to do better the following season. Measure him also by the fact that from one interview to the next he spoke candidly and at length about those championship silvers, regurgitating his disappointment with a polite, friendly smile. Never once was there bitterness or self-pity, just that smile and endless words of respect for his fierce rival and friend.

★★★★

EVERYTHING changed at Sandown on April 25, 2015. It was the afternoon when McCoy finally stopped being a jump jockey, signing off with a handicap hurdle third aboard an animal called Box Office. As appropriate as the name of the horse McCoy partnered was the fact Johnson won the race. He did so on Brother Tedd, the horse who became his very last mount at Newton Abbot on April 3.

In the moments that followed the Sandown race, McCoy was in tears. So, too, was Johnson. The pair had sat next to each other in weighing rooms for the majority of their careers. Johnson was seeing his possibilities suddenly open up. He was also seeing his comrade depart the stage. It was the end of an era and it left Johnson thoroughly overwhelmed.

He is an exceptionally good person and always has been, including back when he made his first giant strides in the sport as a protege of the late David Nicholson, whose widow, Dinah, once described the Johnson she knew then as "the perfect child". A similar character assessment came on the day Johnson was shadowed by

the Racing Post. Jackie, an assistant in a Ludlow petrol station, referred to the frequent pump user as "always very polite" and "a happy, smiley person". The sentiments expressed by Dinah and Jackie would be echoed by countless others.

That particular day Johnson – then still yearning to be champion – was travelling from his Herefordshire home to Ffos Las. When we met for an interview in a hospitality room at Southwell the yearning was over. He spoke of his new pre-race exercise regime and explained why someone at the top of his tree had travelled to one of Britain's bottom-rung racecourses for a single mount in a maiden hurdle. "If Philip has a runner on the moon, I'll go there," he said. He would definitely have given it a good go.

The Philip he referred to was Philip Hobbs, with whom Johnson had an association more deeply rooted than an ancient oak tree. There were perhaps times when someone less loyal could have been wooed away by a tempting offer. This jockey and his trainer proved inseparable, with Hobbs as committed to Johnson as Johnson was to Hobbs. It was entirely fitting that they shared his final race together, both at Newton Abbot, both emotional.

In equine terms, their union will be

▲ Golden moments: Richard Johnson receives a special recognition award at Sandown in April; below from top, winning the Gold Cup on Looks Like Trouble, the Champion Hurdle with Rooster Booster and the Champion Chase on Flagship Uberalles

best remembered for the wonderful Rooster Booster, who like his regular rider was known for a series of valiant near misses until at last he was crowned champion. On his day of days at Cheltenham, Johnson's arms were stretched as he tried to keep the elastic band taut on the approach to the final bend. How different it had been when the then 21-year-old won the 1999 Stayers' Hurdle aboard Anzum, a horse he practically carried up the Prestbury Park hill. Victory on Flagship Uberalles in the 2002 Champion Chase was hardly a walk in the park either.

That was the thing about Johnson. The concept of giving up never entered his head. He was both tireless and fearless, often asking horses for jumps that terrified the watching audience. He would push, scrub and kick for longer and harder than most could possibly manage, even when well into his forties, which he already was when lifting the Cheltenham Gold Cup for a second time.

The first success had come in 2000. His ally on that occasion was a horse who on retirement went to live chez Johnson, which seemed perfectly apt as he was trained by his subsequent father-in-law Noel Chance. Looks Like Trouble became part of the

▶▶ *Continues page 144*

family but in Native River, Johnson joined forces with his perfect match, a supremely courageous, hard-working chaser who embodied so many of the jockey's finest qualities. If anybody ever wanted to see a single contest that defined Johnson, it was the 2018 Gold Cup. Heroic does not do it justice.

★★★★

BACK in that Southwell hospitality room there was further reason to admire him when he spoke with genuine regret about having transgressed the sport's whip rules and incurred a suspension in that extraordinary duel with Might Bite. "I was in the wrong and I was punished with a ban and fine, which was the right thing to do," he said. "I wish I hadn't broken the rules and I was disappointed I did. I don't want racing to be looked at in a bad light."

Take that as your mark of the man. He has always been well aware of his responsibility to the sport. Over what turned into a marathon career for a jump jockey, he carried that responsibility with enormous distinction.

He leaves the stage with his head held high, knowing he completed what he set out to accomplish. The race that meant more to him than any other, the Gold Cup, has his name on it twice. Even more important to him, both before and after McCoy, was being champion jockey. Those four titles were so richly earned.

Bestow upon him all the superlatives you like. Each and every one will be merited. The perfect child became a perfect professional and the ideal role model for all young jockeys. There was nothing tricky about Dickie. Racing has been blessed to have him.

Individuals like Richard Johnson are few and far between. As a sportsman, competitor and person, he was second to no-one.

This is an edited version of an article that appeared in the Racing Post on April 4

▶ Worth the wait: Richard Johnson savours his first championship with Philip Hobbs; inset from left, celebrating after claiming each of his four jockeys' titles

Johnson on . . .

His first championship season It was the best point of my career. I've had lots of highs but it was very special to me. The support through that season was phenomenal and it's a time I will never forget.

Cheltenham highlights To win the four big festival races within four years was the stuff of dreams, but I didn't know how lucky I was. When you're young you don't understand, you think it will carry on forever.

Philip Hobbs It was particularly important to me to finish on one for Philip and Sarah Hobbs who, like Henry Daly, have supported me for over 20 years. I'll never be able to articulate what their loyalty has meant to me.

Family They've given up so much for me. I haven't been around like a normal father would be for things like sports day. I want to be there for them and that's my main priority now.

Sir Anthony McCoy I enjoyed riding against AP. He was a great jockey but also very fair. He helped me a huge amount and I hope I helped him because I wouldn't let him coast along. Unfortunately I could never quite get past him!

Others on Johnson . . .

Sir Anthony McCoy We probably had a similar mindset. He's very hard, mentally and physically, a real tough lad but really genuine and decent. He wanted to beat you and was the hardest man to try to beat but he was always fair.

Philip Hobbs He has been a wonderful ambassador for the sport and also a magnificent role model, but on top of all that his work ethic has been extraordinary. I could never have wished to have anyone else as our jockey. He has been phenomenal.

Henry Daly He's ridden for me for 23 years and never missed a Tuesday morning – what an incredible man. He's as regular as you like and I promise you in all the years we have never had a cross word. He's just an astonishing man – an absolute legend.

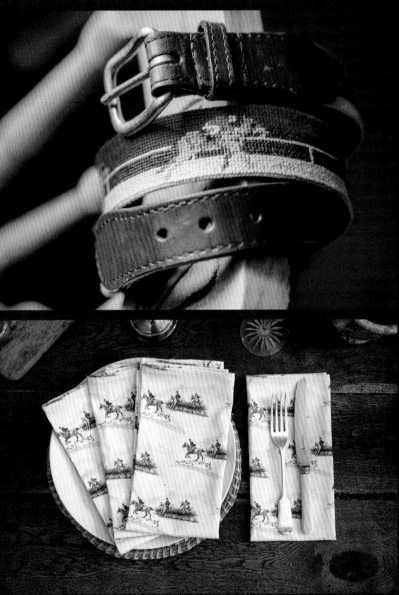

IN THE PICTURE

Seven up as Cartmel legend Tonto's Spirit equals track record

THE returning summer crowds at Cartmel enjoyed a wonderful 'I was there' moment on August bank holiday Monday when Tonto's Spirit scored a record-equalling seventh win at the track in the Peter Beaumont Memorial Handicap Chase.

The Dianne Sayer-trained nine-year-old landed his third success of the season at Cartmel to move level with Soul Magic, who like Tonto's Spirit racked up seven wins from just 12 outings at the Lake District course to set the record in 2013. His first two victories of 2021 had come in the space of three days at Cartmel's late May bank holiday meeting when racecourses were still in lockdown, but a full summer holiday crowd was there to see Tonto's Spirit match the record three months later.

"We're absolutely delighted. He knows where he is and he comes alive here. We love this horse to bits," said Sayer, who trains about 40 miles away at Hackthorpe on the north-eastern edge of the Lake District National Park.

She was also delighted to win the race named in honour of Peter Beaumont, the trainer of 1993 Cheltenham Gold Cup winner Jodami, who died in March 2020 at a time when pandemic restrictions made a fitting send-off impossible. "It's such a poignant race to win as Peter was a wonderful person and I was lucky enough to know him and enjoy his company. It was great to have a runner in the race, let alone win it," she said.

Beaumont's daughter Anthea Leigh is clerk of the course at Cartmel and she explained the reasons for the memorial race. "Poor Dad died 11 days into the first lockdown and the rules were so strict at the time of his funeral," she said. "There were only six of us present at the crematorium. We were only allowed ten minutes outside; we weren't allowed to give a reading. It really was brutal. We still want to celebrate what was a wonderful, happy, successful and kind life, and he loved coming to Cartmel. He would come even without runners."

Sayer's family also has a poignant love affair with Cartmel through Tonto's Spirit. Owned by the trainer's father Arthur Slack, the gelding was originally trained by Sayer's brother Ken Slack, who died in February 2019. "Tonto was one of Ken's all-time favourite horses and now his daughter Anna does all the work with him," Sayer said. "We never go to Cartmel without thinking about Ken and to have a winner with basically one of Ken's horses is just great. It's a very important place for us."

Starman took a leading role in the sprint division as he gave trainer Ed Walker his first Group 1 win in the July Cup and went agonisingly close to another at Haydock

SHOOTING STAR

By Nick Pulford

STANDING at the furlong pole as the July Cup field hurtled towards him, Ed Walker was worried. Very worried. The trainer's concern had started in the preliminaries when Starman, the fast-rising sprinter he felt sure could give him a first Group 1 triumph, appeared to have his mind more on the fillies around him than the job in hand. As the race unfolded, Walker's unease grew and grew.

Reliving his emotions, Walker said: "He wasn't concentrating before the race. If you'd caught me then I'd have been very doom and gloom. Then it wasn't happening in the race. I was feeling sorry for myself at the three pole, thinking it's more bad luck in a big race. I watched down at the one pole and as he came past me I thought 's**t, he's still got quite a lot of ground to make up here'."

In less than 12 seconds from there to the line, Walker went from agony to ecstasy. At the furlong pole Starman still had half a dozen or more rivals in front of him with the runners spread across the track, but Tom Marquand already had him stoked up and the fire was starting to catch light. Hitting the rising ground, Starman proved far too hot to handle as he roared into a late lead and ultimately won conclusively by a length and a quarter from Dragon Symbol.

Reflecting on the turnaround, Walker said: "Tom did a tremendous job and Starman was a very willing companion. He had to be brave and bounce off some horses and force his way through gaps – and he's not a small horse. When he saw daylight and hit the rising ground it very quickly went from 'I don't think this race is happening for us' to 'we're not going to get beaten!' All his best work was at the end and he was well on top at the line."

Ten years into his training career, Walker had his Group 1 victory at last. "It's taken time but it's a great feeling and I always believed so much in this horse," he said. "I put a lot of pressure on myself and on him because the belief was there and it's great when it's vindicated."

★★★★

BELIEF in Starman had grown quickly. Having not started his racing career until July 2020, well into his three-year-old season, Starman had reeled off three wins on the bounce, rapidly reaching a Racing Post Rating of 116 with the last of them in a Listed race at York. His first season ended on a low note when he was only 14th in the Group 1 British Champions Sprint at Ascot, but that was on soft ground and it was already clear he wanted a fast surface.

"He's very fast – and massively talented and exciting. I'm praying he'll win a big one," said Walker as the new season opened, and Starman's reappearance in the Group 2 Duke of York Stakes only added to the sense of anticipation. Against a high-class field that included 2020 July Cup winner Oxted and subsequent Haydock Sprint Cup scorer Emaraaty Ana, Starman showed spirit as well as speed to edge out Nahaarr by a neck.

The obvious next destination was Royal Ascot for the Diamond Jubilee Stakes but the ground went against Starman and he was withdrawn. After the first three days were run on good to firm, the going turned heavy on the Friday and was soft on the Saturday for the Diamond Jubilee. "It's pretty brutal. We've got this horse of a lifetime and we can't run him," Walker said. "He's been to Ascot once before on soft ground and didn't perform; we don't want to make the same mistake again."

The road map after Ascot no doubt would have led to the July Cup and Walker immediately pointed Starman in that direction. At Newmarket he was 9-2 second favourite, with his main market rivals all having run well at the royal meeting. Dragon Symbol, demoted to second in the Commonwealth Cup, was 7-2 favourite, Jersey Stakes winner Creative Force went off 5-1 and Oxted was 11-2 after his King's Stand Stakes success.

The good to firm ground was in Starman's favour but virtually everything seemed to go against him in the race. Slightly caught out as the pace lifted at halfway, Marquand's mount ran into traffic problems with two and a furlongs to run and again about a furlong later, before turning a lost cause into a magnificent win.

"They had me in a bit of trouble at the three pole, where you start running downhill," Marquand said. "As these top-class sprinters were quickening, it all got a bit tight. He's very inexperienced

▸ *Continues page 150*

◄ Flying finish: Starman and Tom Marquand win a dramatic July Cup with an electrifying late burst

compared to a lot of them, but my God he had a turn of foot when he hit that rising ground."

★★★★

JULY CUP glory was also a fairytale for owner David Ward, a big David Bowie fan whose Starman had blown his mind. "This is what dreams are made of," he said. "He's the second horse I've bred and he's probably the horse of a lifetime. We always believed he was seriously talented and he is, but you've got to come to these places against tip-top competition. He's realised everything we wanted him to. I'm just the lucky chap who's managed to come along on the trip."

Next stop on the trip was the Prix Maurice de Gheest at Deauville, where Starman ran well to finish third behind home-trained pair Marianafoot and Tropbeau considering the six-and-a-half-furlong trip stretched his stamina in unsuitable conditions. "We took a bit of a gamble in hoping we were wrong about the ground being too soft for him, but unfortunately we were right," Walker said.

The ground was good to firm for the Haydock Sprint Cup in early September and Starman was back to his best but he fell short by a short head against Emaraaty Ana. Again his connections ran the gamut of emotions as he made his late charge and Walker admitted he did not take the defeat well on the day.

Reflecting more calmly a few days later, he said: "It was similar to the July Cup as there was a period when it looked as though he had no chance, then my emotions did a complete 180 when he was set to win – and then he didn't quite do it. It's amazing what can happen in little more than a minute. It was heartbreaking, a real rollercoaster. Sport is all about fine margins and we were just the wrong side of a great race."

That turned out to be the last we saw of Starman, who was retired to stud after a slight setback ruled him out of the British Champions Sprint won by Creative Force, but his edge-of-the-seat style of racing contributed hugely to the sprint season. With its stomach-lurching twists and turns, ups and downs, this rollercoaster was an exhilarating ride.

'A top career and it's been a great trip' – Battaash bows out

"There comes a time for all of us." The words of Angus Gold, long-serving racing manager to Shadwell Estate, signalled the end was nigh for Battaash's superlative racing career after a lacklustre defeat at Glorious Goodwood. Twenty-four hours later came the inevitable confirmation of the brilliant sprinter's retirement. It was the end of an era.

At Charlie Hills's Faringdon Place Stables in Lambourn there was sadness but also immense pride. "It's been a great trip, a hell of a journey," Hills said. "This weekend has been emotional. We had six years and it was great having a horse like him who kept going for so long. He became very close to everyone at the yard and my family as well. He had 25 starts and was out of the first four just three times. He's had a top career."

Battaash had won on all three outings in 2020 but, having sustained a small fracture over the winter that necessitated having a pin put in a joint, he could not recapture that sparkling form as a seven-year-old.

The crown started to slip at Royal Ascot when Battaash was fourth to Oxted in the King's Stand Stakes and seventh place behind Suesa in the King George Stakes at Goodwood confirmed he was no longer the sprint king. Yet none of the emerging Group 1 speedsters, nor indeed few of the 21st century, could occupy the throne in such commanding fashion as Battaash.

After a wayward youth, he matured into the dominant sprinter of the age, winning the Nunthorpe Stakes twice, the Prix de l'Abbaye and King's Stand Stakes at Group 1 level. He won the Group 2 King George at Goodwood in four consecutive seasons, blitzing the five furlongs in 56.20sec in 2019 to set a course record, and beat the brilliant Dayjur's near 30-year-old mark at York with a scorching 55.90sec in the 2019 Nunthorpe.

That York victory earned a Racing Post Rating of 129, matching his career-best from the 2018 King George. To put that figure into perspective, the only other European-trained sprinters since 2000 to reach such heights are Mozart (2001), Oasis Dream (2003) and Dream Ahead (2011), while the top sprint mark of 124 by Starman in 2021 was bettered on five occasions by Battaash during his career.

Having been gelded as a two-year-old, Battaash was never destined for a stallion career but in late August he went to a new home at Shadwell Stud, having taken a final racecourse bow when parading in front of the stands before the Nunthorpe at York. The following month he was on show again at the National Horse Racing Museum during Henry Cecil Open Weekend in Newmarket.

No doubt there will still be more starring performances to come for the dazzling sprinter who lit up European racing for so long.

▲ Final bow: Battaash and Jim Crowley go to post for the King George Stakes at Glorious Goodwood; inset, Charlie Hills and wife Philippa watch admiringly as the superstar parades in front of the stands at York before the Nunthorpe

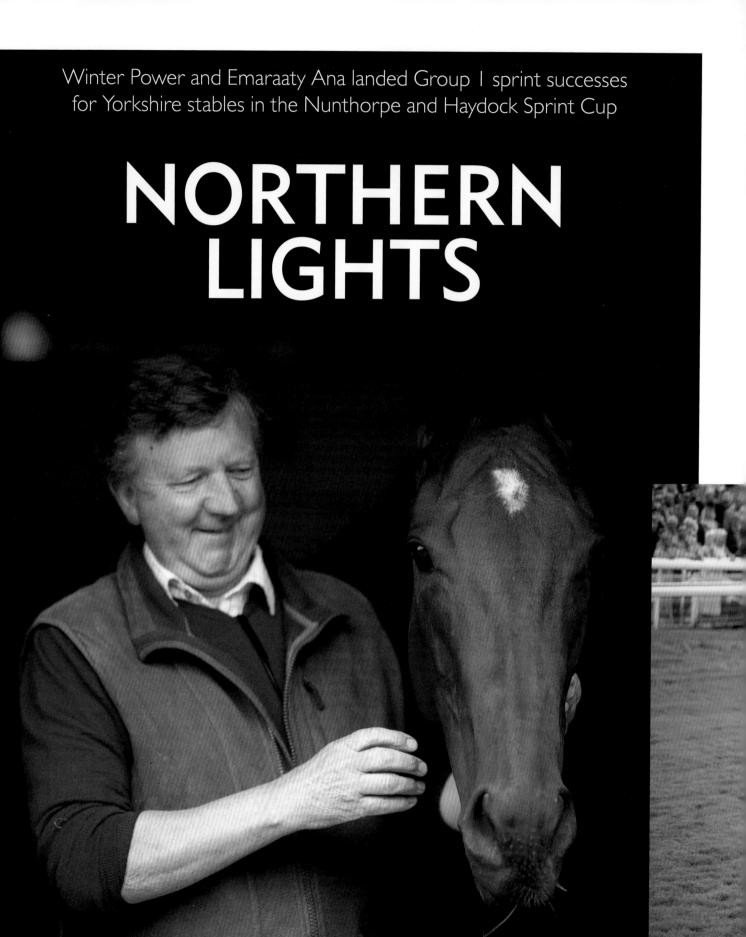

Winter Power and Emaraaty Ana landed Group 1 sprint successes for Yorkshire stables in the Nunthorpe and Haydock Sprint Cup

NORTHERN LIGHTS

By Nick Pulford

IN THE year he turned 60, Tim Easterby enjoyed the most prolific season of his 25-year training career in terms of winners. The biggest and best of them was Winter Power, who left an international cast gasping for breath as she thundered down York's straight in the Nunthorpe Stakes. Victory in the prestigious Group 1 sprint in Easterby's home county set the seal on a tremendous campaign.

Easterby, who trains just 30 miles from the course, took the prize from fellow Yorkshire-based trainer Kevin Ryan, whose outsider Emaraaty Ana got closest to Winter Power at the end to complete a local one-two. A few weeks later Emaraaty Ana grabbed his own slice of Group 1 glory in the Sprint Cup at Haydock,

ensuring that the north came out on top in the region's two biggest speed tests.

Speed is what Winter Power is all about and she won the Nunthorpe with a blistering attack from the front. Before the race there were high hopes for French filly Suesa, fresh from her King George Stakes scorcher at Goodwood, and for US speedball Golden Pal, whose bullish trainer Wesley Ward was adamant this was the best horse he has trained, stating baldly: "If he loses it's my fault." Easterby was quietly confident too, however, and it was his filly who turned on the power where it mattered.

Faced with Golden Pal's speed from the gates under Frankie Dettori, Silvestre de Sousa rode an astute race on Winter Power, allowing the US raider to set the early fractions and waiting for his moment to strike. In two course-

and-distance Listed wins in May and July, Winter Power had led from start to finish, but her only defeat of the season had come when she went off too fast in the King's Stand Stakes at Royal Ascot and the lesson had been learned that a more controlled effort was needed in Group 1 company.

This time Winter Power was quickly away, opening a good lead on most of the field, but her turbo wasn't injected into the race until halfway. Once De Sousa released the brakes she accelerated clear to win by a length and a quarter from the strong-finishing Emaraaty Ana, with Dragon Symbol third and 9-4 favourite Suesa a never-threatening fourth.

"On an easy track like this she gets into fifth gear straight away," De Sousa said. "I could see Frankie on Golden Pal to my left but I had to take over because she was going too well. I decided I had to

stretch them and say, 'catch me if you can'."

There was no catching her as she gave Easterby his seventh Group 1 win, six of them in sprints. "She's just brilliant," the trainer said. "She's a machine, she's a superstar and she's also just right now. It took a long time to get her there. Some horses need a bit of time to come to themselves. When they have ability like she does, you have to be patient."

★★★★

SOMETIMES Winter Power has blown out – in the King's Stand, when last in the Group 2 Flying Childers Stakes as a juvenile and again after the Nunthorpe when she was only tenth in the Flying Five at the Curragh and eighth in the Prix de l'Abbaye on heavy ground – but a relaxed approach with her has paid dividends.

"She just works quietly on her own because she doesn't want to go too quick in the mornings," Easterby said. "She wants to be chilled out at the back, otherwise she's free. She was like that from the start, we had her switched off all the time, but she was an absolute natural."

Easterby's Nunthorpe triumph added to the family legend established by father Peter, who won five Champion Hurdles, and uncle Mick, whose big-race wins include the Nunthorpe in 1976 with Lochnager. Mick still trains in partnership with son David, while Peter is on hand to help Tim after passing on the reins at Habton Grange Stables a quarter of a century ago.

"My dad's still here at 92, watching all the gallops in the morning, watching all the races on the television in the afternoon, asking me what I was playing at if one runs bad. He still knows more than I do," Tim said in a Racing Post interview after the Nunthorpe.

On the handover back in 1996, he added: "Dad never pushed me to do any of this, but it was what I really wanted and you couldn't have had a better man to learn from. He was a legend round here, good to work for, pretty laid-back

▲ Super power: Winter Power (Silvestre de Sousa) holds Emaraaty Ana at bay in the Nunthorpe Stakes at York
◀ Tim Easterby with Winter Power at Habton Grange Stables in North Yorkshire

▶ *Continues page 154*

▼ Fight to the finish: Emaraaty Ana (nearside) edges out Starman by a short head in the Sprint Cup at Haydock

and wouldn't give you a hard time. He just said, 'Do you fancy taking the licence?' and I said yes."

In time the licence will be passed down again, with Tim's older children Emily and William already involved in day-to-day operations and younger son Thomas also taking a keen interest, and the foundations are as firm as ever. After a first century with 118 winners in 2018, Easterby set another personal best with 126 in 2019 and surpassed that again about a month after Winter Power's Nunthorpe.

In a season where the yard's success was spread far and wide, the flying filly's victory on home turf was the most cherished of all. As Easterby said: "We like winning big races down south as well, but we're very much Yorkshire."

★★★★

RYAN has played his part in establishing Yorkshire as a sprinting powerhouse from his Hambleton Lodge base near Thirsk and, while he was disappointed Emaraaty Ana could not catch Winter Power in the Nunthorpe, the Irishman was optimistic his speedster's time would come. "This fella is as good a horse as I've had and I was really confident he was going to run a big race," he said at York. "He's going to get better. He's probably better over six furlongs, but we've been running him over five to get him to settle."

Just over a fortnight later Ryan's

words came to fruition. Running over six furlongs in the Sprint Cup, Emaraaty Ana did indeed get better – by 4lb according to Racing Post Ratings – to land the Group 1 prize from July Cup winner Starman. This time Emaraaty Ana was the one being chased but he managed to hold on by a short head in a frenetic finish.

Ryan was sure he had lost. "I thought he was beat," he said. "You always do, don't you? When he kicked I thought, 'oh f***, this is a long way.' It's always a long last furlong. I knew he'd idle, but the result is the result."

The importance of this result, a 13th Group 1 winner for the stable but the first of 2021, was stressed by the trainer. "When you've had one, you need another, that's what we base everything on now, trying to have the good horses, trying to compete at that level. It's hard to do. A lot of trainers are trying to do it and I'm thankful I can drop in there somewhere."

Ryan also reaffirmed his belief in Emaraaty Ana, who had won the Gimcrack Stakes at York as a juvenile but taken until the age of five to strike at Group 1 level. "He's as good a horse as I've trained," he said again. "He was a great two-year-old. He lost his way a little bit but we were riding him wrong. We were using his speed early in a race and we started dropping him in."

Patience is a virtue when it comes to training sprinters. Ryan and Easterby, two masters of the art, proved that again with northern lights Emaraaty Ana and Winter Power.

Super group of fillies hit the big time

Girl power spiced up the sprint scene in 2021 as a group of fillies and mares went from wannabes to number ones with a string of big-race hits.

Top of the pops was Winter Power with her Group 1 Nunthorpe Stakes success, but in ratings terms Suesa put up the best performance by a female sprinter with her electrifying victory in the Group 2 King George Stakes at Goodwood. The French-trained three-year-old, who had impressed in a pair of Group 3 wins at Chantilly early in the season but then had run too free with no cover in the Group 1 Commonwealth Cup at Royal Ascot, stamped her mark on the division in no uncertain terms at Goodwood, scorching clear for a three-length win to earn a Racing Post Rating of 122.

The yardstick was the consistent but luckless Dragon Symbol, who was second here having previously been demoted to that position after being first past the post in the Commonwealth Cup. Suesa dispatched him with ease, prompting trainer Francois Rohaut to say: "She was incredible. You don't have the impression watching her that she's really accelerating."

The Commonwealth Cup ultimately went to another filly, the US-trained Campanelle, but only after a stewards' inquiry on the day and a later appeal from Dragon Symbol's connections. Most commentators agreed with the reversal of placings after Campanelle was carried across the track by Dragon Symbol, who passed the post just a head in front.

After the result was finally confirmed almost a fortnight after the race, Campanelle's trainer Wesley Ward said: "I felt they made the right call then [at the stewards' inquiry] and they made the right call today. My filly was taken the whole way across the track and otherwise she would have won."

After that reversal, Dragon Symbol continued to find fillies getting in his way in his fruitless quest for a big victory. After his second to Suesa at Goodwood, he was third behind Winter Power in the Nunthorpe and then fourth to Romantic Proposal in the Group 1 Flying Five at the Curragh.

At 16-1 Romantic Proposal was the most surprising of the female sprint winners, returning trainer Edward Lynam to the top level for the first time since his epic days in big sprints with stable stalwarts Sole Power and Slade Power. "It's six years since I had a Group 1 winner, but when you get a bit of a taste for it, it's nice to have another," he said.

THE HOME OF BEAUTIFUL GIFTS & ACCESSORIES I LADIDA-ANDOVER.COM

STAND & DELIVER

Oxted gave trainer Roger Teal and jockey Cieren Fallon another big day in the King's Stand Stakes at Royal Ascot

ROGER TEAL kept the faith. He always believed in Oxted's ability to bounce back from a rocky opening to his 2021 campaign and held firm to his hope that five furlongs was the way. On the opening afternoon of Royal Ascot, in the most furious race of the week, Oxted rewarded his trainer's devotion.

The Group 1 King's Stand Stakes was Oxted's first try at five furlongs but Teal had long felt his stable star could win a big race at the trip to go with his 2020 July Cup success over six furlongs. "We're going to run him in the King's Stand because that's a stiff five and we've been wanting to drop him back for a while," he said. "He's quite aggressive in his races now and this is the right time."

The Lambourn trainer was speaking in May before Oxted finished third in the Duke of York Stakes, his final prep for Royal Ascot. That defeat behind Starman was the five-year-old's third in a row at the start of 2021, following his seventh place on dirt in Saudi Arabia and second in the Abernant Stakes at Newmarket, but Teal was sure Oxted would come good again.

"You have to take your turn in sprints and that's the way it is," he said. "You need an awful lot of luck on the day, being in the right place with the right speed. He'll be back. He's still run to a very high level and I've not lost any faith at all."

Punters took Teal at his word and there was strong late money for Oxted on the day at Royal Ascot, halving his odds to 4-1 second favourite behind 11-8 shot Battaash, the previous year's winner and the fastest sprinter around. This was the day the sprint king's crown started to slip, however, and he failed to burn off the pursuers after taking the lead with two furlongs to run. Having had to weave a path through the pack, Cieren Fallon brought Oxted with a strong run inside the final furlong to take a convincing victory by a length and three-quarters from Arecibo, with US raider Extravagant Kid third and a fading Battaash only fourth.

It was a first Royal Ascot success for both Teal and Fallon, who had broken through together at Group 1 level with Oxted's July Cup the previous summer. "It's a dream come true, a Group 1 at Royal Ascot," Fallon said. "I've been very blessed to sit on a horse like this so early in my career. Harry [Teal, son and assistant to Roger] does all the hard work behind the scenes and I'm very lucky to sit on him on a racetrack."

Recounting his passage to victory, Fallon added: "They went a real solid gallop early on and I didn't panic. I just picked them up when I needed to. He's shown the July Cup wasn't a fluke, he's a proper Group 1 horse."

It was just as exciting for the Teal family, who were shown on camera roaring Oxted home. "It's unbelievable, dreams come true you know, and this horse has been such a wonderful servant for us," the trainer said. "We've dreamed about these days for so long. We had it in the July Cup last year, but a Royal Ascot Group 1? I mean, come on! A yard of our size doing this is amazing."

Next stop was Newmarket for a crack at a July Cup repeat, but again Oxted found Starman too strong over six furlongs and was beaten a length and three-quarters into third. Teal's flyer hung noticeably right near the end and he was sent for a scan after the race. The news was not good.

"He's had a little floating chip for a while, but when he hung in the July Cup we decided to have him checked again," Teal reported a couple of weeks later. "On the MRI scan you could see it had moved slightly, so we decided to have it removed. The operation went well and he's back home safe and sound."

That ended plans to go for the Haydock Sprint Cup and Prix de l'Abbaye later in the season, but Teal was already looking forward to 2022. "We'll probably concentrate on the same races again with the King's Stand, and perhaps start in the Abernant at Newmarket or the Duke of York as a prep," he said.

The faith remains as strong as ever.

DREAM COME TRUE

Dream Of Dreams finally secured Diamond Jubilee glory at the third attempt

TRY, try, try again. The old proverb was apt for Dream Of Dreams, who had twice lost the Diamond Jubilee Stakes by a head but on his third attempt finally got his own head in front – and a bit more – to register a popular and deserved victory. Even though a gallops injury soon ruled him out for the rest of the season, it was mission accomplished at Royal Ascot.

Group 1 honours had been secured for the first time in the Haydock Sprint Cup the previous autumn, but there is something different about doing it at Royal Ascot and for Dream Of Dreams' connections there was a sense of unfinished business in the Diamond Jubilee. As Bruce Raymond, racing manager to owner Saeed Suhail, said after the deal had been sealed: "Winning at Ascot, that was the main one."

There was an element of third time lucky, not least in the strength of the opposition. Dream Of Dreams had gone off 12-1 and 8-1 for his first two attempts at the

Diamond Jubilee, when he was beaten by the higher-rated Blue Point in 2019 and Hello Youmzain in 2020. He put up a brave fight to go so close both times but ultimately the best horse won – not just on the day but on overall form.

This time was different. Dream Of Dreams was 3-1 favourite in a weaker field and had 3lb or more in hand on official ratings. The only Group 1 winner among his 11 rivals was Glen Shiel, who had taken the 2020 British Champions Sprint after finishing runner-up to Dream Of Dreams at Haydock.

Dream Of Dreams stood out on ratings, although perhaps not in the preliminaries. He is not a stereotypical ball-of-fire sprinter and on this occasion was almost worryingly laid back. "He has got more and more relaxed," Stoute said after the race. "He doesn't go to post like a sprinter, does he? I thought he was going to pull up halfway down."

If Dream Of Dreams didn't quite seem to have his mind on the race, Ryan Moore certainly did. "Ryan had it all planned and it all worked out," Stoute related. "He told me what he was doing, and I said, 'kick on'."

★★★★

THAT was just a turn of phrase because Moore's plan revolved around anything but kicking on. His seven-year-old partner was keen to get on with things when the stalls opened – in contrast to his demeanour on the way down – but Moore soon restrained him near the back of the farside group.

The key was to be close enough to make a telling thrust in the final furlong. Dream Of Dreams has staying power and his victory over seven furlongs in the Group 2 Hungerford Stakes in 2020 summed up the type of sprinter he is; not one with electrifying speed but with the ability to travel well and keep on to the end.

In his first two attempts at the Diamond Jubilee he had been caught out of his ground somewhat by fast, classy sprinters. Against lesser opposition, he had every chance of being able to strike from a more favourable position. Moore executed his plan to perfection.

Art Power proved best of the nearside group and led going to the final furlong, hotly pursued by the strong-travelling Glen Shiel on the other side. Moore never let Glen Shiel get too much of a run on him, however, and made it a three-way battle at the furlong pole. With three cracks of the whip, he forced his way into the lead with half a furlong to go and the others could find no more. The winning margin was a conclusive length over Glen Shiel with Art Power another three-quarters of a length behind.

Stoute was delighted. "Any winner here is a great thrill, particularly a Group 1, but this fellow has just been touched off twice, so I'm pleased for him. He deserves it," he said, before touching on the physical and mental qualities that had brought Dream Of Dreams his royal moment at last. "He's fully developed and strong now. But it's his mind – he's really, really chilling. He's more relaxed, and a little better."

Stoute's point was backed up by Racing Post Ratings. Having run to 121 and 120 in his first two Diamond Jubilees, Dreams Of Dreams raised his game to 122 to secure victory. That was the same as his Sprint Cup triumph and only 1lb behind his best two performances in his seven-length Hungerford win and his Windsor prep for royal success. Tellingly, all four of those high-rated wins came with soft in the going description, a word absent in his first two attempts at the Diamond Jubilee. As Moore said: "A stiff six [furlongs] with cut in the ground, it's perfect for him."

★★★★

FINALLY it had all fallen right for Dream Of Dreams, who extended Stoute's record haul at Royal Ascot to 82 winners. He was the last runner of an otherwise fruitless meeting for the 75-year-old trainer, whose resurgence in recent years has come in the face of fierce competition from the generations below him. "I thought I wasn't going to have a Royal Ascot winner this year," he admitted. "It's been tough – it's always been tough, but it's tougher."

There was a tough moment still to come with Dream Of Dreams, who aggravated an old ankle injury during routine exercise in Newmarket shortly before the July Cup and was stood down for the rest of the season.

The good news is that he is expected back at the age of eight in 2022, and no doubt a Royal Ascot defence will be top of the agenda. Like his trainer, he will carry the fight to the young ones again.

IN THE PICTURE

McGuinness lands first Group 1 as A Case Of You flashes home in Abbaye

IT WAS simply a case of waiting. Ado McGuinness felt all year he had a potential first Group 1 winner on his hands in A Case Of You and he was finally proved right in the Prix de l'Abbaye, the last top-level sprint of the European season. With the heavy ground and low draw in his favour, the three-year-old got up in a thrilling finish to deny Air De Valse by a short head.

It was third time lucky in a Group 1 for A Case Of You (*nearside*), who had pulled off a shoe in the Commonwealth Cup at Royal Ascot and finished fast but just too late in the Flying Five at the Curragh, falling half a length short of Romantic Proposal at the line.

Emboldened by that display, McGuinness supplemented A Case Of You for the Abbaye at a cost of €25,200. "The Flying Five was his first

time over five furlongs and he's just got better and better," McGuinness said. "I knew he'd definitely improved because I've got a good sprinter at home and he can't lay up with him."

Even with that level of confidence going into the race, coming out on the other side with his first Group 1 win still took time to sink in with the trainer.

Speaking a few days later back home on Off

The Ball, McGuinness said: "You say to yourself, 'Am I dreaming, am I dreaming?' You never think it might happen to you. You'd often be sitting at home watching these races saying, 'God, wouldn't you love to be there, and I'm very privileged that I was."

Winning jockey Ronan Whelan was glad to be there with another Group 1 chance after the agonising defeat in the Flying Five. "I was a bit gutted after last time. He flew home at the Curragh and I thought in another few strides I might have won," he said. For a few moments after the Abbaye, Whelan feared the worst again. "I knew I'd hit the line pretty good and I looked up to the screen, but I wasn't sure," he admitted. "When they called it out I didn't know whether to smile or cry. To ride a winner here is unbelievable."

Going to that next level with A Case Of You was important for McGuinness, whose yard in Lusk, County Dublin, has been on the up for several seasons. "We're always looking to improve on quality," he said in the summer. By the autumn he had a sprinter of proven Group 1 quality.

Picture: EDWARD WHITAKER (RACINGPOST.COM/PHOTOS)

BACK ON COURSE

Cheltenham, March 16: The behind-closed-doors opening day of the Cheltenham Festival, 12 months on from the packed crowds just before the first lockdown

HAD you been here the noise would have been wonderful. Even without you, and my God you were missed, the sound was still sweet.

From their vantage point on a structure named after one heroine of Ireland they roared approval for two more. Honeysuckle and Rachael Blackmore were accepting their tickets to immortality in the Unibet Champion Hurdle and on the steps of the Dawn Run Stand the reduced Irish invasion reacted with joy.

They might have liked to get closer than the Cheltenham infield but that would have been against the rules. At this behind-closed-doors festival all the staff caring for Ireland's horses are living in a pop-up hotel that, like the grandstand that commemorates Dawn Run, is situated in the Best Mate enclosure. Only if they have a runner that afternoon are those workers allowed to cross the track and enter the posher bits. What they had and where they were was more than enough.

"The atmosphere is brilliant," said Kate Tracey, one of those brought in from Britain to join the Willie Mullins team for the week. "It's bizarre and surreal, but there's such a collective feel among the Irish yards to share the successes. I think we're attempting to bring as much atmosphere as possible to try to make it the event that it is."

In the Champion Hurdle the sun shone on the right horse.

Honeysuckle and her magnificent jockey gave this day, this festival and this sport the performance, the result and the story it needed. In strange, surreal circumstances we would never want repeated, the horses and their humans rode to the rescue.

LEE MOTTERSHEAD

Lockdown kept racecourses virtually empty in the early months of the year but crowds gradually built up from May as normality began to return. The Racing Post charted the twists and turns

Carlisle, May 17: Step three on the roadmap out of lockdown allows up to 4,000 spectators in England, with four courses in action on the first day back. Carlisle is quickest out of the gates at 1pm

FOR a moment it was just like old times as the first spectators on a British racecourse this year filtered through the turnstiles. After queuing outside for the gates to open, the early racegoers all appeared to have a spring in their step, thrilled at being back on familiar territory and in a familiar routine.

Friends and family brought together for a day at the races – a simple pleasure but one they have been prevented from doing for so long. The sight of hand sanitiser stations and social distancing signs soon brought the here and now back into focus, but it was still a day to savour as racing rediscovered its heart and soul.

It was also a memorable one for Workington-based couple Craig Hamilton and Louise Williams, who brought five-month-old son Mikey to the track for the first time.

"It's great to be here as it's Mikey's first day at the races and hopefully he'll be a lucky charm," Craig said. "It's the first time he's seen so many people as we've been in lockdown since he was born and he's been taking it all in.

"Today is also Louise's surprise birthday present. It's nice to have some normality again and get dressed up and do something. We normally go racing seven or eight times a year, but haven't been for nearly two years now. We love horses and have really missed the atmosphere."

Carlisle general manager Molly Dingwall said: "We've been dreaming about this day for so long and are thrilled to be the first racecourse in the country to welcome the public back. There's nothing like having a crowd, it changes the atmosphere of the day. We're in the entertainment business and love seeing people enjoying themselves."

ANDREW DIETZ
▸▸ *Continues page 164*

THE RETURN OF CROWDS

Redcar, May 17: Across the Pennines, Redcar gets under way 20 minutes after Carlisle

YOU know something special must be happening when there are hordes queuing in the sunshine just minutes before the first race – at Redcar.

Absence really does make the heart grow fonder, an absence of 14 months that ended joyously as racegoers finally returned in a healthy number – and hopefully for good this time, after a couple of abortive trials last autumn. Racing has been almost exclusively behind closed doors since March of last year and the last spectators admitted here had been in October 2019, so there was plenty of pent-up demand.

A phased return meant numbers were capped at 850 and Mark and Sandra Keelty, from Coulby Newham, Middlesbrough, led the charge when the gates opened.

"We've been club members here for a long time and it's just brilliant to be back after so long," Mark said. Sandra added: "We've really missed the atmosphere and seeing friends, so we're just thrilled to be getting back to some kind of normality."

The new normal for friends John Baxter and Chris Varley was a trek from West Yorkshire, so desperate were they to get back on course. Baxter, from Bingley, said: "This was the nearest course to home and we just couldn't wait to get back racing." Varley, from Haworth, added: "We set off at quarter past seven this morning, had our breakfast on the seafront, and now we just want to see some live racing – it's much better than watching it on the telly!"

DAVID CARR

Royal Ascot, June 15: As part of the government's Events Research Programme, Royal Ascot is allowed to have 12,000 racegoers each day. That makes the opening-day crowd the biggest since the 2020 Cheltenham Festival

JUST over four hours after those handsome gates were finally opened, two musicians from the Band of the Grenadier Guards commenced a trumpet fanfare.

All around the parade ring paying customers joined in applause until Frankie Dettori began to blow them

kisses and triggered even more acclaim. The applause was joined by cheers and under a sumptuous sun the jockey who loves this place more than any other soared off Palace Pier's back after winning the Queen Anne.

In that moment, and so many others, this was a perfect day at Royal Ascot.

Twelve months ago the world's most famous racecourse staged what was a royal meeting in name only. There were no royals, no racegoers, no atmosphere. Flat racing is never finer than at Ascot but the soul of these five days extends beyond what happens on the track. It demands the pomp, the pageantry and the people. Thank goodness, all three have returned.

First through the gates at 10.32am were, according to their name badges, a Mr and Mrs Michael Birch. Many of the 12,000 people permitted to attend seemed to follow soon after, including another married couple, Rebecca Johnson and Brian Mann, both dressed largely in red and yellow stripes.

▲ Cartmel on July 19, so-called Freedom Day
▼ The biggest crowd since Cheltenham 2020 was allowed at Royal Ascot

Palace Pier's jockey enjoyed the star miler's second Royal Ascot triumph so much more than the first, gained in near silence and with hardly anybody present to see it happen. Last year Dettori sank three espressos before racing to get his blood pumping. Not this time.

"I think I probably needed Valium this morning, I was so excited," he said. "You can't imagine how it feels to see the colours and hear the people screaming. I'm so pleased. What can you say? Ascot with people is amazing."

LEE MOTTERSHEAD

Cartmel, July 19: The final step out of lockdown removes restrictions in England and the Lake District course is the first in action on 'Freedom Day'

AROUND 5,000 spectators at Cartmel made up the largest racecourse crowd outside of pilot events since March 2020 on the day lockdown restrictions were eased across England.

The lifting of restrictions in England could not have come soon enough for racecourses and on-course bookmakers ravaged by the pandemic – and, of course, racegoers starved of live action.

That the great reopening started at Cartmel, before evening meetings at Windsor and Beverley, was particularly apt as the picturesque track is a firm favourite with summer holidaymakers, who turned out in force on a sweltering day.

While limitations remained in place at the other afternoon fixture at Ayr in Scotland, the shackles were off in the Lake District. No cap on crowds, no essential pre-booking, no social distancing and no face masks. What better place on so-called Freedom Day to run wild and free?

A day at Cartmel is unique. You can bring your dog – or your kids if you don't have one – and a BBQ, but the most important thing you need is a sense of fun.

That is something that has been in short supply for nearly the last year

and a half, but in this idyllic setting on a gloriously sunny day, it was hard not to think brighter days lie ahead.

Bernadette O'Donnell and Mick Dowson were among the first to make the most of the scrapping of one of the more contentious restrictions – vertical drinking.

"We've not been racing since before Covid and it's been tough because it's our social thing and we regularly go to different racecourses," Bernadette said. "We can't understand why we couldn't as we're outside and not getting close to people. We've been vaccinated and it feels safe."

ANDREW DIETZ

Leopardstown, September 11: Ireland finally starts to ease restrictions, with a crowd of 4,000 permitted for the first day of Irish Champions Weekend

WELCOME to the new normal, or the start of the same as it ever was era. Whichever you prefer. Day one of Irish Champions Weekend was the stage for the biggest crowd on an Irish

▼ Back on track at Carlisle, Redcar and Leopardstown; previous page, empty stands as the Cheltenham Festival gets under way

racecourse since the second day of February in 2020. It felt abnormal, yet the outcome of the big race turned out to be very normal indeed.

Aidan O'Brien won it for a tenth time, nothing unusual about that, but to see three of the top thoroughbreds in training accelerating into sixth gear in front of a live audience was nothing short of extraordinary. It was an Irish Champion Stakes that will live long in the memory. It was in the Fantastic Light v Galileo mould.

St Mark's Basilica won it but, boy, did he have to work for his fifth Group 1 in a row. It was everything we wanted and more. And the more was not just in the race, but after it too.

"It's incredible," O'Brien said of having crowds back. "The way they clapped when he was leaving the parade ring after the race – amazing. You miss all that stuff. You think when people aren't at the races that they might not have been following it but they are."

DAVID JENNINGS

THE HORRIBLY

Racing was rocked by the negative publicity
surrounding the Gordon Elliott and Panorama cases

By Lee Mottershead

EVERY now and again a 100-1 shot pops up from nowhere. Sometimes the odds are even bigger, for racing is a sport full of uncertainty, one in which we can never be sure exactly what lies around the corner. There are shocks like Foinavon, Mon Mome and Norton's Coin we gladly celebrate. In 2021 the sport was stained and scarred by something that was simply shocking. Even now, as these words are written

months after the story broke, none of it makes sense.

So wildly unbelievable was the image of Gordon Elliott sitting astride a dead horse, many people simply did not believe it. On that Saturday evening in February, as Twitter users reacted to a photograph posted a little earlier, there were numerous claims that what we were seeing had been maliciously manipulated.

It could not possibly be real, they said. It had quite clearly been Photoshopped, they said. Elliott would never have done that, they

said. Then he said it was real and that he had done it. In that moment everything changed for Elliott. It was terrible for him. For racing it was even worse.

Ireland's number-two jumps trainer, the man who had orchestrated the career of Grand National legend Tiger Roll, had been at Fairyhouse when he discovered the photograph was in the public domain. At 7.29pm on that Saturday evening the Irish Horseracing Regulatory Board tweeted it was "aware of an image circulating on social media". At

11.17pm Elliott posted his own tweet, in which he said he had been in communication with the IHRB and was "cooperating fully with their investigation".

At that point there was no admission. That came at around the same time 24 hours later but it failed to name the horse who the picture showed deceased on one of the Cullentra gallops, his four legs stiff and outstretched. In one hand Elliott was holding a phone to his right ear. With his other hand he was making a sideways 'V' gesture. He had a leg

PERFECT STORM

either side of the horse, on whose back he was sat. The horse was Morgan, a four-time winner who had last run at Wexford in June 2019. Elliott was smiling.

In that Sunday night confession, Elliott sought to contextualise the image with an explanation that to most observers appeared to stretch credibility. "At what was a sad time, which it is when any horse under my care passes away, my initial reaction was to get the body removed from where it was positioned," he said in the statement.

"I was standing over the horse waiting to help with the removal of the body, in the course of which, to my memory I received a call and, without thinking, I sat down to take it. Hearing a shout from one of my team, I gestured to wait until I was finished."

Elliott's Cheltenham Festival aspirations could not have been more finished. As racing figures moved quickly to express revulsion, so did the BHA. British racing's governing body determined that pending the outcome of the IHRB investigation it would prevent Elliott making entries in Britain.

★★★★

WITH the start of the festival imminent, this unprecedented crisis had come at the worst possible time. As a result of Covid restrictions there would be no spectators at the festival. The BHA and Cheltenham's owners, the Jockey Club, were adamant on no account did they want Elliott at jumping's biggest celebration. It would have been a public relations disaster.

Over the coming days things deteriorated for Elliott and the sport. On the morning of his 43rd birthday, stable star Envoi Allen and seven other horses owned by Cheveley Park Stud were taken away and moved to other leading Irish yards. "I have never in all my life seen so many grown men cry," said jockey Keith Donoghue. "It was horrific stuff altogether."

That same day, friends of Elliott contacted IHRB senior medical officer Dr Jennifer Pugh, concerned for his wellbeing. "They put me into a car and drove me to her," he later recalled. "At that stage, I didn't know where I wanted to go or what I wanted to do, but Jennifer made me look at things a bit differently, helped me to see I'd be okay, no matter how bad things got."

Elliott was not the only villain.

In the early days of the scandal, a video emerged showing amateur jockey Rob James climbing on to the back of a dead horse. James and Elliott had combined to win at the 2020 festival with Milan Native. Neither would be part of the festival that followed. At separate IHRB hearings, Elliott was suspended from having runners for a year, with six months of that sentence suspended, while head lead Simon McGonagle, who took the picture, was suspended for what amounted to two months. James served twice that amount.

Those of us who went to Cheltenham did so fearing it would be grim. By then the atmosphere had become toxic. As Elliott's supporters understandably rallied around him, some turned

▸▸ *Continues page 168*

their ire on his critics. It felt as though a divide had grown between British and Irish racing. At the end of those four days in the Cotswolds there certainly was a divide. Ireland had won 23 of the 28 races. Three of the winners competed in the name of Denise Foster, brought in to hold the training licence during Elliott's time in the sin bin. Three others were horses who had been removed from Cullentra, two of them owned by Cheveley Park.

Even in his period of exile, Elliott was at the heart of a controversy, when in July the BBC's Panorama documentary series broadcast an episode named 'The Dark Side of Racing' that examined what happens to some horses at the end of their racing careers. The programme showed distressing scenes of thoroughbreds in a British abattoir and claimed three horses previously trained by Elliott had met their end there. Simon Munir and Isaac Souede, the owners of one of the animals, Cheltenham winner Vyta Du Roc, ended their association with Elliott.

★ ★ ★ ★

THE revelations – later followed by a welcome BHA ruling that will prohibit British-trained horses from racing if still eligible for the human food chain – added to the sport's horribly perfect storm.

In January it was revealed Viking Hoard had been sedated prior to a contest at Tramore for which he had been heavily laid to lose.

Then in June trainer Stephen Mahon had his licence suspended for only four years by the IHRB after being found guilty of badly neglecting horses in his care, 13 years after he received just a four-month suspension and €1,000 fine over a previous sickening offence.

Those truly were animal welfare cases. Elliott's treatment of Morgan was plainly not, yet it was the story that attracted far more attention than any of the others. It is a story that will surely never completely

'I will spend the rest of my life paying for moment of madness'

Irish racing investigating Elliott social media picture

Racing Post Wednesday, March 3, 2021

Elliott: I still hope Envoi Allen wins the Gold Cup some day

BHA urges swift investigation into 'shocking' Elliott social media picture

By Lewis Porteous

GORDON ELLIOTT has said he will be "cooperating fully" with an investigation by the Irish Horseracing Regulatory Board into a picture posted on Twitter which appears to show the Grand National and Gold Cup-winning trainer sitting astride a dead horse sprawled in the sand on a training gallop.

The BHA yesterday urged the Irish authorities to act quickly to confirm how the "shocking

picture" of the trainer originated.

The image, posted on Saturday night from an account unconnected to the County Meath-based trainer of dual Grand National winner Tiger Roll and a host of Cheltenham

Festival favourites, was widely circulated on the social media platform, leading the Irish Horseracing Regulatory Board (IHRB) to tweet that "an investigation was taking place".

Elliott responded on Twitter with the statement: "I'm aware

of a photo in circulation on social media. The IHRB have been in contact with me regarding this photo and I will be cooperating fully with their investigation."

The IHRB chief executive **Continues page 2**

Gordon Elliott: aware of a photo in circulation on social media

Cheveley Park stars moved from Elliott

Envoi Allen among festival contenders divided between De Bromhead and Mullins

By Peter Scargill

CHEVELEY PARK STUD had no option but to remove eight horses, including superstar Envoi Allen, from Gordon Elliott due to the "shocking" photograph of the trainer sitting on a dead horse and the damage it could do to the organisation's reputation, managing director Chris Richardson said yesterday.

Sir Gerhard, Classic Getaway and Grangeclare West have joined Willie Mullins, with Ballyadam, Malone Road, Quilixios and Gally Billy accompanying Envoi Allen to Henry de Bromhead's stable.

Cheveley Park are the first major owner to leave Elliott's yard after the trainer confirmed the viral image of himself **Continues page 2**

Racing has been besmirched by Elliott and must make its revulsion clear

▲ Media frenzy: Gordon Elliott was in the headlines for all the wrong reasons over the infamous photo that led to his six-month suspension

go away, even now Elliott is once again training winners in his own name.

Prior to his return in September he spoke to the Racing Post's Ireland editor Richard Forristal. He was open and apologetic. "From now on, I have to prove that the impression people have of me from the picture does not reflect who I am," Elliott said. "For myself, for my family, for my staff and, most of all, for the industry and its supporters, I need to step up and prove to everyone that I am not a monster."

Elliott is not a monster. There are many very good people who spoke up for him. They cannot fathom what made him do something so incredibly callous and stupid but they are equally adamant it was not a fair representation of the person they know.

Yet the damage was done to the reputations both of Elliott and the wider sport. Lovers of racing always confront its critics by arguing nobody loves horses more than those who work with them. That remains no less true but some

outside the sport may now find it harder to believe. If people who have no connection to racehorses could not conceive of acting with the gross insensitivity so graphically displayed by Elliott and James, how could people who spend most of their waking hours with horses?

We must all move on, for the past cannot be rewritten. The tragedy for Elliott – a truly brilliant racehorse trainer – is that while he may be forgiven, this brief part of his past will never be forgotten.

Gordon Elliott gave an exclusive interview to the
Racing Post in the week of his return from suspension

'I'm sorry for what I did. A chance to move on is all I'm after'

By Richard Forristal

"IT'S something I have given a lot of thought to," says Gordon Elliott from across the table in the kitchen of his converted home at Cullentra House in County Meath. "How am I going to be received when I go back racing? Going racing is something I've always loved doing. I probably go racing more than most trainers because I'm a people person. I suppose I just hope people will forgive me and let me move forward by going back to doing what I think I do best, training winners."

In sitting on Morgan, who had collapsed and died on the gallops in 2019, one of horseracing's most recognisable figures undermined the central ballast of the sport's justification. Elliott's indiscretion betrayed our insistence that thoroughbreds are privy to regal lifestyles and afforded similar dignity when they die in our service. Here was a Gold Cup and Grand National-winning trainer, who had single-handedly threatened the dominance of Willie Mullins' empire, involved in a crass, juvenile incident. As much as anything, it suggested an abject failure on his behalf to grasp the responsibility that comes with such success.

"It's true," the 43-year-old admits when that point is put to him. "I don't think I realised the impact that something I would do could have. You pick up a paper and see a famous soccer player or whoever, and I don't think I thought of myself in that way. But then you look at what happened, you find yourself in nearly every paper across the world for the wrong reasons, it makes you realise the position I'm in.

"From now on, I have to prove that the impression people have of me from the picture does not reflect who I am. For myself, for my family, for my staff and, most of all, for the industry and its supporters, I need to step up and prove to everyone that I am not a monster."

✷✷✷✷

HOW did he end up in a situation where it was deemed acceptable to sit on a dead animal, and what does that say about the culture at the yard? The incriminating photo was taken by his head lad Simon McGonagle,

➤ *Continues page 172*

who is also one of his oldest friends and was hit with an effective two-month suspension for taking and disseminating the picture on Snapchat in 2019.

"That's the sort of thing I have had to reflect on," says Elliott. "But what happened was a moment of madness, and if I hadn't sat on the horse, there wouldn't have been a picture for Simon to take in the first place, so the first mistake was mine. We've been friends since we were 12 or 13 years of age and we both have to live with what happened, but we were always going to stand by each other.

"Everyone knows we all celebrate our good days, because we have to work to get them. I've always worked hard to get the owners I have, and you don't get them by sitting at home. We are in the entertainment business, and having a meal or a drink with an owner is usually how I meet my new owners. I wasn't born with a silver spoon in my mouth, so I have to go out and attract owners.

"Now, since this all happened, I've had to look at every aspect of my life, and it's certainly changed because I'm now more aware of what is expected of me, but I'll continue to work to attract new owners because I want to get back to where we were before all this."

Given the sheer magnitude of what Elliott had built in the decade and a half since he burst on to the scene by sending out Silver Birch to win the 2007 Grand National, with more than 1,800 winners amassed, including 32 at the Cheltenham Festival, the scale of the toll that fleetingly threatened to be inflicted upon him was staggering. He puts the number of lost horses arising out of the affair down to just a dozen, but some of the departed epitomised the pinnacle of his ambition.

Envoi Allen, Sir Gerhard and Quilixios, all unbeaten at the time, were among those taken away by Cheveley Park Stud on March 2.

The names speak for themselves. All stars in the making.

Envoi Allen and Sir Gerhard cost £400,000 apiece, and they joined Elliott's closest rivals on a free transfer. They weren't just horses, they were dreams going up in a puff of smoke.

"That was the lowest point throughout it all," he concedes.

With the Cheltenham Festival two weeks away, did he fear the damage would be ruinous?

"I didn't know what was going to happen, or where it was all going to end up," he says. "If you were listening to just a tenth of what people were telling you . . . like, some people wanted me banned for life.

"I had worked very hard to source those horses, and then they were gone. Just like that. When Envoi Allen was here, there wasn't a night I didn't lie in bed thinking about him. And now that he's gone, there still isn't a night I don't lie in bed thinking about him, but I have never had a cross word with any of the owners who left. I still speak to them all and the gate is always open. I understand completely why they had to go. Having said that, I still have a brilliant bunch of owners here who have stuck by me and want to support me and want to see me get back to where I was."

★★★★

THE Cheltenham Festival came and went without him. By then, Denise Foster had been drafted in to take over at Cullentra. For Elliott, those four days

at Cheltenham did not make for an easy watch. Sir Gerhard, Quilixios and Galvin all won for different stables. Foster had three wins, including Tiger Roll's return to form in the cross-country.

He says: "When Quilixios won the Triumph Hurdle, Henry de Bromhead rang me to say, 'Well done', and he made a point of acknowledging me on television, which was decent of him. And Sir Gerhard hadn't crossed the line in the Champion Bumper when I got a text from Willie Mullins.

"As much as it is so competitive here in Ireland, we all have each other's backs, and I guess through things like that you find out a bit more about who your real friends are. Others had their own agendas, and everyone is entitled to their opinion, but I was disappointed with some people. I shouldn't have done what I did – I will never shy away from that – but I'm a human being who made a mistake."

When the picture emerged, rumours abounded as to its origins. Elliott insists he doesn't know who put it into the public domain, but he does believe it was an orchestrated attempt to damage him. "I don't know who put it out there, and I had never seen the picture before it went online," he says. "When you look at how it turned up just before Cheltenham, so long after it was taken, I do feel it was malicious."

On the day that the Cheveley Park horses departed, Elliott's friends, recognising his fragile state, reached out to the IHRB senior medical officer Dr Jennifer Pugh. "They

put me into a car and drove me to her," he recalls. "At that stage, I didn't know where I wanted to go or what I wanted to do, but Jennifer made me look at things a bit differently, helped me to see that I'd be okay, no matter how bad things got. She came down to the yard three or four times as well and spoke to the staff individually and collectively.

"I went to bed that night, after seeing Jennifer the first time, thinking to myself, 'Right. All of my staff are sticking by me, so I need to stick by them, and get strong for them'. I promised them that, if they stuck with me, I'd stand by them, and not one member of staff has left. I really couldn't say enough about how good they have been throughout all of this."

One unexpected source of succour came from Sir Alex Ferguson, who reached out on the Tuesday of Cheltenham. By then, Elliott had watched Black Tears win for Foster and Galvin score for Ian Ferguson, so the full extent of his suspension was starting to crystallise.

The Manchester United icon likened the thirst for a scalp Elliott encountered to the outrage that descended when Eric Cantona launched himself into the Selhurst Park crowd to kick a Crystal Palace fan in 1995. Ferguson reminded Elliott that some things are worth fighting for, and for him to ignore the noise and concentrate on working towards rebuilding his career.

"That's all I can focus on now," concludes Elliott. "I know all this has set me back, but I have proved I can train horses at every level, and it's all I want to do. I made a mistake, I understand that, and I am sorry for what I did. A chance to move on is all I'm after now."

He will get that chance, and don't bet against him making the most of it. As Sir Alex might say, he has never played for a draw in his life.

This is an edited version of an article that appeared in the Racing Post on September 6

▶ Gordon Elliott returns to the track at Punchestown on September 14; he saddled a winner the next day at Sligo (bottom)

A golden hue envelops the Warren Hill gallops
on a misty September morning in Newmarket
EDWARD WHITAKER (RACINGPOST.COM/PHOTOS)

FIRST LADY

Lady Bowthorpe turned tears to smiles
with her popular Group 1 breakthrough in
the Nassau Stakes at Glorious Goodwood

By Nick Pulford

FOR a long time it seemed Lady Bowthorpe would be thwarted by Lady Luck at every turn. Having fought back from an injury that almost ended her career and taken her place among the elite at last, this brave lady suffered another gut-wrenching slice of ill fortune at Newmarket, bringing tears of frustration to the eyes of trainer William Jarvis. Then finally, gloriously, everything came right and she was a Group 1 winner. It was quite a day.

That day came at Goodwood on July 29 when she lined up for the Nassau Stakes. Three weeks earlier Lady Bowthorpe had gone close in the Falmouth Stakes, finishing a luckless fourth in that Group 1 mile, and this time jockey Kieran Shoemark left nothing to chance. Keeping her away from any trouble around the outer, he coolly produced her with an irresistible run in the final two furlongs to take the prize decisively by a length and a half. It was a first Group 1 for Shoemark and Lady Bowthorpe's owner Emma Banks and only the second in Jarvis's long career, coming 27 years after Grand Lodge's victory in the St James's Palace Stakes.

It was a great underdog story for a 28-horse stable that sits among Newmarket's biggest operations but rarely has the chance to compete with them for the top prizes, let alone beat them. Jarvis left no-one in any doubt about what the Nassau triumph meant to him – as well as to his staff, Banks and Shoemark – and he revelled in the memories when he looked back a few weeks later.

"It was a very special day," said the master of Phantom House Stables, "and after the Falmouth it was a feeling of relief and unbelievable joy. The applause that the racegoers and my fellow professionals gave us was very gratifying and the whole experience was lovely. My son Jack was there and my grandson Zander, and my partner Linda, and two of my godchildren as well, Harry Eustace and George Smyly. Zander's not yet a year old, so he won't remember the day, but I certainly will.

"We're a small stable in Newmarket. I don't know if we punch above our weight, but we do okay. We had a lovely party afterwards. I was very proud of the whole team at Phantom House and delighted for Emma, who's been a very loyal supporter of the stable in recent years. It made into a nice story, especially with Kieran riding his first Group 1 winner, and I was thrilled for him as well."

★★★★

WHILE Shoemark made sure he was well in control of Lady Bowthorpe's fate, Jarvis had to find his own way to keep himself in check as the race unfolded. He had long felt the step up to a mile and a quarter would suit his mare but some nervousness was understandable after almost three decades of waiting for another Group 1 winner.

"If you asked Linda, she would probably say I was a bit anxious but I felt in control," he said. "I was confident she would stay the trip. I never watch a race with my owners, I just wander around and smoke a cigarette or two. I listen to the commentary and glance at the big screen occasionally, then have another walk around."

Up in the stands, Banks sat with Luca and Sara Cumani of Fittocks Stud. Lady Bowthorpe's breeders Paolo and Emma Agostini of Scuderia Archi Romani keep her dam Maglietta Fina there and the Cumanis have continued to take a keen interest in her career. The former trainer, who counts two Derby triumphs on his big-race roll of honour, was a reassuring presence. After the race, the owner related: "Half a furlong out Luca looked to me and said, 'You've got it', If Luca Cumani tells you that, of course you've got it."

Glorious Goodwood was a fitting place for the Lady Bowthorpe story to take its most thrilling twist because it was where Jarvis and Banks were first introduced seven years earlier. Banks, the noted celebrity agent whose clients include Kylie Minogue and Katy Perry, was there

▸*Continues page 178*

as a guest of the Earl of March, and as it happened Jarvis was saddling a runner for her uncle and aunt, Michael and Rosalind Banks. "She came down from the box and I met her for the first time with Michael and Rosalind," the trainer recalled. "She enjoyed the experience, she slightly compared it to going backstage, and soon after we bought a cheapish horse, Lackaday, who won for her. That was her first horse."

Lady Bowthorpe was more expensive, being picked up as a yearling for 82,000gns, and yet her remarkable story almost ended after chapter one. She finished fourth on her debut at Yarmouth as a juvenile in September 2018 but then disaster struck. "I was galloping her towards getting another run into her, but then she fractured her cannonbone on the gallops," recalled Jarvis. "It could easily have been a career-ending injury but thanks to the skill and expertise of the Newmarket Equine Hospital and their surgeons, she was able to come back into training. She's got five screws in her cannonbone."

****

IT WAS almost a year before she was ready to race again and the delay left her playing catch-up. After a long climb up the ranks, she won the Group 2 Dahlia Stakes at Newmarket on her first run of 2021 and it was time to try her in the toughest class. "We threw her in the deep end in the Lockinge," Jarvis said. "She was an outsider there but was the only one to give Palace Pier a race, although I wouldn't for one minute say she gave him a fright. I thought she could compete in Group 1 company and she confirmed she could."

Further confirmation came with her strong run in the Falmouth, although she had to settle for fourth after a troubled passage behind Snow Lantern, Mother Earth and Alcohol Free, beaten only a length. Opportunity had knocked but then the door was slammed shut, bringing emotion bubbling to the surface for Jarvis.

"I think the crying after the Falmouth was slightly exaggerated," he said. "I was called 'cry baby' on the Heath for a few days by my fellow trainers, but I can take that. I still feel she was probably the best horse in the Falmouth."

There was only three weeks to wait for the next chance – a mere blink of the eye for Jarvis after the long years since Grand Lodge – and the Nassau was the perfect stage for Lady Bowthorpe to prove just how good she was. Banks now had a different kind of star on her books, and one who had captured the hearts of the racing public.

"Grand Lodge was very special and he had a following, but not as big as this mare has," Jarvis said. "Even on Newmarket Heath, people know who she is and it's lovely that they look out for her, and I'm often asked 'how's the mare?' She's got a big following and it's great. It's really special to have a mare as good as this."

The long gap between his two stars had been testing at times but Lady Bowthorpe was worth the wait.

▲ Glorious success: trainer William Jarvis with Lady Bowthorpe at Phantom House Stables in Newmarket; inset, a day to remember from the winning line to the presentation

'Claire's totally dedicated to her'

William Jarvis gives a lot of credit for Lady Bowthorpe's development to Claire Harkness, who has looked after the Group 1 winner from day one.

"This mare takes a little bit of managing, she has to go in the stalls last with a blindfold, and in the stables at home she gives Claire quite a hard time on occasion," the trainer said. "But they have a wonderful bond; she even takes Polos from Claire's mouth.

"Claire's very good with her and they have a great affinity. She's a wonderful person to have, she's totally dedicated to Lady Bowthorpe, she talks to her all the time, she keeps her relaxed at the races, and she's a very big influence on the success we've enjoyed with Lady Bowthorpe."

Aloeride bridges the gap between grazing, feed and the nutrients horses need to thrive. Goes well beyond fantastic digestive support and building physical condition. RING us for a trial of 120 servings, secure 40% PREMIUM straight out of the gate.

+44 (0)1858 464550

ALOERIDE
.com

Best British Aloe Vera by far

After his first Group 1 win on Lady Bowthorpe in the Nassau Stakes, Kieran Shoemark spoke openly about addiction, redemption and loyalty

'I put my family through hell – but I hope I've repaid them in some small way'

By Peter Thomas

THE story of Kieran Shoemark had the potential to become a tragedy. A tragedy of talent wasted, opportunities squandered, youthful promise unfulfilled, or perhaps far, far worse. Racing has had its share of those tales but they become no easier to bear for their familiarity.

'Young man does well, discovers booze, disappears down the pan,' is not a new plot line. Throw in the modern predilection for drugs and you have all the ingredients for something dark and with an unhappy ending. Which was why the final chapter of the Nassau Stakes, with its groundswell of tears, jubilation and communal outpouring, made for such a joyous occasion.

Not that the 24-year-old jockey was the only player in this ultimately uplifting narrative. Shoemark highlights the part of Emma Banks, the forthright music agent whose act of loyalty gave him his shot at redemption, and he points to William Jarvis, the Newmarket trainer who waited 27 years to back up the almost forgotten potential of his own salad days. But for sheer weight of pathos and dramatic tension, the rider's own contribution was every bit their equal.

To see Shoemark sitting quietly, stylishly, waiting to pull the pin on the explosive power and pace of Lady Bowthorpe in the coveted Goodwood Group 1, it was hard to imagine the contrast with the all-too-recent years of his alcoholism and drug abuse, which led to a failed test, a six-month ban and a career on the brink.

All of that was traumatic for the rising star who had missed out by just one winner on landing the 2017 apprentice championship, but while he's frank in revisiting the devastation visited upon his own life, these days, with a clear head and an awakened conscience, it's the people he dragged down with him who now receive all the sympathy they deserve, which goes some way to explaining the intensity of the feelings that surfaced as he crossed the line in the Nassau.

"I celebrated as we passed the post," he explains, "but after that it was just relief, for the first Group 1 of my career, of course, and for all the hard work and support that had gone into it, but mostly for my family. I put them through so much and it was a shame they weren't there to see it happen, but I know how special it would have been for them just watching at home on TV.

"I put them through hell. I wasn't aware of it at the time and I don't like to talk about it now, but I know full well what I did to them. I was so wrapped up in it all, twisting and turning, and they lost their son for four years – we had no relationship at all – but they stuck by me through everything and I'm so grateful for it.

"I hope that win repaid them in some small way, but of course they're parents, so me staying clean and sober now is all they want as repayment, and the things I achieve along the way are a bonus. Being able to repay them with love, by spending time with them, means so much to me, and they deserve it all."

★★★★

THOSE long-suffering parents, Niamh and Ian, brought up Kieran, his brother Conor, a former jump jockey, and sister Eva in the heart of National Hunt country in Stow-on the-Wold, Gloucestershire, which is hardly surprising given that Ian was an accomplished jump jockey himself (like his own father Bill), having abandoned the Flat career that saw him bag a winner for the Queen on his first ride, on Insular, trained by Ian Balding.

There was no parental encouragement for the two boys to ride, but Kieran was always determined to pursue a career in the saddle, and eventually his dad bowed to the inevitable and backed his choice. The youngster enjoyed successful stints in Australia, became a fixture at Roger Charlton's Beckhampton yard and rode a winner – Atty Persse in the King George V Handicap – for Godolphin at Royal Ascot in 2017, but by the following year his life had begun to unravel. By the end of 2018 he had begun a six-month ban for a positive drugs test. He had lost his bearings, risked his career and hurt those closest to him, and something had to change.

"I still go to Alcoholics Anonymous meetings and talk to people in the fellowship most days," says Shoemark, less than three years down the line but with his life back on the rails and his work back at the highest level. "I have a lot of friends there, you meet people from all different walks of life and I get a lot of advice and try to give some."

But while curing his dependencies was something he could do outside the racing bubble, resurrecting his professional standing relied very much on an often conservative industry stretching out a hand of forgiveness. Luckily, in his corner was Banks.

"I think it was the owner's call to keep me on Lady Bowthorpe in the Nassau," says Shoemark, who still recalls the flak he received on social media after being beaten on the mare in a muddling Duke of Cambridge Stakes and a Falmouth characterised by the kind of ill fortune that left Jarvis in tears.

"She could have had anybody she wanted, so what a vote of confidence. I know Lady Bowthorpe isn't the most straightforward – she can be keen down to the start, she has a blind on and has 'Yarmy' [Steve Dyble] down at the stalls to help her – and I think Emma probably had in mind that I knew her very well, but she'd told me already that she's a very loyal person.

"Racing isn't always like that but Emma is a strong, independent woman who has got where she is by her own efforts and has every right to make her own decisions and not listen to anyone else. I'm not quite Lady Gaga and she has bigger problems than mine to deal with, but her loyalty made the win even sweeter."

★★★★

BANKS must have heard the sirens calling in the lead-up to the Nassau, with Jarvis later reporting to his jockey that agents had been on the prowl to see if the ride on his stable star might become available.

"He told me he got quite a few phone calls saying that they should be looking for another jockey, although he didn't tell me that until afterwards," recalls Shoemark, "but you know when you're not seen as a Group 1 jockey there are going to be other people looking for the ride, so I'm grateful to him for sticking with me, even though he was quite upset after the Falmouth.

"He's quite an emotional guy and I understand why he was in tears after Lady Bowthorpe was beaten at Newmarket and in tears after she won at Goodwood, but he's so well liked and respected and he thoroughly deserved the reception he got. I just hope it doesn't take me 27 years to ride my next Group 1 winner."

This is an edited version of an article that appeared in the Racing Post on August 16

In National Racehorse Week the
Racing Post highlighted the work
of the British Racing School in
giving ex-racers a new life

'People care – and the love for old racehorses still shines through years down the line'

By Peter Thomas

TOUCH THE SKY was once a very hot property. Although expectations would have been managed at Lordship Stud, as a son of Derby winner Sea The Stars and Oaks winner Love Divine he might have been expected to turn out pretty useful, with a long-term value to match.

That was then, though, and this is now. The blue-blooded gelding spent two seasons on the sidelines with injury, won a couple of Class 4 handicaps for David Elsworth and was finally retired at the age of five, having reached a handicap mark of 85 that did scant justice to his pedigree. Then he was sold, for the princely sum of £1.

The buyer was the British Racing School in Newmarket, where the contented underachiever is now enjoying his second career as a schoolmaster to the jockeys, trainers and stable staff of the future. It may not be quite the stuff of legend, but it's an honest living for a potential superstar who never quite made the grade. Most

importantly, it guarantees him a home for life and the endless devotion and care of a small army of admirers.

"We buy all our horses for a pound, for insurance purposes," explains Grant Harris, chief executive of the BRS, "but to us he's invaluable, like all of the horses we have, because without them we couldn't do this. We're a charity, so we can't afford to pay for horses like him, but he was a six-year-old living out his days in a field at Lordship Stud and they didn't know what to do with him, so owner Trevor Harris asked if we'd like to give him a go, and he's been a great success."

At the other end of the scale is Andrew, the only crossbreed in a yard of some 80 thoroughbreds, currently standing contentedly in his box, serenely devoid of any inferiority complex and renowned as a "bombproof" member of the teaching staff.

Then there's Poetic Rhythm, once famous as Fergal O'Brien's first Grade 1 winner in the 2017 Challow Hurdle – now tacked up, with trainee Lucy Hughes in the

saddle, ready to begin the day's lessons.

These are just a few on the long list of ex-racers who have been recruited for second careers in the low-pressure environment of the BRS. Some are model employees, sweet-natured and docile; others have a naughty streak that makes them ideally qualified to prepare their young riders for some of the greater challenges in a racing yard; all of them are fit to do the job in return for a life of certainty, security and an endless supply of Polos.

'George', as Poetic Rhythm is affectionately known, isn't a saint, but he seems to have taken to his new job with relish. He likes a buck and a kick before and after his stint on the all-weather strip – just to remind everyone that he was once a bit of a star, presumably – but Hughes, an 18-year-old soon to continue her training with Cheshire-based Oliver Greenall, is wise to his ways and happy to indulge him.

"He was keen, but that's fine," she says. "I like going quick and it's

▸ *Continues page 184*

good to get the opportunity to ride a horse as good as him. You definitely fall in love with them. Poetic's one of my favourites – he can have his off days, but he loves a cuddle and the more you ride them the more of a connection you get and the more they understand you. We're all horse lovers here and it's nice to be part of the way racing treats horses like him when they've finished racing."

Poetic Rhythm is one of many success stories the school has written as a major rehomer of retired racehorses. His owner Chris Coley had enjoyed his successful racing career but was aware his best days were behind him and was keen to find him a new role that would satisfy his innate competitive instincts and offer him a good life into the bargain.

"Poetic Rhythm was just the kind we like," Harris says. "He'd had a few back issues, was sliding down the handicap and struggling to win, but he was in good shape and I remember him arriving. Chris drove up here and was in buckets of tears and took loads of photos, but he knew George would be ideal for us, so we took him in and checked him out."

★★★★

THERE was never any danger of George being put into work that didn't suit him or, worse, threatened his wellbeing. The selection procedure sees to that, as Zoe Hammond, quality assurance manager at the school, explains. "As soon as the phone rings, we look up the horse's form on the Racing Post website to see if they're hard-pullers or have any other awkward traits. That doesn't necessarily relate to what they're like at home but at least it gives us some idea," she says.

"Then we'll contact the people and arrange to have the horse on a six-week trial. It used to be four weeks but now we get the instructors to ride them on every facility and then get the more experienced students to do the same: indoor, outdoor, round canter, straight canter, in behind, on their own, so we have a really good idea what they're like."

The school takes all types, so that students, who may ride 50 individual horses on their course, can gain as much experience as possible. Types like Falmouth Harbour, a 16-rated gelding who beat just four horses in four runs for Paul Cole. "I went to see some students down there and came back with him," Harris recalls. "The owner was delighted and so were we!"

Types like Heart Of A Hunter, who is barely three weeks out of training with Tony Carroll and is out in a field learning to relax; like Brief Goodbye, the former John Berry-trained horse who, at the age of 21, is described as a "naughty old man" who has never quite shed the habit of trying to get rid of unsuspecting riders.

"The students need to ride plodders and difficult ones," says Hammond's husband Mike, yard instructor and former point-to-point trainer, who spends much of his morning charging along beside the straight gallop in a minibus, encouraging and cajoling riders via a walkie-talkie.

The students seem to derive great benefit, experience and no small degree of excitement from a spin on the livelier steeds, just as the owners and trainers who send them here derive a huge amount of satisfaction from knowing they have done a good thing.

▲ School life: Shay Halton riding Touch The Sky at the British Racing School; previous page: main picture and inset top middle, Lucy Hughes on Poetic Rhythm; inset top left, British Racing School chief executive Grant Harris; inset top right, yard instructor Mike Hammond

"We had a horse arrive recently called Sussex Road," Mike says. "His claim to fame is that he was rated 46 over fences, the lowest-rated chaser in the country, but when he was advertised on Facebook, I rang and asked if we could have him. The trainer, Aytach Sadik, had already been offered a couple of grand for him but he went away and thought about it and phoned back a few days later. When he came to look round the place, he said it was a privilege for his horse to live here."

With a non-racing agreement signed, each horse is guaranteed a life out of serious competition, but with its instincts to gallop satisfied provided it has the physical wherewithal. Some of the old-timers loafing out in the fields would still lead the rest a merry dance on the all-weather given half a chance, but there comes a time when their enthusiasm has to be kept in check.

"The majority of our horses have quite a few miles on the clock," Harris says. "They'd be aged six to 25 and they'd have their niggles, but they're not injured, they're just like you and

▶ *Continues page 186*

me, they're middle-aged horses."

"The aim is to keep them for as long as we can," Zoe says. "We had a couple we've just rehomed at the age of 25 and they'd still have been doing indoor work with the absolute beginners and maybe one little canter a day, but if it's hot we don't do much with them at all."

★★★★

THE symbiosis between owners, trainers and the BRS is obvious, but there are other areas in which these semi-retired horses help to complete the circle of racing life. The school is the first port of call for the Royal Veterinary College when it wants to carry out studies on anything from saddles and shoes to stride patterns and provides the results in return; SIS trialled its tracker system here and the quid pro quo consisted of five sets of numbered saddlecloths; and when a blood donor is required by Rossdales Equine Hospital, there's one place they will be sure to contact.

"There was a regally bred broodmare that needed a caesarean in February and we sent a horse down there that was a perfect blood match," remembers Mike with no little pride. "He stayed down there for a week so they could take blood from him whenever they needed."

These are horses who begin their lives giving sporting pleasure in return for bed, board and kindness, and carry on serving and helping to perpetuate racing, while being treated like family pets. Even the people who passed them on for £1 rarely forget them.

"Whenever I see Trevor Harris at the races, the first thing he asks is how Touch The Sky is, and a lot of former owners will visit when they're at the races in town," Harris says. "They turn down money in return for peace of mind, and they love to stay in touch with the horse that's now keeping people in the industry busy and giving a lot of pleasure."

"What it shows you is that the sport cares, people care and most of them want to do the right thing," Zoe says. "The love for old racehorses shines through years down the line."

This is an edited version of an article that appeared in the Racing Post on September 17

'Amazing feedback from the public' as 130 yards open up

THE inaugural National Racehorse Week was held from September 12 to 19, showcasing the care and attention given to thoroughbreds during their racing careers and beyond.

The initiative was born out of an idea put forward in the Racing Post in 2019 by trainer Richard Phillips, who suggested creating a single event that the entire racing industry could get behind to celebrate the animals who power the sport and provide entertainment for millions. Phillips' Adlestrop stables in the Cotswolds was among 130 yards that opened their doors to the public and he was delighted with the response.

"From my point of view it went really well and I've spoken to a few other trainers, all of whom have been very positive and have asked how we can do it again and how we can do it better," Phillips said. "We've had amazing feedback from the public. People we've never met before have emailed to say what a fantastic time they had. I know I'm not the only trainer who has had that feedback.

"It's a good way of engaging with the public and promoting what we know we do every day, which is to look after racehorses' welfare, every day of the year, 24 hours a day. It's an opportunity for everyone, including racehorse trainers and their staff, to show that point off."

The week was bookended by open days in Malton and Epsom on September 12 and the Henry Cecil Open Weekend in Newmarket on September 18-19. Great British Racing funded more than 50 per cent of the national campaign – with additional financial support from the Racing Foundation, the Sir Peter O'Sullevan Charitable Trust, Godolphin, Racecourse Media Group and a generous private donation from the late Andy Stewart – and the Racing Post ran a series of in-depth articles on the lives of racehorses from early days to racing and retirement.

The Malton open day, already well established as a popular attraction, resumed after its loss to Covid in 2020. The event is a huge fundraiser for Racing Welfare and Nicola Strong, head of communications and marketing, said: "We sold more tickets in advance than we normally have people on the day. There is obviously a huge appetite for in-person events. National Racehorse Week is a really great initiative, allowing people to see not just the horses but also the stable staff who work so hard to look after them."

Organisers of the Newmarket Open Weekend said it was the most successful staging of the event since its revival in 2012, attracting almost 3,000 people.

THE
BIGGER
PICTURE

A foal by Arc winner Waldgeist out of Date With Destiny at Newsells Park Stud in Hertfordshire with her handler Carey Plummer, who holds her mother

EDWARD WHITAKER (RACINGPOST.COM/PHOTOS)

'She embodied everything there is to love about jump racing'

Racing lost one of its own in April when amateur rider Lorna Brooke died following a race fall

RACING went into deep mourning for amateur jockey Lorna Brooke, who died on April 18 aged 37 following a heavy fall at Taunton ten days earlier. Brooke was airlifted to Southmead Hospital in Bristol after falling from Orchestrated, trained by her mother Lady Susan Brooke, and was taken into intensive care with a suspected spinal injury, but due to complications she was placed in an induced coma and died two days later.

News of her death was announced in a statement by the Injured Jockeys Fund (IJF), which read: "It is with deep sadness that we have to share the tragic news that Lorna Brooke passed away yesterday. Her family thank everyone for their kindness in the last ten days, particularly the staff at Southmead Hospital, who were so professional."

Brooke rode 17 winners – plus 40 in point-to-points – including the first running of a ladies' chase in Britain or Ireland at Fairyhouse in 2015 aboard Moonlone Lane. She had her first winner under rules in 2007 and her last in October 2019.

Evan Williams, one of the trainers she won for, said: "Racing is built on hard-working people with a passion for horses like Lorna and she was an absolute joy to deal with. She rode a winner for me aboard Dashing Doc at Newton Abbot. He was a very tricky horse and professional jockeys couldn't win on him but Lorna was definitely up for the challenge. She was far more optimistic about his chances than I was but she always looked on the bright side of life. Even if she was on an outsider, it didn't matter and she always gave 100 per cent.

"It's so devastating to think poor old Lorna has gone – words can't describe it. She was what makes this sport great. It's not just about the big prizes at big meetings, it's about the Lornas of this world."

Brooke made her debut under rules on Hag's Way as a teenager in February 2002 for her mother and celebrated her first winner aboard Super Nomad in the Ludlow Gold Cup Hunters' Chase in April 2007 before the pair followed up at the track in March 2008. Her biggest victory came in the inaugural running of the Ladies Handicap Chase at Fairyhouse in 2015 with 25-1 shot Moonlone Lane for Paul Stafford. Behind her in second, third and fourth were top riders Katie Walsh, Lizzie Kelly and Rachael Blackmore.

That race was the brainchild of Fairyhouse manager Peter Roe, who recalled: "Paul Stafford rang me to say he had no jockey for his horse. Lorna was recommended as a really good old-fashioned amateur rider. I told Paul about Lorna and he said he'd be happy to use her.

"So over comes Lorna to ride a horse with absolutely no form, a rank outsider who looked to have no chance whatsoever, yet all she kept saying was how much she appreciated being asked to ride in the race. She said she'd always wanted to ride in Ireland and she was absolutely thrilled to be able to tick off that box. Then she ends up winning the bloody thing. It was just unbelievable. She gave the horse an absolute peach of a ride."

Brooke was the first jockey to sustain fatal injuries while race-riding under rules in Britain or Ireland since Tom Halliday in July 2005. A period of silence was observed at every meeting in Britain after her death was announced and jockeys wore black armbands.

Professional Jockeys Association chief executive Paul Struthers said: "This is a devastating reminder of the dangers our brave men and women face. Lorna was an incredibly hard-working, popular member of the weighing room and, while her licence was as an amateur, she was a professional in every other sense. We have lost one of our own and she'll be sorely missed."

Jockey Lucy Gardner rode alongside Brooke for years, first as an amateur herself, and said: "She was always happy. She just loved her horses and loved racing. Lorna and her mum were a team together similar to myself and my mum [Sue Gardner]. They did everything for the love of the sport and of each other. This will affect everyone. It's something nobody is going to forget for a long time and nobody is going to forget her."

Amateur jockey David Maxwell said: "Our hearts are broken in the amateur ranks. Lorna and her mother embodied the family spirit of racing and a bit of our hearts are missing now. At times like this you get a real sense of how tight-knit the racing community, but especially National Hunt, really is."

Amateur Jockeys Association chief executive Sarah Oliver, who put Brooke forward for the Fairyhouse ride on Moonlone Lane, said: "Lorna was blessed with a vivacious, bubbly personality and her smile lit up the racecourse wherever she went. Her thirst for racing was unquenchable – she embodied everything there is to love about jump racing. Her loss is keenly felt in the weighing room and beyond. One thing is for certain, Lorna will never be forgotten."

Reporting by Jonathan Harding, Sam Hendry and David Jennings

◄ Happy day: Lorna Brooke lifts the trophy after winning the Ladies Handicap Chase at Fairyhouse in 2015 on 25-1 shot Moonlone Lane

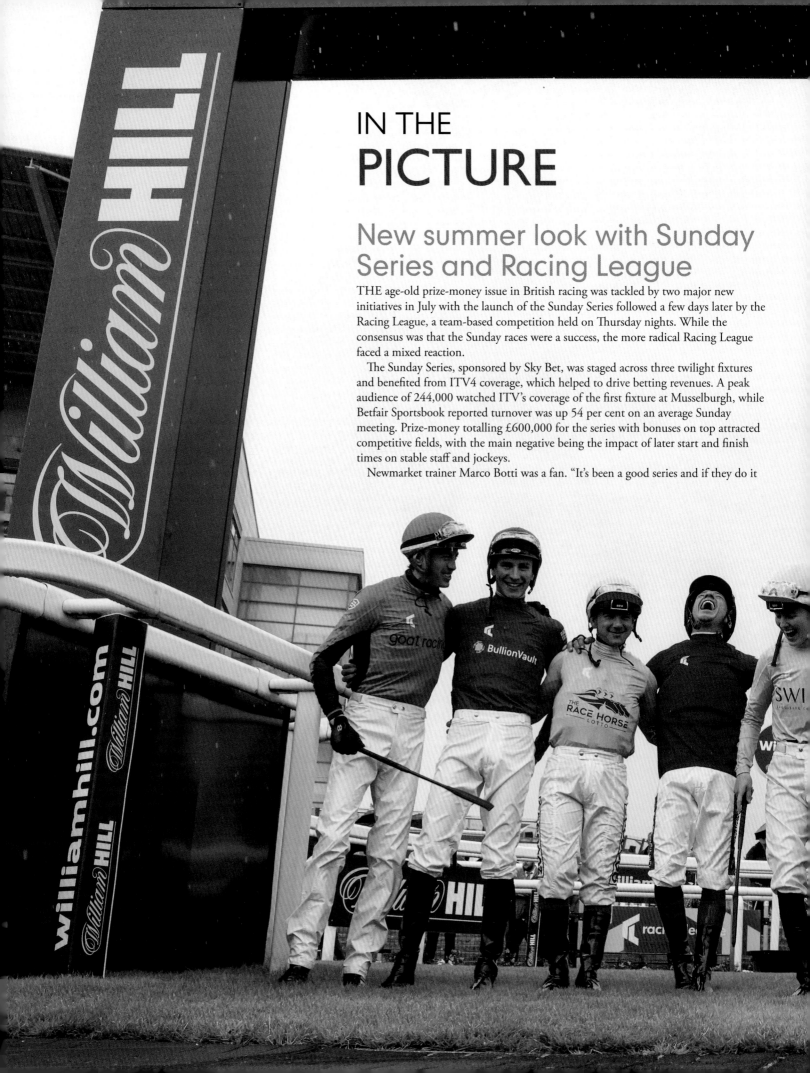

IN THE
PICTURE

New summer look with Sunday Series and Racing League

THE age-old prize-money issue in British racing was tackled by two major new initiatives in July with the launch of the Sunday Series followed a few days later by the Racing League, a team-based competition held on Thursday nights. While the consensus was that the Sunday races were a success, the more radical Racing League faced a mixed reaction.

The Sunday Series, sponsored by Sky Bet, was staged across three twilight fixtures and benefited from ITV4 coverage, which helped to drive betting revenues. A peak audience of 244,000 watched ITV's coverage of the first fixture at Musselburgh, while Betfair Sportsbook reported turnover was up 54 per cent on an average Sunday meeting. Prize-money totalling £600,000 for the series with bonuses on top attracted competitive fields, with the main negative being the impact of later start and finish times on stable staff and jockeys.

Newmarket trainer Marco Botti was a fan. "It's been a good series and if they do it

again next year, we'll have another go," he said. "We don't run many horses on a Sunday unless there's a reason and when it's good prize-money the staff are happy to make the effort."

The Racing League (*pictured*), sponsored by William Hill and broadcast by Sky Sports Racing, also offered good prize-money with a total value of £1.8 million across six consecutive Thursday nights at £50,000 per race. The novel concept involved 12 teams, comprising 30 horses each, putting one runner in each of the six races per night. Instead of their usual owners' silks, horses ran in team colours under names such as Team Swish.

The first winner at Newcastle on the opening night was Saluti, who earned nearly ten times as much as he had when scoring at Nottingham a few weeks earlier. His jockey Paul Mulrennan said: "It can't be anything but good. Look at the prize-money this horse has been running for on his last three runs – buttons. Tonight he's won £25,000."

Yet there were complaints about the team concept and whether it works in racing, the selection process for the trainers and the competitiveness of the races, with a sizeable proportion falling short of the 12-runner maximum field. Scheduling was an issue too, with Thursday nights on Sky not offering the same shop window for the sport as the Sunday Series did with terrestrial coverage.

Those gripes were countered by support in many quarters, with leading northern trainer Tim Easterby saying: "I'm pro-Racing League because the prize-money's great. It's the same with Sunday evening racing. I wasn't really into it at all but when I saw the prize-money I thought we've got to welcome it."

Picture: JOHN GROSSICK (RACINGPOST.COM/PHOTOS)

KNOCKOUT PUNCH

GOING into the mid-September big weekend featuring the St Legers at Doncaster and the Curragh among a multitude of Group 1 races, Johnny Murtagh could not have been in a better mood. Already enjoying a season that had brought high-profile victories at Royal Ascot, Glorious Goodwood and in the Ebor at York, he had high hopes of more success over the weekend.

"I'm sitting here, the sun is blazing down and we're coming into the biggest weekend of the year. We've had a great year, so at the minute it's a great life. There's no better game in the world when things are going well," the trainer said in a Racing Post interview published on the Saturday.

By the end of that afternoon, however, Murtagh was feeling very different. Champers Elysees was sixth in her bid to land the Matron Stakes at Leopardstown for the second year in a row, while Ottoman Emperor was beaten almost 17 lengths into last place in the St Leger at Doncaster. Things definitely weren't going well.

Then the pendulum swung again in Murtagh's favour and on the Sunday he claimed his Classic breakthrough with Sonnyboyliston in the Irish St Leger. Having won the Ebor the previous month, the horse named after a world heavyweight champion landed another knockout punch for the trainer just when he was on the ropes.

"Racing is a great game, it's a great leveller. You can never get too high and you can never get too low. On Friday I was very bullish, but I have to admit I was pretty deflated last night," Murtagh admitted as he stood in the winner's enclosure. His only Irish St Leger in a stellar riding career had come on Jukebox Jury in 2011 in a tooth-and-nail dead-heat with Duncan and Sonnyboyliston fought just as hard to secure Murtagh's first Classic as a trainer.

Sent off 4-1 second favourite, Sonnyboyliston had the other market principals around him as he launched his attack with two furlongs to run. Search For A Song, 100-30 favourite to complete a hat-trick in the race, was first to wilt and 6-1 shot Baron Samedi could never quite land a telling blow as hard as he tried in third, but Melbourne Cup winner Twilight Payment had the lead and refused to throw in the towel. It took every ounce of strength for Sonnyboyliston and his young rider Ben Coen to force their way to the front at the furlong pole and hold off the brave resistance of Twilight Payment by three-quarters of a length.

"It means a lot to win a Classic on your local track," said Murtagh, who rode 15 Classic winners there and now trains on the Curragh. "This horse never disappoints and he did very well to win. It looked like a proper race and he had a good position all the way. He got into a battle, but he never lacks in a battle."

★★★★

THE trainer also knows a good jockey when he sees one and he has found a gem in Coen, who at the age of 19 crowned his first proper season as stable jockey with his maiden Group 1 winner. "Ben is very good on the big day, very cool and strong in a finish. He's everything we need and a huge addition to the yard," Murtagh said.

Coen, who had also been on board for Sonnyboyliston's hard-fought head victory in the

those countries themselves in 2022 for the Saudi Cup and Melbourne Cup. With £667,089 in prize-money, the club was already well in profit.

"There'll be a nice payout for the members now," Clarke said, "and, as I'd always say, take some money, put good profit in your back pocket, and we can buy a couple of yearlings and continue on from here. There'll be money there to pay for them now. It doesn't always happen that way!"

****

THINGS certainly kept happening for Murtagh and Coen throughout 2021. Sonnyboyliston was the stable star with his Irish St Leger and Ebor triumphs but Ottoman Emperor, despite his Classic disappointment, gave them a big moment at Glorious Goodwood with victory in the Group 3 Gordon Stakes and there was a prized first Royal Ascot success for trainer and jockey with Create Belief in the Sandringham Handicap.

Murtagh, who registered 43 Royal Ascot winners in his distinguished riding career, could not have been more delighted after his filly romped home by five and a half lengths down the straight mile.

"I was very successful at this track as a jockey – I love the place," he said. "This is where I want to be. I'm a born winner and I want to be on the big stage. To come back as a trainer means the world. Training is a much tougher game. You're with the horses all the time, I'm responsible for 25 staff and huge thanks to them. It's a magical day."

Magic was everywhere for Murtagh and his team in 2021. Every month he seemed to have a new trick for the big Flat festivals, and he saved the best for his home crowd at the Curragh. Sonnyboyliston was the Classic ace up his sleeve.

Ebor, had gone to Doncaster the previous day hoping for Classic success on Ottoman Emperor and the pendulum had swung for him too. "I really wanted to get this Group 1 winner. For it to be a Classic and for Johnny is unbelievable," he said. "They turned it into a real staying race and this lad keeps improving and finding a way to win. Every day we step him up he keeps on finding and it's a day I'll never forget."

Exactly a year earlier Sonnyboyliston had won the Northfields Handicap on the same card, with subsequent Group 1 Tattersalls Gold Cup winner Helvic Dream in third, and this

was a new peak on his climb up the ranks. It had been an even longer journey for Kildare Racing Club, which started as a shared ownership venture in the mid-1980s simply as a bit of fun among friends. Joint-founder Liam Clarke, a Curragh-based bloodstock agent, bred Sonnyboyliston as part of a different group but the "big and raw" youngster went into the colours of Kildare Racing Club after being bought back through Murtagh for €26,000 as a yearling. It proved a wise call as Sonnyboyliston gradually developed into easily the best horse the club has ever had.

Over the years the venture had continued with the odd Flat horse or jumper spread among the various acquaintances Clarke has made during his long stint in the sport. "We've got people from all over Ireland, plenty from England too, friends and clients from buying horses. Some of them have got involved with horses we've had over the years, maybe buying a quarter share or something," he said.

Now they had a valuable commodity on their hands and were turning down multiple offers from Australia, as well as from a Saudi owner, with the intention being to take Sonnyboyliston to

THE
BIGGER
PICTURE

The Colin Bowe-trained winner Ya Boy Ya (James Kenny) is on the far side at the first fence as the leaders vie for position in the 2m4f beginners' chase at Kilbeggan on June 6
PATRICK McCANN (RACINGPOST.COM/PHOTOS)

Bargain buy Skyace completed a remarkable rise to the top with Grade 1 victory at Fairyhouse in April

SKY HIGH

A £600 castoff from Willie Mullins' powerful Closutton operation seems an unlikely Grade 1 winner, yet within 18 months of her sale to trainer Shark Hanlon that is exactly what Skyace became after a remarkable rise from obscurity.

The mare's progress was so swift and sure, in fact, that by the time Hanlon pitched her into Grade 1 company at Fairyhouse in April he was bullishly confident of victory. "I'll give you a story, 'Shark Hanlon wins his first Grade 1 with Skyace'," he told the Racing Post the day before the Mares Novice Hurdle Championship Final. "I rang the lads who own her in Dubai [Birdinthehand Syndicate] and I told them she's a certainty and to have what they like on her. That wouldn't usually be my way, especially in a Grade 1, but I couldn't be more confident in this mare. I think she'll give me my first Grade 1 win and if she does it would be absolutely mighty."

She did, and it was. Skyace, who had gone from maiden hurdle success the previous June to Grade 3 winner by October, handled the jump up to the top level with aplomb to land a half-length victory. Filling the next three places were the Mullins-trained Gauloise, Hook Up and Glens Of Antrim, as Skyace confirmed the massive improvement she had made since leaving their company at Closutton.

"Everyone wants to train a Grade 1 winner and to do it is great," Hanlon said. "It's also great for racing. Anyone out there now can say 'right, she's a small-priced filly, let's put together a syndicate and go and have some fun'."

★★★★

LOOKING back on his trip to Ascot sales in November 2019, Hanlon said: "I went over to buy this mare and I rang the lads in Dubai to tell them I'd love to have her. They asked me how much I thought she'd make and I said 15 grand. When they looked at the form they said not to come home without her. I opened the bidding at £600 and there wasn't another bid. I was shocked but thrilled.

"I don't know why she was so cheap as she'd been placed in three bumpers for Willie Mullins. The group of lads who bought her asked me if she had three legs or four, but I told them she'd be fine."

Hanlon waited more than six months to run Skyace but she got off the mark immediately in a maiden hurdle at Tipperary in late June 2020 and followed up at Gowran Park three weeks later. A few disappointments followed and she was 66-1 when she lined up for a Grade 3 mares' novice hurdle at Down Royal at the end of October. The odds were upset in no uncertain fashion as Skyace won by a head from the Gordon Elliott-trained 6-5 favourite Queens Brook, a £160,000 purchase whose only previous defeat under rules had been in the Champion Bumper at Cheltenham.

Skyace overturned another hotshot, the Mullins-trained Finest Evermore at 8-13, in a Listed mares' novice hurdle at Punchestown in December. "The funny thing about it is that her form is very good, but because she was bought very cheaply people seem to be stunned by her the whole time," Hanlon said after that win.

Confidently the trainer put her away for the big spring festivals and she produced the most stunning moment of all at Fairyhouse, sandwiched between a good fourth in the Grade 2 mares' novice hurdle at Cheltenham and an early fall at Punchestown.

Her Grade 1 breakthrough was the ultimate vindication of Hanlon's abilities as both a talent spotter and trainer. "Not many people have improved one off Willie Mullins. In fact, it's usually the other way around," Hanlon said as her winning run gathered momentum. "But Willie has been nothing but a gentleman and has sent a text to say 'well done' every time she's won."

★★★★

THERE was another Mullins link with Skyace's Fairyhouse triumph as she was ridden by Jody McGarvey, whose only previous Grade 1 success had been for Closutton on Great Field at the 2017 Punchestown festival. Having made it two on Skyace, McGarvey quickly moved on to three when Janidil led home a Mullins 1-2-3 in the Grade 1 novice chase later on the card.

Just as it was for Hanlon, this was a big day for McGarvey, who had been on board for all of Skyace's previous wins. "It's unbelievable. Coming to this meeting with the good rides I had was very exciting. For it all to click into place like it has, it's a dream come true," the rider said.

"I've been riding a long time now. I'm 30 years old. You appreciate it that bit more when you're not a regular in the winner's enclosure. It's a day I won't forget."

That was the magic of Skyace, the mighty mare who cost virtually nothing but was worth the world to her connections.

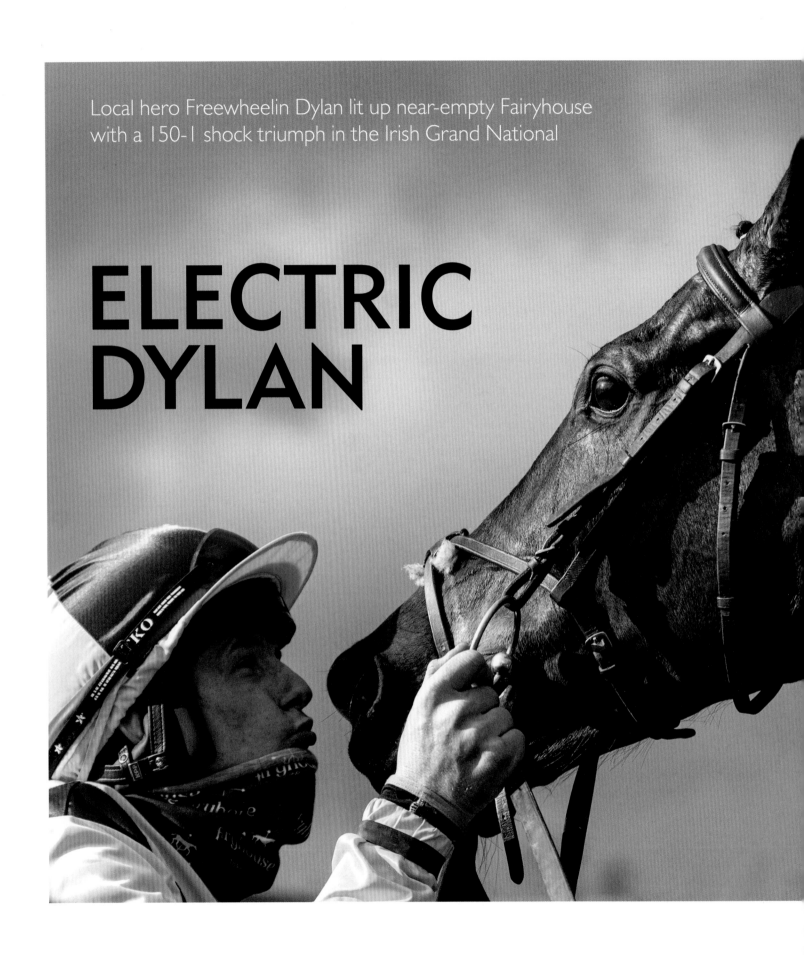

Local hero Freewheelin Dylan lit up near-empty Fairyhouse with a 150-1 shock triumph in the Irish Grand National

ELECTRIC DYLAN

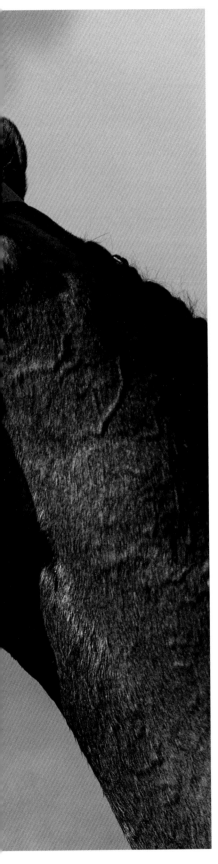

TURNING into the straight in the Irish Grand National, Ricky Doyle could hardly fathom what he was feeling from his mount Freewheelin Dylan and hearing from his rival jockeys behind him. "I could hear them slapping in behind me," he said afterwards, "and I was thinking to myself, 'no way am I going this easy in an Irish National on this lad'. I couldn't believe it."

Around a near-empty Fairyhouse and for those watching on television at home, there was a similar sense of disbelief. Freewheelin Dylan was a 150-1 shot for Ireland's richest jumps race, a rank outsider in the 28-runner field, and yet here he was cruising with three fences to jump. It wasn't an illusion: Doyle's mount really was travelling like the winner and he was about to finish the job.

Dermot McLoughlin, Freewheelin Dylan's trainer, could see it too. "I was fairly relaxed about it until they turned in," he said. "I was enjoying it up until then. It was nice to see a horse jumping fences like that and enjoying himself. He was loving it. But when he turned in I knew he had a chance and I started to get a bit excited."

Freewheelin Dylan continued to enjoy himself on the run to the line. He did not put a foot wrong over the last three fences, nor did he falter in his relentless gallop, and he came home in front by a length and a quarter from Run Wild Fred, one of the Gigginstown runners. The 9-2 favourite Latest Exhibition, a Grade 1 performer, was fourth, with other fancied runners from the big stables well beaten.

It was the biggest upset in the long and storied history of the famous race, which was established in 1870 and had lost what should have been the 150th anniversary edition when Covid caused its cancellation in 2020. The biggest-priced winner in the race's previous century and a half was Liberty Counsel at 50-1 in 2013. "It will be easy to talk to BoyleSports about next year's sponsorship anyway," joked Fairyhouse manager Peter Roe after Freewheelin Dylan had smashed that record.

Freewheelin Dylan's triumph brought happiness all round. The weighing room turned out to applaud Doyle's return to the winner's enclosure, which would have been thronged with racegoers in normal times, and Latest Exhibition's trainer Paul Nolan was among those heartily clapping in the shock winner. In an era of dominance by the big stables, this was an old-fashioned underdog story to warm the heart.

★★★★

McLOUGHLIN trains in Boreen, less than four miles from Fairyhouse, and Freewheelin Dylan is owned by Sheila Mangan, his head groom. She was far from deterred by the long odds and doubled down every time her horse's price lengthened, starting with odds of 66-1 and 100-1. "Then he went 150-1 and I said, 'Ah, for f***'s sake, I have to have a bit of that as well,'" Mangan told the Racing Post. "So I backed him at 66-1, 100-1 and 150-1. We got a nice few quid and it'll pay for a party."

McLoughlin had always dreamed of winning the local showpiece, having heard all the stories about his late father Liam's victory as a jockey on Kerforo in 1962. The other claim to fame for McLoughlin snr was that he was the first rider to win on Arkle, the greatest chaser of all time and winner of the Irish Grand National in 1964.

"This is a race I always wanted to win," said the 47-year-old trainer. "We've been coming here since I was a young boy. My father won the race, and my uncle Peter was second in it, and it's a race I've always wanted to have runners in, let alone a winner. I've been training for about ten years now and I set out my stall to find a horse to run in the Irish National."

For Doyle, victory on his first ride in the race was a special feeling. "This is the best day of my life by far, I can't believe it," said the 26-year-old, whose tally of 17 winners at the end of the season was a personal-best. "I was delighted just to be riding him. Because of the way he jumps, I couldn't wait for the race. Dermot McLoughlin, what a man."

Doyle is recognised as one of the hardest-working members of the weighing room, often seen mucking out and driving horseboxes for his boss Conor O'Dwyer, and he was keen to acknowledge the support that had helped him to his biggest day. "My career got off well on the Flat and then slowed up a good bit, and since I went to Conor he has put so much trust and faith in me. This is thanks to him and his owners and the staff in the yard for helping me."

Having written another famous chapter in Fairyhouse's history, McLoughlin's mind soon turned to Aintree's Grand National in 2022. "I'd say Aintree would suit him," he said. "Jumping is his forte and all he does is keep galloping. Once he gets top of the ground, that's all that matters to him. He's not overly big either, so he might have a nice racing weight in it too, like he had at Fairyhouse."

McLoughlin has experience of Aintree, having sent 100-1 shot Vics Canvas to finish third behind Rule The World in the 2016 National. Whatever the odds, Freewheelin Dylan will be hard to dismiss.

By James Stevens

SOMETIMES a racehorse doesn't need to be the best to capture the imagination of racing fans. In fact, it can be done without winning a race. That was something Celerity had managed after no fewer than 105 winless runs, which gave her a place in the history books for the biggest losing run ever by a horse in Britain and Ireland and thrust her into the spotlight in a Racing Post feature article.

The seven-year-old mare was dubbed the new Quixall Crossett, the serial loser who became a cult hero of the jumps game in the north in the 1990s and early 2000s. His losing run had stretched to 'only' 103 outings. But on a damp August Friday at Haydock, the one-time €800 purchase provided one of the most heartwarming stories of the season by doing what Quixall Crossett had never done. On her 106th outing, Celerity finally got off the mark.

Celerity was sent off 33-1 for a six-furlong fillies' handicap that evening and even her most optimistic supporters could not have expected she would produce such a confident and assured victory, although she had shown some promise by finishing third on her previous two starts and Erika Parkinson, who had ridden her in an apprentice handicap at Thirsk a fortnight earlier, was able to claim 7lb this time.

"She'd hit a bit of form going there and she looked really well," recalled Lisa Williamson, who trains Celerity at her small yard on Kelsall Hill just outside Chester. "But in truth, we went to Haydock with no expectations at all. We said to Erika to ping the gates and let her be happy. We wanted her to go in front for as long as she could. I said she'd probably tire in the final furlong and finish last."

In the first few strides Parkinson followed the instruction to the letter as Celerity cannoned out of the gates and breezed into the lead by a couple of lengths. In her

CELERITY
THE CELEBRITY

bright yellow visor she continued to roll on in front and gradually increased her advantage. "The long-standing maiden is five lengths clear at halfway," said commentator Stewart Machin with a tinge of surprise in his voice.

With two furlongs to run it seemed the old familiar story would unfold as the well-fancied Dandys Gold and Laura Pearson took aim at the leader, while 6-4 favourite Verreaux Eagle was still in a stalking position under champion jockey Oisin Murphy.

But they didn't eat up the ground in the manner expected and, with Celerity still in front, Williamson held her breath in the final furlong. "I thought I was going to faint," she said. "I heard the crowd and I just couldn't watch, so I turned around."

As Parkinson asked for more, this time Celerity was able to deliver. There was no tiring in the final furlong, no sign of finishing last, as a comfortable winning margin of a length and a quarter raised cheers from the Haydock crowd. After crossing the line, Parkinson stood tall in her irons with a bright smile lighting up her face. It was impossible for those watching not to smile too; after a racing career of 1,953 days, Celerity was a maiden no more.

★★★★

"I WAS listening and in the final half-furlong I turned around to watch the finish," Williamson said. "Everyone was going mental and so was I. It was definitely my best moment in racing. I'm a small trainer and we train low [rated] horses but we have a great little yard and that was an amazing day.

"The atmosphere at Haydock was unbelievable. She got a huge round of applause, it was incredible. I had loads of messages, including from David Evans, who we bought her off. My phone never stopped pinging. There were so many 'well done' messages and people appreciating that we never gave up, which is true. Erika gave her a fantastic ride and everything fell into place on the day. I suppose it was meant to be after the Racing Post article on the day of the race. To me it was an absolute fairytale."

Owner Rick Heath was on a staff outing at Haydock on that fantastic Friday and it was an occasion he won't forget in a long time. It was by far his best experience on the racecourse, but perhaps the last time his work colleagues will be listening to his tips.

"We fancied our other horse in the race, Isabella Ruby, and we didn't have a penny on Celerity," Williamson said. "Rick said to the people at the staff do to put a fiver on Isabella Ruby and not Celerity. We thought the six furlongs was more Isabella Ruby's trip. Rick had told 16 women to back the other horse, so he wasn't the most popular. We had a laugh about it.

"But he said that win was his best moment too. After the race he called me and said 'I'm in the car park, I'm on my own, I'm just having a moment.' He couldn't believe what had happened. He was very humble – he thanked me and I thanked him."

Celerity started life in Ireland, where she had three runs as a two-year-old for Darren Bunyan before moving to Britain to join David Evans. She got close to that much-desired breakthrough for her second yard, once finishing a half-length runner-up at Ffos Las, but was a 24-race maiden by the time she joined Williamson late in her three-year-old season.

The waiting went on. Celerity would often run well but by the time of her breakthrough win she had been runner-up on seven occasions and third in eight races. Somewhat frustratingly, she had a habit of saving her best efforts for better races, in particular running well in big handicaps at Chester. One example was a creditable fifth in 2019, beaten just under three lengths when a whopping 16lb out of the handicap.

Williamson can pinpoint the reason for Celerity's turnaround as a seven-year-old. "We took her on a proper break this year, which I think made all the difference. I took her away from the yard to a bit of land I've got and going to that new environment helped her. She came back a different horse."

Celerity has always been a favourite at Williamson's yard and her popularity now extends far wider after her Haydock heroics, which means a lot to those at the beating heart of the story.

"She has to go out at a certain time every day," her trainer said. "She weaves and box walks if she isn't out by 8am. If you don't take her out she'll drive you nuts. She's a great ride, though. At the races she sweats and you can't do anything with her when you get her there. You just put the saddle and bridle on and leave her to it. She's quite a character.

"The support she's had means a lot to us. It's a big team effort and I'm here every day, mucking out and doing my bit. I'm a hands-on trainer and driving the lorry home from Haydock certainly brought everything back down to earth. It was fantastic to do it, though."

Fantastic indeed. Celerity wasn't exactly an overnight sensation but she had turned into quite a celebrity.

This is an edited version of an article that appeared in the Racing Post Weekender on August 25

Having racked up the longest losing run ever, Celerity finally put her name in lights by getting off the mark at the 106th attempt

THE
BIGGER
PICTURE

Maydanny, trained by Mark Johnston and
ridden by Jim Crowley, wins the Golden Mile
Handicap at Goodwood on July 30
EDWARD WHITAKER (RACINGPOST.COM/PHOTOS)

Our selection of the horses and people likely to be making headlines in 2022

NATIVE TRAIL

GODOLPHIN and Charlie Appleby had a pair of top-class three-year-old colts in 2021 with Adayar and Hurricane Lane, and by the autumn they had showcased two of the best prospects for next year's Classics too.

Native Trail and Coroebus both won impressively on Future Champions Day at Newmarket in October, putting themselves at the head of the betting for the 2,000 Guineas. Coroebus moved to favouritism after his two-length success in the Group 3 Autumn Stakes but was usurped just over half an hour later when Native Trail scored his second Group 1 victory in the Dewhurst Stakes.

How they come through the winter will be crucial, but Native Trail had the edge on their autumn performances judged on Racing Post Ratings and Topspeed. His RPR of 121 at Newmarket was up to scratch for a good Dewhurst winner, albeit just below the 122 he had achieved in the Group 1 National Stakes at the Curragh, and kept him ahead of Coroebus on 116.

Like Adayar and Hurricane Lane, one is a Godolphin homebred and one was a sales purchase, in Native Trail's case from the breeze-ups in April for 210,000gns. He was an impressive specimen when he arrived at Appleby's Moulton Paddocks yard and the trainer continues to be wowed by him.

"It was one of those occasions that as they were walking around the paddock I was gaining more confidence," Appleby said after the Dewhurst. "I just thought he was the standout and I think we've got a fantastic horse on our hands for next year's Guineas. He's 540kg and came in at that weight from the breeze-ups. He warms into the race and does it all the right way round. Once he met the rising ground the one thing this horse wasn't going to do was stop galloping. It was very similar to his win in the National Stakes and his acceleration, when he's really given the office, is quite remarkable."

Coroebus also has an excellent turn of foot, and possibly his is more instant, which leaves plenty of room for debate.

"I've never put them anywhere near each other at home," Appleby said. "Native Trail is a harder horse to assess. Coroebus travels for fun, but this horse does it in a different manner. I can't see him [Native Trail] going further than a mile."

Those giant strides look set to take Native Trail a long way.

APPRECIATE IT

BEFORE Appreciate It, Willie Mullins' last three winners of the Supreme Novices' Hurdle were Vautour, Douvan and Klassical Dream, who all went on to rate higher than 170 on RPRs and between them won nine Grade 1s after their novice hurdling seasons.

Yet Appreciate It stands above them at this stage judged on his RPR of 165 for his stunning 24-length victory in the Supreme. What might he achieve if he makes the same sort of progress in the senior ranks as those illustrious predecessors?

"The way he finished the race he looks as good as any of them," was high praise from Mullins when asked to compare Appreciate It with his recent Supreme winners. The accolade was thoroughly justified after a perfect four-race campaign that featured two other Grade 1 victories on the way to Cheltenham.

The best of those was another wide-margin win, by nine lengths from Irascible, in the Future Champions Novice Hurdle at the Leopardstown Christmas meeting, which earned an RPR of 156, and he was not far off that level in his Grade 1 success at the Dublin Racing Festival.

That meant he went to Cheltenham already close to the ten-year average RPR for Supreme winners. While victory was expected for the 8-11 favourite, the manner in which he achieved it was not. "You'd have to think that was a Vautour-like performance, wouldn't you?" Mullins said. "The way he destroyed them up the hill was fantastic. He was awesome."

Awesome is as awesome does. Appreciate It has the stamp of a special one.

GALVIN

GORDON ELLIOTT lost several stars during his suspension and for a time Galvin was among the departed. The seven-year-old has returned to the fold, however, and could be one of the flagbearers as the trainer tries to rebuild his reputation.

Owned by Ronnie Bartlett, Galvin left Elliott's yard before the Cheltenham Festival and was saddled by Ian Ferguson to win the National Hunt Chase. The County Antrim handler, who had done the pre-training with the young Galvin, then sent him back to resume his career with Elliott once the six-month suspension was over.

Galvin was one of the early post-suspension winners for Elliott, landing a Grade 3 chase at Punchestown in October, and that strengthened his position as a Grand National fancy.

Elliott has a strong association with the National, of course, after he burst on to the scene with Silver Birch in 2007 and won twice more with the hugely popular Tiger Roll in 2018 and 2019.

Galvin clearly has plenty of stamina and jumping ability given his Cheltenham success over 3m6f and he will have age on his side if he turns up at Aintree as an eight-year-old next spring. National winners of that age used to come along roughly once every ten years (Red Rum 1973, Corbiere 1983, Party Politics 1992, Bindaree 2002) but four eight-year-olds have won in the past six runnings.

Winning jockey Jack Kennedy had Aintree on his mind after the National Hunt Chase, saying: "He has a bit of class and stays very well, so I think the National would be right up his street."

BOB OLINGER

THE Ballymore Novices' Hurdle was billed as one of the races of the 2021 Cheltenham Festival between Grade 1 winners Bob Olinger, Gaillard Du Mesnil and Bravemansgame. The big three duly filled the places, but really there was only one horse in it.

Bob Olinger turned it into a rout, bursting clear up the home straight under Rachael Blackmore to win by seven and a half lengths. "The manner in which he did it, he has a massive future," Blackmore said. "An awful lot of people have thought a lot of this horse and it's great that he could really stamp what he's made of."

With Gaillard Du Mesnil going on to win another Grade 1 at Punchestown – in Bob Olinger's absence – and Bravemansgame finishing second in a Grade 1 at Aintree, the form of the Ballymore is rock solid. So is a Racing Post Rating of 163 for Bob Olinger over hurdles, which leaves him well set to take high rank as a chaser.

Trainer Henry de Bromhead is one of those who has long thought a lot of the exciting six-year-old. "We've always liked him," he said. "We took him away to work with our Cheltenham horses before he ran in a bumper and he worked better than a lot of them that day. That told us plenty about him."

A few weeks later, as he looked forward to sending Bob Olinger over fences, De Bromhead told us a bit more. "We think he's good. Very, very good. He's got gears and he stays. What more could you want?"

What indeed.

JOE TIZZARD

HAVING got married in the summer, Joe Tizzard looked forward to another big life change with the long-planned taking of the reins from father Colin at the family's Venn Farm Stables in Dorset.

The yard has one of the most powerful jumps strings in Britain, although there is room for improvement after a disappointing 2020-21 campaign brought only 37 winners and 11th place in the final standings.

That was the first time the yard had finished outside the top half-dozen in six campaigns and this is a big season as the team set out to recapture past glories.

Tizzard, 41, who retired from race-riding in 2014 and then took an increasingly prominent role as assistant to his father, is relishing the challenge. "We had a quiet season by our standards last term, but we hope to be back where we're used to being," he said. "We're set to have a busy winter and we're hoping it'll be a big season."

The stable could not produce a Grade 1 winner last term but there were promising signs from Albert Bartlett Novices' Hurdle runner-up Oscar Elite, Fiddlerontheroof and The Big Breakaway – second and third to Monkfish in the Brown Advisory Novices' Chase – and Eldorado Allen, who was twice best of the rest behind Shishkin, including in the Arkle Chase.

Native River, who won the Grade 2 Cotswold Chase and was fourth in the Cheltenham Gold Cup, will be the senior figurehead of a refreshed team. "We've got some lovely young horses," Tizzard said. "We've got 32 unraced horses, including this year's stores. We didn't have too many bumper horses last season, so we're looking forward to them. The team is really good."

Tizzard snr, who built up his stable from a part-time operation alongside his dairy farming business, produced 32 Grade 1 wins and popular stars such as Native River, Cue Card and Thistlecrack.

A joint training licence was considered but Tizzard snr, 65, said: "Joe's been doing more and more and he deserves his name at the top."

It will still be a collective effort, though. "We're all a team and have always worked like that," Joe said. "Dad's still up there every morning by my shoulder, so it's a lovely position to be in."

HISTORY

WHAT can we learn from History? Quite a lot actually, although there is still plenty we don't know – and that's the exciting part.

We know the Aidan O'Brien-trained filly is well bred, coming from one of the last crops of the late, great Galileo and out of a sister to top-class miler Mohaather, and we know the Coolmore partners were so keen to acquire her as a yearling that they went to 2,800,000gns, which made her the second most expensive lot at Book 1 of the 2020 Tattersalls October Sale.

History is a quick learner herself, finishing runner-up on her first two starts but getting much closer the second time, and then winning a Gowran Park mile maiden by two and a half lengths. Those three runs came six weeks apart and Wayne Lordan, who rode her at Gowran and the time before, was encouraged by her progress.

"History feels like she's improving the whole time," he said after her win. "She quickened up like a smart filly. Going to a mile was a help and her trip in time will be a mile to a mile and a quarter."

We also know History's form is solid – Panama Red, who beat her second time out, won a Listed race on her next run – and that the Group 1 Prix Marcel Boussac was being strongly considered for her final start at two until a slight setback ruled her out.

The unknown is what lies in store for her as a three-year-old but it will be interesting to find out more.

SEAN O'KEEFFE

COMING down the hill in the Martin Pipe Conditional Jockeys' Handicap Hurdle, Sean O'Keeffe was waiting for his moment to strike on the strong-travelling Galopin Des Champs. He moved alongside the leaders off the home turn, but then waited some more. Finally, going to the last, he went to the front and took the race by the scruff of the neck, scoring by two and a quarter lengths.

It was a first Cheltenham Festival winner for O'Keeffe, but the 22-year-old had ridden like an old hand. Willie Mullins, who entrusted the youngster with the ride that sealed the trainers' award for him in the last race of the festival, was impressed.

"Sean was very cool on the horse," Mullins said. "He did everything right. He slotted in and bided his time. When things opened up he still waited and waited and that's a real sign of a good pilot in the making."

O'Keeffe had ridden out his claim in style the previous autumn with victory on Dromore Lad in the Cork National and has continued to be much in demand even without a weight allowance. Over the summer he formed a fruitful alliance with Jessica Harrington, including a Grade 3 win on Exit Poll, and teamed up again with Mullins to take the Munster National with Ontheropes.

Thirty-nine winners on home turf in 2020-21 was a personal best and, with support from a number of big yards, he looks to be in a good position to improve on that tally.

INSPIRAL

THADY GOSDEN has seen plenty of Classics stars around Clarehaven Stables over the years, but there wasn't one for him to accompany into the winner's enclosure in his first season as joint-trainer alongside father John. Inspiral could be the one to give him that special feeling.

The 1,000 Guineas falls on the opening Classic weekend in the calendar and, all being well, the Cheveley Park Stud homebred will head across Newmarket from Clarehaven to the Rowley Mile with a leading chance. Four wins in four starts stamped her as one of the best two-year-old fillies and Gosden jnr was excited at the prospect of even better to come at three.

"She's got plenty of class," he said after her third win in the Group 2 May Hill Stakes at Doncaster. "She's an exceptional filly, but she's got plenty of frame to fill into, so we're hopeful she can mature nicely over the winter into next year." Frankie Dettori was in full agreement, saying: "She's a work in progress and I think she can get better over the winter. At the moment she's all frame and she'll be a very exciting filly next year."

The excitement level rose a notch further when Inspiral rounded off her juvenile campaign with a Group 1 success

in the Fillies' Mile at Newmarket, an important test over the Guineas course and distance. Having beaten Properous Voyage by three and three-quarter lengths at Doncaster, the gap narrowed to two and a half lengths over the same filly but it was still comfortable enough.

"Inspiral is the real deal, no doubt about it, and she just keeps improving," Dettori said. "Before the race I thought she may need a mile and a quarter by now but she travelled so well and finished off so well that hopefully she can go to the Guineas next year and then perhaps further."

The Cheveley Park filly has a Classic pedigree – by 2,000 Guineas winner Frankel out of 1,000 Guineas runner-up Starscope – and the stud's Richard Thompson is excited too. "Having a homebred like this, trained by Thady and John and ridden by Frankie, is what we live for and dream about," he said.

"She looks special. We've won the Fillies' Mile a couple of times and the Guineas a few years ago now, and it would be absolutely fantastic if she was good enough to compete in the Guineas."

MOSTAHDAF

SHADWELL ESTATE will be concentrating its energies around homebreds rather than sales purchases following the death of Hamdan Al Maktoum and this John and Thady Gosden-trained colt could be one of the flagbearers.

From a good Shadwell family and by Frankel, Mostahdaf took his record to five wins from six starts with a smooth success in the Group 3 Darley Stakes at Newmarket in October. His sole defeat came in a disappointing display in the Group 1 St James's Palace Stakes at Royal Ascot, but that may well have come too soon in his career and he looks set to thrive at a higher level as a four-year-old.

His half-sister Nazeef certainly did that for the Gosden stable, going from Newmarket handicap success at three to dual Group 1 winner at four in the Falmouth and Sun Chariot Stakes in 2020, as well as Royal Ascot victory in the Group 2 Duke of Cambridge Stakes.

John Gosden showed his high regard for Mostahdaf when he revealed there had been thought of sending him back into Group 1 company at the end of his three-year-old campaign. "We've always thought him a mile-and-a-quarter horse. I was going to leave him in the Champion Stakes but I was overruled by the management and that's why he's here," he said after the Darley. "He's a classy horse and we've always thought he's one for next year."

ADAM FARRAGHER

PROMISING apprentice Adam Farragher was quick to make his mark after arriving in Newmarket from Ireland in June and looks poised to do even better in his first full season in Britain.

Farragher, 21, from west Cork, gained a plum apprentice role with William Haggas, having previously been with Curragh trainer Mick Halford. With his experience and support on the increase, Farragher was pleased with how the move had worked out. "I wanted to give something different a go," he said. "I was really hoping to come to Mr Haggas and I'm really grateful he took me on. I can't believe the opportunities I'm getting."

Looking to next season, he added: "I'll try to hold on to my claim and use that to build contacts and hopefully get some nice winners for the boss."

Given the good impression he has made already, Farragher's claim is likely to be in high demand.

DISCOVERIES

IN 2017 Jessica Harrington discovered she had a highly talented two-year-old called Alpha Centauri and the following year turned the Niarchos family's filly into a champion miler with four Group 1 victories. In the process many people discovered Harrington was just as good at training top Flat horses as she was at handling elite jumpers.

Discoveries. Now along comes Alpha Centauri's sister, who achieved more than her illustrious sibling as a juvenile and could fly just as high at three. With Harrington's Group 1 winner Alpine Star in the family too, the stars appear to be aligned again.

Harrington enjoyed a golden run of form in the autumn and Discoveries was one of those who shone brightest with Group 1 victory in the Moyglare Stud Stakes. Alpha Centauri had been a disappointing favourite in the Curragh race four years earlier but there was no denying Discoveries, who fought off Agartha by three-quarters of a length.

That was a turnaround in form from their previous meeting in the Group 2 Debutante Stakes over the same course and distance three weeks earlier, when Discoveries was beaten four and a half lengths in third, and it was largely explained by the better ground on Irish Champions Weekend. "The going came up soft in the Debutante but she wants top of the ground," Harrington said.

Discoveries earned a Racing Post Rating of 110 in the Moyglare, 4lb better than Alpha Centauri's mark as a juvenile, and hopes are high, even if she will have to improve a stone to match her sister at three. One ambition will be a trip to Royal Ascot for the Coronation Stakes, won in record time by Alpha Centauri in 2018 and by their half-sister Alpine Star two years later.

"How can I be so lucky to have three fillies out of the one mare all win Group 1s? That's the most amazing Niarchos family," Harrington said as she stood with Discoveries after the Moyglare. "She's a lovely filly and completely different to Alpha Centauri. She's not as big as Alpha but has done a lot of growing, has a lovely temperament and isn't as feisty. Alpine Star looked completely different again."

What they have in common is innate ability. It will be fascinating to discover how far the latest family member can go.

DAVE LOUGHNANE

HELSHAW GRANGE STABLES, run by Dave Loughnane and his wife Sarah, took significant steps up in 2021 and hopes are high that the Shropshire yard will continue to climb the ladder.

Winning numbers have been rising since Loughnane started out in 2016, but now the quality is on the up too. Go Bears Go became the yard's first Group 2 winner in the Railway Stakes at the Curragh in June and went close to Group 1 success back there a couple of months later when third in the Phoenix Stakes, beaten a length. With Hello You later scoring in the Group 2 Rockfel Stakes at Newmarket, the stable has a strong core of high-level performers.

That is what Loughnane wants, more than increasing his string from around 70, as he explained in the summer. "People say to me of course you'd want more, but I'm happy with this number as I can treat every horse as an individual," he said. "For me that's key – if you have too many you can't give them the attention they each warrant."

He added: "It's my dream to be known as a trainer of good horses. For me it's about quality and you can see we're definitely upping the quality throughout the string."

That ambition is helped by the backing of Amo Racing, which is run by football super agent Kia Joorabchian and owns Go Bears Go and Hello You as well as the Richard Hannon-trained Derby and St Leger runner-up Mojo Star.

Loughnane has another important connection with Amo's retained rider Rossa Ryan, whose star is on the rise at the age of 21. He was in the saddle on both of the stable's Group 2 winners and winning the Railway together was a particularly sweet moment. The trainer and jockey both hail from Galway, with Loughnane having started out working in the jumps yard of Ryan's father David.

"I couldn't be happier for Rossa," Loughnane said after the Railway. "The connection between us goes back a long way. For us to come back here to the homeland and do something like that is very special."

More special times should lie ahead for both of them.

JONBON

FOR the first time since 1998 Nicky Henderson did not have any runners in the Grade 1 novice hurdles at the Cheltenham Festival in March but he expects to be back with a bang next year after assembling a strong team.

Jonbon is one of the most exciting prospects, having long carried the weight of expectation as the next big thing at Henderson's Seven Barrows yard. A brother of eight-time Grade 1 winner Douvan, he was bought for £570,000 by JP McManus in November 2020 shortly after winning his only point-to-point by 15 lengths and made a successful debut for Henderson in a Newbury bumper last March.

"We're very lucky to have him and he's bred to be good, looks good and everything he's done in one point-to-point and bumper has been very good," Henderson said at his annual owners' day.

Expanding on his team in the novice hurdle division, Henderson said his other big hope is I Am Maximus, another once-raced bumper winner in the 2020-21 season. In his case he beat My Drogo, who went on to land the Grade 1 Mersey Novices' Hurdle.

"Those two are top of the bunch, but it's a very strong bunch," he said. "I think this will be an exciting division for us and then next year I hope I'm talking about novice chasers again because the Jonbons and I Am Maximuses will be going over fences."

With Britain desperate to turn back the Irish tide, many will be looking to Henderson's new generation for salvation.

MY DROGO

DAN SKELTON is as honest as he is talented. "When I started off I was probably an owner-breeder's worst nightmare," he confessed in a Racing Post interview in January. "I was a young fella desperate for winners and going flat out. Now they can look at me in a different light. With the horses we have now, we'd be letting them down if we trained them the way we used to."

One of those horses is My Drogo, and he might turn out to be the best of the lot. As a homebred in the ownership of Richard and Lizzie Kelvin-Hughes, he also proves the point of how Skelton's methods have changed, tilting his yard towards quality and a long-term outlook that has encouraged owner-breeders to come on board.

Skelton does not hide his ambition for My Drogo. "We're a long way off the Gold Cup, but it's a dream," he said at the end of the six-year-old's novice hurdling campaign. "He has an awful lot of ability and the owners just want to make him into the best possible chaser we can."

The project could not have got off to a better start. After

finishing second at 50-1 in a Cheltenham bumper in October, beaten by Nicky Henderson's highly regarded I Am Maximus, he made rapid progress through the novice hurdling ranks, starting with a maiden victory at Newbury. From there he went straight up to Grade 2 level and won the Kennel Gate at Ascot just before Christmas, with next-time-out Betfair Hurdle winner Soaring Glory in third.

My Drogo was even more impressive when he returned from an 11-week break to score another Grade 2 win at Kelso in early March, winning by nine and a half lengths in a good time. Having been kept out of the fray at Cheltenham, he went to Aintree instead and stepped it up again to round off an excellent season with victory in the Grade 1 Mersey Novices' Hurdle.

That was over two and a half miles and confirmed him as a fine staying prospect, as well as the best British-trained novice of the season with a Racing Post Rating of 156.

"I felt relief after winning," Skelton admitted. "He's a very good horse. Ultimately we want to build up to going down the staying chase route. The team has done a great job with him. He's very exuberant at home, always doing more than necessary, so you have to turn the dials down, not up."

There is, however, no dialling down the excitement of where My Drogo might end up.

TRIPLE TIME

ON THE day Emaraaty Ana gave him a Group 1 triumph in the Haydock Sprint Cup, trainer Kevin Ryan dared to dream of more top-level success in 2022 with one of the undercard winners.

Two hours before the big race, Triple Time landed the Listed Ascendant Stakes by a length and a half under an assertive ride by Andrea Atzeni, who took him to the front early in the mile contest and then held the challengers at bay with some comfort.

Ryan did not attempt to hide his enthusiasm for the Frankel two-year-old, who races in the Emaraaty Ana colours of Sheikh Mohammed Obaid. "We thought

he was very special in the spring," the trainer said. "He has loads of speed and he's a long-striding horse, that's why Andrea let him go to the front."

Having been beaten on his first

two starts, Triple Time had broken his duck over the Haydock mile a month earlier with a runaway win on soft ground and Ryan was pleased to see him cope with different conditions in the Ascendant.

"It's very fast ground and he'd won on very soft – it's a sign of a good horse that he could adjust," he said. "He's taken a bit of time and he's taken racing to learn the job – physically he was there but mentally he took racing."

As for next year, Ryan added: "He has identified himself as a very talented horse. He's going to be very exciting. Ten furlongs is probably as far as he wants to go and we think of him as a Guineas horse."

MONMIRAL

MONMIRAL did not go to Cheltenham but ended up as the highest-rated juvenile hurdler in Britain or Ireland after rounding off a perfect season for Paul Nicholls with victory in the Grade 1 Anniversary 4-Y-O Hurdle at Aintree.

That made it five wins out of five for the French recruit, who comes from the family of popular Cheltenham Festival-winning chase mare La Landiere, and there was huge excitement at what the future might hold.

"There's a long way to go but he was bought to be a chaser and ultimately that's where he'll end up," Nicholls said. "He has got an engine and there's lots to look forward to."

A winner in France as a three-year-old, Monmiral was purchased for an ownership group of John Hales and his daughter Lisa, Ged Mason and Sir Alex Ferguson, and he made a winning debut for them at Exeter in November before following up in the Grade 2 Summit at Doncaster and another juvenile event at Haydock.

Nicholls said he was "itching" to run Monmiral in the Triumph Hurdle, but the owners, who know a thing or two about top-level racing, were not so keen and the decision was made to skip Cheltenham for Aintree.

Explaining that choice at the time, Nicholls said: "John Hales and the other guys aren't interested in the Triumph Hurdle – they're interested in chasing. If you're going to be serious about chasing in the future, you have to mind him a bit. He wasn't purchased for a Triumph Hurdle."

Monmiral came up against Triumph runner-up Adagio at Aintree and beat him by seven and a half lengths, going up to a Racing Post Rating of 151 as he continued the progressive profile that had brought improvement with every run.

All the signs are that Monmiral will do much more yet.

A PLUS TARD

YEARS from now, it will remain a staple quiz question for racing fans: name the three horses who completed the holy trinity for Henry de Bromhead at the 2021 Cheltenham Festival. Most will recall the names easily. "Honeysuckle, Put The Kettle On and Minella Indo," they'll shout.

Ask a different question – name De Bromhead's Gold Cup one-two that year – and people will scratch their heads for 'the other one' to go with Minella Indo. As they say, no-one remembers the runner-up.

That is the fate of A Plus Tard, beaten a length and a quarter into second by Minella Indo, but there is time for him to change the narrative. At seven he was the youngest of the Gold Cup principals – a year below Minella Indo and at least two years junior to the others in the first five – and it was only his 11th chase run.

There were question marks about A Plus Tard's stamina before the Gold Cup, and he was ridden accordingly, but he proved he

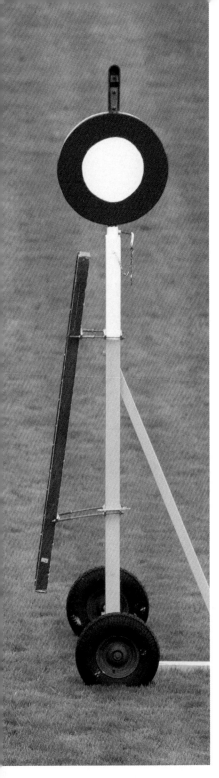

stayed the trip and his determined effort up the hill might have succeeded with a better jump at the last.

With that experience behind him, plus more to be gained this season before Cheltenham, A Plus Tard could well move up to the top step of the podium. His Racing Post Rating of 178 in last season's race was good enough to win a typical Gold Cup and he sets the standard just as much as his stablemate.

It is certainly not too late for A Plus Tard.

TATSUMAKI

WINNING a valuable sales race can be all about the moment – grab the big prize, job done – but Tatsumaki may well have bigger days to come given his style of victory in the £150,000 Tattersalls October Auction Stakes at Newmarket.

The Marco Botti-trained colt went into the six-furlong race unbeaten and came out with that record intact and his reputation enhanced after an impressive five-length success. Fearby, a Listed winner and Group-placed, was sent off 15-8 favourite and finished best of the rest in the 28-runner field but he could not live with Tatsumaki's acceleration.

Neil Callan, back in Britain after a long stint in Hong Kong, was easing down on Tatsumaki before the line, which is a rare sight in these highly competitive contests. "Fair play to Neil, who's always said this colt was the best he's sat on since he came back from Hong Kong," Botti said. "He could well get further and even make up into a Guineas horse as he wasn't stopping."

Tatsumaki's £81,000 first prize was a significant dividend on the 16,000gns paid by owner Ahmed Bintooq at the yearling sales. "Not many horses, especially two-year-olds, win three races in a row, and in a big race like that, so we're very happy," said Bintooq, who is in partnership with bloodstock agent Alessandro Marconi.

One of the new generation of owners from Dubai, Bintooq, 33, added: "Hopefully he's a better horse when he's three. I have two or three runners every year, and [Tatsumaki] is the best I've owned so far. Horses like this doesn't come around very often."

GREAT AMBASSADOR

ED WALKER produced top sprinter Starman in 2021 and has high hopes Great Ambassador will follow in those footsteps. The son of Exceed And Excel started on that path by winning the Listed Garrowby Stakes at York in September – as Starman did 12 months earlier – and either side of that success he was unlucky not to win a big handicap.

Having been taken out of the Wokingham at Royal Ascot due to the soft ground, the four-year-old made it to Glorious Goodwood and Ayr's big autumn meeting but was compromised by the draw both times. He was best of those drawn in single figures when third in the Stewards' Cup (the first two were drawn 23 and 22) and came from stall one to finish second in the Ayr Gold Cup to Bielsa, who raced on the opposite side from the highest draw in 25.

"These big sprint handicaps are so exasperating. I've no doubt he'd have won at Goodwood and Ayr with a better draw," said Walker, who was also frustrated that Great Ambassador did not get his favoured fast ground on either occasion. It was soft at Goodwood and good at Ayr, whereas it was good to firm for the Garrowby and for Great Ambassador's other turf win in a Newmarket handicap in July.

Even so, Great Ambassador ended the campaign on a Racing Post Rating of 116 – the same as Starman the year before – and Walker is excited. "He's a special horse with loads of speed," he said. "I think he's very smart and could probably be competitive at the highest level next year. You can see what an upward trajectory he's on. Who knows where he'll end up?"

AHOY SENOR

FOUR years after winning the Grand National for Scotland with One For Arthur, Lucinda Russell enjoyed another big moment at Aintree in April with Ahoy Senor's Grade 1 victory in the Sefton Novices' Hurdle and there is the promise of more exciting days for this impressive young prospect.

Ahoy Senor was a 66-1 shot for the three-mile contest at Aintree, having had only one previous run over hurdles, but he made a mockery of those odds with a seven-length success over Bravemansgame, who had won the Grade 1 Challow Novices' Hurdle and finished third in the Ballymore at Cheltenham.

The six-year-old's victory was no surprise to Russell. "Of course I backed him. I don't do very big bets but 66-1 was quite insulting," she said. "This was only his second hurdles run but we had such confidence in him at home."

Ahoy Senor came out of the British point-to-point scene and, having won over two and a half miles for Philip Rowley, was bought by Russell for £50,000 in November 2020. He was second in a bumper at Ayr on his debut for the yard and went back there to land a maiden hurdle in March before heading on to Aintree.

"Isn't he just a super horse?" Russell said at Aintree. "He just gallops and jumps. I saw his point-to-point win and he did the same. He ran so well over two miles four at Ayr and we knew he'd keep on galloping. I can't believe we managed to get him beat in a bumper but jumping takes him to another level. I can't wait for him to go chasing. I'd like to think next season is going to be really exciting with him."

As a cold snap bites in the first week of 2021, trainer Ciaran Murphy's string return home via the stream after cantering at his Charlestown base near Mullingar, County Westmeath

PATRICK McCANN (RACINGPOST.COM/PHOTOS)

A-Z of 2021

The year digested into 26 bite-size chunks

A

D

A is for angry no more. Gary Bardwell, once known as the Angry Ant in his race-riding days, finally won the Leger Legends race for retired jockeys at the eighth attempt. The 53-year-old, twice champion apprentice and winner of two Chester Cups and an Ayr Gold Cup, was delighted, saying: "This is up with the best of all my big winners. I've got all my family here – my wife, brothers, kids and grandkids – and it's a special day."

B is for bargain buy. One bid was all it took for Shark Hanlon to take home Skyace from Ascot sales in November 2019 for just £600 and within 18 months he had turned the castoff out of Willie Mullins' yard into a Grade 1 winner. "I don't know why she was so cheap," said Hanlon, who had budgeted to spend up to £15,000 on her.

C is for changing of the guard. Frankel replaced his late father Galileo at the top of the sire standings after Adayar became his first Derby winner and Hurricane Lane added further Classic success. Galileo, champion sire 12 times and for the previous 11 years in a

row, died in July at the age of 23.

D is for drama, drifting and demotion. Dragon Symbol was first past the post by a head from Campanelle in a ding-dong battle for the Commonwealth Cup at Royal Ascot, but his wayward course cost him Group 1 victory as the stewards reversed the placings after an inquiry.

E is for eye of the needle. Faced with a split-second decision on Adayar in the Derby when a gap appeared on the rail with two and a half furlongs to run, Adam Kirby took the daring route to victory. "When that little sliver opened up I didn't think twice about getting in there," Kirby said after his life-changing success on only his second Derby ride.

F is for fifty-somethings. Age is just a number to Frankie Dettori, who won Classics on Mother Earth and Snowfall at the age of 50, and to Kevin Manning, 54, who set the tone with his 2,000 Guineas victory on Poetic Flare, becoming the oldest jockey to win a British Classic since Lester Piggott landed the 2,000 Guineas on Rodrigo De Triano in 1992 at the age of 56. Joe Fanning

joined the party, winning the Gold Cup at Royal Ascot on Subjectivist at the age of 50.

G is for green wall. Irish trainers utterly dominated the Cheltenham Festival, thrashing the home team 23-5 and taking home 11 of the 13 Grade 1 prizes as well as seven of the nine handicaps. When Minella Indo took the Gold Cup on the Friday, he was the tenth winner in a row for Ireland, a run that included seven one-twos for the raiding party.

H is for holy trinity. The triple crown of Champion Hurdle, Champion Chase and Gold Cup had been an unattainable feat until Henry de Bromhead wrote his name in history with Honeysuckle, Put The Kettle On and Minella Indo. As if that were not enough, he then became the first trainer to win all three top jumps races (Champion Hurdle, Gold Cup, Grand National) in one season with Minella Times' victory at Aintree.

I is for inspirational. That description was apt for both the concept and the reality of National Racehorse Week, held for the first time in mid-September, as 130 yards across Britain took part. "It was just how I

visualised it," said a delighted Richard Phillips, the trainer who first suggested the idea in the Racing Post in 2019.

J is for Jubilee jubilation. After two head defeats in the Diamond Jubilee, Dream Of Dreams finally landed the Royal Ascot sprint at the third attempt. "Any winner here is a great thrill, particularly a Group 1," said trainer Sir Michael Stoute, "but this fellow has just been touched off twice, so I'm pleased for him. He deserves it."

K is for kin. Family ties are strong in racing and there were special moments at the end of the jump jockeys' championships. Harry Skelton was propelled by brother Dan to his first British title, overhauling title-holder Brian Hughes in the final fortnight, while Paul Townend celebrated his fourth Irish crown alongside sister Jody, who became champion female amateur for the first time.

L is for late scare. Oisin Murphy's lead in the British Flat jockeys' championship looked secure with a week to go but the nerves were jangling as William Buick came with a storming run. Murphy had just enough in hand to hold

on for his third title, but it was mighty close.

M is for Mr Aintree. Trevor Hemmings died in October aged 86, having etched his name in Grand National history by becoming the race's joint most successful owner with the memorable victories of Hedgehunter (2005), Ballabriggs (2011) and Many Clouds (2015). Oliver Sherwood, trainer of Many Clouds, said: "He was Mr Aintree, wasn't he? He loved the place."

N is for nickname. Denise Foster was not widely known before, but her name – invariably accompanied by her nickname 'Sneezy' – had six months in the spotlight when she took interim charge of Gordon Elliott's stable during his suspension. Three Cheltenham Festival winners – Black Tears (Mares' Hurdle), Tiger Roll (Cross Country Chase) and Mount Ida (Kim Muir Handicap Chase) – went down in her name in the record books, although without the 'Sneezy' attached.

O is for out on his own. Colin Keane roared to a record total in the Irish Flat jockeys' championship, setting such a

blistering pace that he passed Joseph O'Brien's old mark with three weeks left in the season.

P is for photograph. The image of Gordon Elliott sitting astride a dead horse will haunt him and racing for years. Having served his six-month suspension, he said on his return: "From now on, I have to prove that the impression people have of me from the picture does not reflect who I am. I need to step up and prove to everyone that I am not a monster."

Q is for quarantine nightmare. Cieren Fallon spent four days in a hotel so he could ride The Lir Jet in the French 2,000 Guineas, only for the horse to be withdrawn. Among the rides he missed back home was Oxted in the Duke of York Stakes, but that part of the tale had a happy ending when he got back on board next time to win the Group 1 King's Stand Stakes, his first Royal Ascot success.

R is for Rachael. Few jockeys make such an impact that they become known by something other than their surname. We have had Frankie, AP and Ruby, and now there's Rachael, who became a

familiar presence through her boundary-pushing achievements and a household favourite with her well-supported Grand National triumph on Minella Times.

S is for sixteen and Snowfall. The Oaks winner recorded the biggest winning margin in the Classic's history when she powered home by 16 lengths under Frankie Dettori. "I've won many Classics, but not as easy as this one," he said. "I was like a hot knife through butter and had everything completely beaten coming around Tattenham Corner. I pulled up at the stables and everyone else pulled up by the winning post."

T is for tears. William Jarvis was visibly upset after Lady Bowthorpe's luckless fourth in the Falmouth Stakes at Newmarket's July festival but gained glorious reward later

that month with her Group 1 victory in the Nassau Stakes at Goodwood. Having waited 27 years for a second top-level success in his long career, Jarvis could have been forgiven tears of joy on this occasion.

U is for utter silence. After a crowdless Arc in 2020, 15,000 racegoers were allowed into Longchamp for the 100th running of the great race, but you could hear a pin drop in the moments after German outsider Torquator Tasso passed the post in front for a massive 72-1 upset.

V is for veterinary requirements. Stringent new rules for the Melbourne Cup caused a rethink for many of the potential raiding party. Among those disappointed was Charlie Fellowes, who was told by the vets that Prince Of Arran, runner-up

in 2019 and third in the two years either side, would not be eligible to run. With that option removed, Prince Of Arran was retired at the age of eight with career earnings of £2,042,180. "He's been a superstar for me and has taken me places I could only have dreamed of," Fellowes said.

W is for welcome back. Racegoers were gradually allowed back on course in increasing numbers as lockdown restrictions eased and an important step was taken on May 17 when courses in England were allowed crowds of up to 4,000. Carlisle was the first to get going and among those in attendance was Peter Dixon, who spoke for many when he said: "It's amazing to be at a sporting event again. I've missed being able to go to the races or watch football and rugby live."

X is for ex-racers. Altior and Battaash, two Lambourn legends stabled barely a mile apart for more than six years, were retired within weeks of each other in the summer after stellar racing careers in their respective spheres. Nicky Henderson's ace two-mile chaser went off to happy retirement with ITV Racing

pundit Mick Fitzgerald, while Charlie Hills's super sprinter headed to his new home at Shadwell Stud.

Y is for You'resothrilling, the remarkable Coolmore broodmare who produced her third Classic winner when Joan Of Arc, her seventh foal, won the Prix de Diane. The other two were dual Guineas winner Gleneagles and Irish 1,000 Guineas scorer Marvellous, while Happily (like the others by Galileo) was a dual Group 1 winner. "To have already produced four Group 1 winners at only 16 years of age is truly remarkable," said Coolmore's James Mockridge.

Z is for Zambia. Barney Curley, the legendary punter and trainer who died in May aged 81, devoted much of his energy in his later years to his charity Direct Aid For Africa and Frankie Dettori and Jamie Spencer were among those who turned out in his honour for a fundraising raceday at Bellewstown in September. Spencer, who like Dettori was mentored by Curley, said: "I hope he's best remembered for his charity work in Africa. Anybody who has been fortunate enough to witness his work in Zambia will tell you how fantastic it was."

RACING POST ANNUAL AWARDS

Our pick of the best of 2021

HORSE OF THE YEAR (FLAT)
St Mark's Basilica
Unbeaten campaign across three countries for Aidan O'Brien

HORSE OF THE YEAR (JUMPS)
Honeysuckle
Imperious Champion Hurdle winner on both sides of the Irish Sea

RACE OF THE YEAR (FLAT)
Irish Champion Stakes
Small field but big on quality as St Mark's Basilica beat Tarnawa and Poetic Flare in a thriller

RACE OF THE YEAR (JUMPS)
Queen Mother Champion Chase
Tremendous battle up the hill with Put The Kettle On toughing it out

RIDE OF THE YEAR (FLAT)
Adam Kirby, Adayar, Derby
Chance ride and he took it with courage and conviction

RIDE OF THE YEAR (JUMPS)
Rachael Blackmore, Minella Times, Grand National
Nerveless nine minutes and 15 seconds that changed the world

RISING STAR
Marco Ghiani
The 22-year-old Italian impressed as he took the British apprentice title

COMEBACK OF THE YEAR
Jack Kennedy
Gold Cup glory on Minella Indo after all the injury and despair

SURPRISE OF THE YEAR
Torquator Tasso's Arc
German outsider stunned the big names in the 100th running

UNLUCKIEST HORSE
Dragon Symbol
Form figures of 22234 in successive Group 1s including demotion at Royal Ascot

MOST IMPROVED HORSE
Skyace
The £600 castoff improved 2st on Racing Post Ratings in her climb to Grade 1 success

DISAPPOINTMENT OF THE YEAR
Home defence at Cheltenham
The most one-sided festival ever as Ireland won almost everything

BEST 'I WAS THERE' MOMENT
Lonsdale Cup
Great race, great ovation for Stradivarius in front of a buzzing York crowd

▲ Memorable moments: clockwise from top left, St Mark's Basilica, Honeysuckle, Rachael Blackmore, Marco Ghiani, Torquator Tasso, Dragon Symbol, Skyace and the finish of the Lonsdale Cup

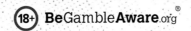

STAY AHEAD OF THE FIELD WITH

RACING POST
MEMBERS' CLUB

ACCESS PREMIUM CONTENT AND FEATURES

FIND OUT MORE AT
RACINGPOST.COM/MEMBERS-CLUB

THE
BIGGER
PICTURE

Love Is Golden, trained by Mark Johnston and ridden by Franny Norton, en route to an all-the-way success in a 1m4f handicap at Chester's behind-closed-doors May festival
EDWARD WHITAKER (RACINGPOST.COM/PHOTOS)

Khalid Abdullah and Hamdan Al Maktoum, two titans of racing and breeding on a global scale, died in 2021. In these articles their impact is assessed by senior Racing Post writers Julian Muscat and John Randall

'Magic thoroughbred dust at the tips of his fingers '

KHALID ABDULLAH 1937-2021

PRINCE KHALID ABDULLAH epitomised better than anyone the maxim that horses should speak for themselves. No owner said fewer words than the Saudi Arabian prince, whose totem racehorse Frankel could not have spoken more eloquently on his behalf.

The vast majority of racing fans nominate Abdullah's stupendous champion as the best racehorse they have seen – and many of those had previously declared they would never again see the like of Dancing Brave, who carried Abdullah's silks with rare distinction in 1986.

The man who entered the sport with his inaugural yearling purchases in 1977 has left it demonstrably the richer, his legacy enshrined in Juddmonte Farms, the breeding concern that made Abdullah a serial winner of awards defining excellence.

Abdullah's homebreds landed all five British Classics in a ten-year spell from 1990. The full set in France was completed five years later, but Juddmonte Farms reached its apogee in 2003 when it was the leading owner in Britain and France while simultaneously landing Eclipse Awards in the US as top owner and top breeder.

Such riches prompted informed commentators to describe Juddmonte Farms as the model operation. It is one without peer, its achievements rendered more remarkable by the fact it started from scratch. A series of astute, mostly private purchases of fillies and broodmares established the platform from which the majority of its contemporary horses descend. Very few yearling purchases have been made in the last 30 years; they were simply not necessary.

Abdullah's development of the Juddmonte brand saw the operation expand significantly from his original purchase of Cayton Park Stud, in Berkshire, in 1982. As his broodmare band grew he took steps to ensure there was sufficient pasture for their produce.

In the end a mature Juddmonte Farms embraced four substantial properties in Britain, two in Ireland and the 2,500-acre Juddmonte Farms, south of Lexington, in Kentucky.

Until Frankel, the best horse Abdullah owned was unquestionably Dancing Brave. Bought as a yearling by James Delahooke for $200,000 and trained by Guy Harwood, Dancing Brave's big-race triumphs in 1986 numbered the 2,000 Guineas, Eclipse, King George VI and Queen Elizabeth Stakes and Prix de l'Arc de Triomphe.

But the most rewarding horse for him personally was Frankel, whose 14-race unbeaten career represented near-unparalleled achievement. There was an equally

▼ The greatest: Khalid Abdullah with Frankel, along with his racing manager Teddy Grimthorpe (left), Sir Henry Cecil and jockey Tom Queally after the 2011 Sussex Stakes

poignant human side to the Frankel story: his trainer Sir Henry Cecil, who was suffering from stomach cancer, died eight months after Frankel closed out his unbeaten career in the Champion Stakes in October 2012.

Frankel was named after Abdullah's US trainer Bobby Frankel, who lost his own battle with leukaemia in 2009. Many of the trainer's best wins were gained for Abdullah, notably Empire Maker's Belmont Stakes triumph in 2003. It says much about Abdullah that he funded state-of-the-art medical treatment for both Cecil and Frankel to help their fight against illness.

In the last five years of his life Abdullah owned two great champions, Arrogate and Enable. Arrogate is the only horse since Frankel to be the overall world champion twice on official ratings, and he achieved that distinction with three consecutive hugely valuable victories in late 2016 and early 2017.

The Bob Baffert-trained grey confirmed himself a champion as a three-year-old in the $6m Breeders' Cup Classic and continued his purple patch in the new year by trouncing the field in the $12m Pegasus World Cup at Gulfstream Park and outclassing his rivals in the $10m Dubai World Cup.

Enable achieved immortal fame by winning the Prix de l'Arc de Triomphe in 2017 and 2018, and becoming the first horse to win the King George VI and Queen Elizabeth Stakes three times. Trained by John Gosden, Enable also numbered the Oaks, Irish Oaks, Breeders' Cup Turf and Eclipse among her 15 victories.

A publicity-shy individual who was made an honorary member of the Jockey Club in 1983, Abdullah always credited his senior staff for Juddmonte Farms' achievements. That may have some truth to it but the fact remains very little happened at Juddmonte without Abdullah personally sanctioning it. He had magic thoroughbred dust at the tips of his fingers.

JULIAN MUSCAT

Title HRH Prince Khalid bin Abdullah Al Saud of Saudi Arabia

Born 1937

First winner Charming Native (trainer Jeremy Tree), Windsor, May 14, 1979

First Group winner Abeer (1979 Queen Mary Stakes)

First Group 1 winner Known Fact (1979 Middle Park Stakes)

Unbeaten champion Frankel (14 races 2010-12 including ten Group 1s, notably 2011 2,000 Guineas, Sussex Stakes, Queen Elizabeth II Stakes, 2012 Sussex Stakes, Juddmonte International, Champion Stakes)

Overall world champions (from 1995, official ratings) Frankel (2011, 2012), Arrogate (2016, 2017), Enable (2019 joint)

Overall European champions (official ratings) Dancing Brave (1986), Warning (1988), Zafonic (1993), Frankel (2011, 2012), Enable (2019 joint)

Derby winners Quest For Fame (1990), Commander In Chief (1993), Workforce (2010)

King George VI and Queen Elizabeth Stakes winners Dancing Brave (1986), Enable (2017, 2019, 2020)

Prix de l'Arc de Triomphe winners Rainbow Quest (1985), Dancing Brave (1986), Rail Link (2006), Workforce (2010), Enable (2017, 2018)

Dubai World Cup winner & Pegasus World Cup winner Arrogate (2017)

Breeders' Cup Classic winner Arrogate (2016)

Breeders' Cup Turf winner Enable (2018)

Other British Classic winners Known Fact (1980 2,000 Guineas), Dancing Brave (1986 2,000 Guineas), Toulon (1991 St Leger), Zafonic (1993 2,000 Guineas), Reams Of Verse (1997 Oaks), Wince (1999 1,000 Guineas), Special Duty (2010 1,000 Guineas), Frankel (2011 2,000 Guineas), Enable (2017 Oaks), Logician (2019 St Leger)

Irish Derby winner Commander In Chief (1993)

Champion owner in Britain 2003, 2010, 2011

Champion breeder in Britain 1993, 2003, 2004, 2010, 2011, 2012

'A proper horseman with a sharp eye '

HAMDAN AL MAKTOUM
1945-2021

HAMDAN AL MAKTOUM was a colossus of the turf whose investment of billions of pounds made the deputy ruler of Dubai a major global player in the sport for four decades.

He and his brothers, especially Sheikh Mohammed, transformed British racing through sheer weight of money, and their horses, studs and other assets made them the world's most powerful owners.

The multiple champion owner and breeder operated under the Shadwell banner, and his long list of stars included Nashwan, Dayjur, world champions Sakhee and Invasor, and Erhaab, Nayef, Battaash and top fillies Salsabil and Taghrooda. He also bred Istabraq.

Unlike some owner-breeders, he was a proper horseman with a sharp eye. He recognised all his horses – they all had Arabic names – and knew their pedigrees, and there were many stories about him going around evening stables and noticing things the trainers and grooms had missed.

Brought up in a horse-loving culture, Hamdan's interest in thoroughbreds was nurtured when attending an English Language school in Cambridge in the late 1960s, watching the racing at Newmarket from the silver ring. A decade later he followed Sheikh Mohammed's lead by starting to purchase yearlings at the sales.

He first attracted attention when paying 625,000gns for Ghadeer, a son of Lyphard, at Tattersalls in October 1979. This more than doubled the European record for a yearling at auction.

With money no object, Derrinstown Stud in Kildare was the first stud he bought, from Arkle's owner Anne Duchess of Westminster in 1983. Shadwell Estate in Norfolk and Shadwell Farm in Kentucky were purchased the following year. Sheikh Hamdan also bought many

Title His Highness Sheikh Hamdan bin Rashid Al Maktoum

Born Dubai, December 25, 1945

First winner Mushref (trainer Tom Jones), Redcar, July 30, 1980

First Group winner Ghadeer (1981 Premio Carlo Porta)

First British Group winner Princes Gate (1982 Westbury Stakes)

First Group 1 winner At Talaq (1984 Grand Prix de Paris)

Top-rated horse Dayjur (RPR 136 three times)

Overall world champions (official ratings) Sakhee (2001 as joint-owner), Invasor (2006)

Overall European champions (official ratings) Dayjur (1990), Sakhee (2001 as joint-owner)

Derby winners Nashwan (1989), Erhaab (1994)

King George VI and Queen Elizabeth Stakes winners Nashwan (1989), Taghrooda (2014)

Prix de l'Arc de Triomphe winner Sakhee (2001 as joint-owner)

Dubai World Cup winners Almutawakel (1999), Invasor (2007)

Breeders' Cup Classic winner Invasor (2006)

Other British Classic winners Nashwan (1989 2,000 Guineas), Salsabil (1990 1,000 Guineas, Oaks), Shadayid (1991 1,000 Guineas), Harayir (1995 1,000 Guineas), Mutafaweq (1999 St Leger as joint-owner), Lahan (2000 1,000 Guineas), Haafhd (2004 2,000 Guineas), Eswarah (2005 Oaks), Ghanaati (2009 1,000 Guineas), Taghrooda (2014 Oaks)

Irish Derby winner Salsabil (1990)

Champion owner in Britain Win-money only: 1990, 1994. Total prize-money: 1995, 2002, 2005, 2009, 2014, 2019, 2020

Champion breeder in Britain 1989, 1994, 1995, 2001, 2005

▲ Hamdan Al Maktoum after the 2014 Oaks with his homebred Taghrooda, who went on to win the King George VI and Queen Elizabeth Stakes

blue-blooded mares including the Queen's Height Of Fashion, who became the dam of Nashwan, Nayef and Unfuwain. He appointed Angus Gold as his racing manager in 1987, and spoke to him almost every day.

In 1989 Nashwan, a half-brother to his King George runner-up Unfuwain, became the only horse to win the 2,000 Guineas, Derby, Eclipse and King George in the same year, and also the first homebred Classic winner for any of the Maktoum brothers. Nashwan is still perhaps the most famous of Sheikh Hamdan's horses because of the prestige of the races in his unique four-timer. He was responsible for making Sheikh Hamdan champion breeder for the first time.

Dayjur was the greatest sprinter of modern times and his RPR of 136 makes him, by that criterion, the best of all the horses to carry Sheikh Hamdan's blue-and-white colours. As a three-year-old in 1990 Dayjur scorched home in the King's Stand Stakes, Nunthorpe, Haydock Sprint Cup and (at odds of 1-10) Prix de l'Abbaye, although he is best remembered for throwing away victory in the Breeders' Cup Sprint by jumping a shadow.

In that same year, triple Classic winner Salsabil proved herself the best filly Sheikh Hamdan ever owned. Purchased as a yearling, she landed the 1,000 Guineas and Oaks, became the first filly in 90 years to win the Irish Derby, and also took the Prix Vermeille, but she disappointed when favourite for the Arc.

The creation of Godolphin in 1992 changed the focus of the Maktoum brothers' racing empires. Dubai's new flagship stable became Sheikh Mohammed's main priority, and some of Sheikh Hamdan's promising youngsters were transferred to race under the Godolphin banner.

Some of his horses with Godolphin's trainer Saeed bin Suroor continued to run in his own colours, as Almutawakel did when winning the 1999 Dubai World Cup, but others ran in Godolphin's royal blue with Sheikh Hamdan retaining an interest, like Mutafaweq in the 1999 St Leger and Sakhee as a four-year-old.

His investment in the sport included not only bloodstock – hundreds of horses in training, plus stallions, broodmares, yearlings, foals and Arab horses – but also new studs and stables and the refurbishment of old ones, the creation of employment, better training facilities for all at Newmarket, and funding for veterinary research, race sponsorship and charity donations.

JOHN RANDALL